PRAISE FOR
ROGUE WAVES
AND JONATHAN BRILL

Jonathan Brill has spent his career navigating the tensions between anticipating the future and adapting to the present. His book offers an actionable framework for driving change instead of being blindsided by it.

—Adam Grant
#1 *New York Times* bestselling author of *Think Again*
and host of the TED podcast *WorkLife*

Seemingly crazy ideas, which first appear as distant specks on your business horizon, can grow into giant waves that sink your company. Jonathan Brill's *Rogue Waves* is an indispensable guide for staying ahead of these storms. Drawing on a wide range of useful examples, Brill offers valuable lessons on how to navigate strategically rather than passively through rapidly changing markets.

—Safi Bahcall
Wall Street Journal bestselling author of *Loonshots*

Rogue Waves is the rarest of important business books. It's a page turner. Brill's captivating examples of resilience cross fields and industries—even centuries. If you need to lead through uncertainty, this is a must-read. Unless, of course, you prefer to leave your future up to fate.

—Alison Sander
Director of the BCG Center for Sensing & Mining the Future

In *Rogue Waves*, Jonathan Brill makes a profound contribution to the science of decision-making and the psychology of leadership.

—Philip Zimbardo
Professor Emeritus of Psychology at Stanford University,
principal investigator of the Stanford Prison Experiment,
and *New York Times* bestselling author of *The Lucifer Effect*

Brill is the Michael Porter of resilient growth. In *Rogue Waves*, he shares the same step-by-step approach that he has used to help my firm and our clients repeatedly ride the waves in 46 countries. Absolutely vital.

—David Frigstad
Chairman of Frost & Sullivan

Rogue waves are coming at us with unnerving frequency as the world wrestles with major economic, sociopolitical, and technological shifts. Jonathan Brill walks you through the awareness, behavioral change, and cultural change your organization must implement to take advantage of the opportunities embedded in these shifts. Turn the future to your advantage with Jonathan Brill's practical tools. Don't miss this book if you want to surf the next wave.

—Mauro F. Guillén
Dean of Cambridge Judge Business School and
Wall Street Journal bestselling author of *2030*

Jonathan's commonsense approach and scenario-planning toolkit have not only helped us get out in front of, thrive, and benefit from change but instilled a team culture that enables us to survive and mitigate against volatility. *Rogue Waves* is the twenty-first century's answer to *Competitive Strategy*. Essential reading for any strategy or policy team!

—Nicholas Butts
Head of Global Strategy and Trade at HP and board
member of the Harvard Kennedy School Fund

Timely and desperately needed, *Rogue Waves* is practical advice from the best in the field. It's the new standard on resilient growth strategy. Highly recommended for business leaders who need to go beyond VUCA.

—Ansgar Baums
Head of Government Relations for Europe,
the Middle East, and Africa at Zoom

If you face disruption, *Rogue Waves* is your secret weapon.

—Dorie Clark
Thinkers50 Thinker, faculty member at Duke University
Fuqua School of Business, and author of *Reinventing You*

Jonathan Brill isn't Nostradamus, but for the world's top business and government leaders, he's the next best thing. In *Rogue Waves* you'll learn the powerful tools to turn the future to your favor.

—Bronwyn Syiek
Board Director of Oxford University Press and
International Personal Finance Plc

ROGUE WAVES

ROGUE WAVES

**FUTURE–PROOF
YOUR BUSINESS**

to

SURVIVE & PROFIT

from

RADICAL CHANGE

JONATHAN BRILL

New York Chicago San Francisco Athens London Madrid
Mexico City Milan New Delhi Singapore Sydney Toronto

1 2 3 4 5 6 7 8 9   LCR   26 25 24 23 22 21

ISBN   978-1-264-25715-7
MHID   1-264-25715-5

e-ISBN   978-1-264-25716-4
e-MHID 1-264-25716-3

Library of Congress Cataloging-in-Publication Data

Names: Brill, Jonathan, author.
Title: Rogue waves : future-proof your business to survive and profit from radical
    change / Jonathan Brill.
Description: New York : McGraw Hill, [2021] | Includes bibliographical references
    and index.
Identifiers: LCCN 2021014003 (print) | LCCN 2021014004 (ebook) |
    ISBN 9781264257157 (hardback) | ISBN 9781264257164 (ebook)
Subjects: LCSH: Business forecasting.
Classification: LCC HD58.8 .B7528 2021 (print) | LCC HD58.8 (ebook) |
    DDC 658.4/062—dc23
LC record available at https://lccn.loc.gov/2021014003
LC ebook record available at https://lccn.loc.gov/2021014004

McGraw Hill books are available at special quantity discounts to use as premiums and sales promotions or for use in corporate training programs. To contact a representative, please visit the Contact Us pages at www.mhprofessional.com.

To Rebecca, Sarah, Lora,
Margot, Kathy, and Masha—
the ladies in my life

CONTENTS

CONTENTS

PART III
CULTURE CHANGE

INTRODUCTION

*Is the biggest wave you've seen
the biggest one you'll see?*

Rogue waves routinely sink even the largest ships.[1] These hundred-foot-tall walls of water pop up out of nowhere when smaller waves collide, shocking the sailors they kill. But for experts who study and model ocean behavior for a living, they're increasingly forecastable. When ships' captains know the places and the conditions in which they're likely to form, they can prepare.

The same is true in business. Our world is becoming more volatile. Phenomena like pandemics and financial crises, artificial intelligence and automation, social unrest and trade wars are colliding to unleash massive, unexpected waves of change. The companies that understand how these changes will impact them can profit from the chaos.

But the processes that most enterprises rely on were built for a different, less volatile time. They presume that you can deliver reliable compound growth, year after year after year, if you reduce risk, improve your efficiencies, and keep your products up to date. When those assumptions are put to the test, they frequently fail. To survive and thrive today, you need to lean into risk and leverage it, setting your organization up to benefit when the next wave hits.

It's admirable to save your crew if your ship sinks, but the fact is that you're the captain, and you're not likely to get another command. Your challenge is to ride the wave and emerge stronger.

Investors, boards, and leaders are all reassessing their organizations in the wake of years of disruption. They're demanding resilience, adaptability, and growth—and wondering if you're the right person to make the necessary changes. Some organizations trade in ambiguity and uncertainty, and there are best practices and behaviors that they've mastered . . . but they aren't the ones taught in business school.

WHY BUSINESS SCHOOL STRATEGY KEEPS FAILING

There are two primary schools of strategic thought. The first, the Competitive Strategy school, suggests you can outperform your industry by sustaining a protectable advantage. The Blue Ocean school believes that the key is to find new markets, thereby making the competition irrelevant. Both are necessary, but not sufficient. Neither matters when the game gets knocked off the table—the board, the pieces, and the rules all go overboard when the rogue wave hits.

The esteemed Harvard Business School professor Michael Porter laid out the foundational questions every manager must ask in *Competitive Strategy*:

1. What is driving the competition in my industry or in the industries I am thinking of entering?
2. What actions are competitors likely to take, and what is the best way to respond?
3. How will my industry evolve?
4. How can my firm be best positioned to compete in the long run?[2]

These are useful thoughts. After all, Porter is perhaps the most cited business scholar today. Monitor Deloitte, the consultancy he cofounded, is filled with Harvard faculty, who recruit their best students. This leads to an awkward question: Why did this esteemed consultancy, populated by the world's smartest competitive strategists, implode?

Economic rogue waves swamped Monitor as they sang the strategy gospel to CEOs. First, there was a bankruptcy caused by a combination of the 2008 financial crash and an exodus of clients alarmed by stories of shady dealings with dictators. More recently, many of its top partners appear to have been forced to walk the plank as business softened in the face of the Covid pandemic.

Some have argued that Monitor Group failed to create new value—the Blue Ocean strategy—as larger competitors, like McKinsey, consolidated a challenging market. But perhaps something else was at play. As any sailor can tell you, blue oceans only exist during fair weather. When the clouds come, the seas turn black. Several central case studies in the classic *Blue Ocean Strategy*—Curves, JCDecaux, and Cemex—had very, very bad years in the face of the 2008 financial crisis and Covid-19. Its primary example, Cirque du Soleil, went bankrupt as other entertainment companies flourished.

Carl Icahn, a strong adherent of Porter's industrial logic,[3] is the captain of corporate raiders and one of the most successful investors in history—clearly, a man who knows something about business. In 2005, Icahn was in the process of taking over Blockbuster Entertainment, which operated 9,000 video rental stores and a nascent but rapidly growing video streaming service that competed with Netflix. In the early 2000s, Netflix's top executives purportedly visited Blockbuster at the company's Dallas headquarters, offering to sell Netflix for $50 million. The existential debate must have made its way to Icahn. He was faced with the question of the looming digital disruption posed by broadband internet, but his actions would indicate that he considered such a threat as elusive as Melville's great white whale.

Icahn subsequently installed *his* CEO, a seasoned executive who had previously led 7-11 stores but knew little about entertainment. What happened next was more than a shift away from online but a doubling down on the historically successful brick-and-mortar strategy. Shortly after, Blockbuster went bankrupt, and Icahn reportedly lost $200 million.[4]

The irony is that while Blockbuster was collapsing, Netflix was scaling up its video streaming service, a move that led to hypergrowth from 2010 to 2020. It became the number one performing stock of that decade.[5] What Icahn missed was that the new entrant wasn't what Porter might call a "substitute product." Broadband internet was more than that. It was a sea change: a substitute industry that was faster, better, and cheaper. The Blockbuster–Netflix battle was shaped by how their respective teams defined and readied themselves for the emerging wave.

While I was at HP in 2019, Icahn started buying up shares of the company. Working with his acolyte, Xerox CEO John Visentin, he was attempting a "Jonah eats the whale" acquisition of Xerox's much larger competitor. As Icahn stated in his letter to investors, the "industrial logic of combining these two great American businesses"[6] was impeccable. What he missed was that HP had invested in a range of resilience strategies to future-proof itself, while Xerox had gutted less profitable businesses and sold off longer-term investments to maximize its share price. When Covid-19 came, Xerox's main line of business, office copiers, disappeared. HP, on the other hand, was ready to grow—with equipment that helped people work from home and technology to drive medical diagnostics in a post-Covid world.

No one knows what the future holds or how HP will execute with an evolved executive team, but it had considered the possibility of—and was resilient to—a simultaneous pandemic, activist shareholder, and market decline. As a result, HP's year-over-year earnings per share were stable for 2020, while Xerox's were down over 60 percent.[7] Xerox had failed to imagine what would happen if the world woke up one day and simply didn't need office printers.

None of this is a knock on Porter (or on W. Chan Kim and Renée Mauborgne, who wrote *Blue Ocean Strategy*). I've certainly benefited from their frameworks, and this book stands on their broad shoulders. What I'm pointing out is the difference between the academy and the real world, and the danger of letting dogma overfocus your thinking. Business leaders, caught in the headlights of the competitive environment, are often blind to the bigger opportunities and threats of systemic change.

Monitor, Cirque du Soleil, Icahn, and Xerox weren't alone in failing to identify the pandemic as a threat. Eight of the 10 largest publicly traded companies in America failed to name pandemics as a source of risk in their SEC filings. The two companies that *did* recognize the threat were Apple and CVS Health.

Even Carnival Cruise Lines, which frequently deals with epidemics on its ships, failed to identify the impact of disease spreading at ports of call. It's not as though global disease outbreaks are a rare event, after all. They are in books on enterprise risk. They've been on the cover of magazines. Respiratory diseases, such as SARS and MERS, nearly stopped the global economy twice in the past 20 years. Polio existed in the United States during the childhood of most Fortune 500 CEOs,[8] and in Europe in the twenty-first century.[7] HIV still ravages the world. I've personally sat in meetings with Fortune 100 leaders in which people like Bill Gates and epidemiologist Larry Brilliant tried to raise the alarm.

Strategy is tough stuff, and even the big names get it wrong. But not having a strategy isn't an option. What leaders often miss is that radical changes can well up from the ocean or fall from the skies—they can come from different levels of the system in which they operate. When they do, the world, customers, and their expectations change—not just the competition.

This reminds me of the blacktail deer that live in the forest behind my house. Much like Bambi, they wander through the sun-dappled woods, fattening themselves in its cool green shade. They're oblivious to the fact that, historically, massive forest fires have burned their source of sustenance every eight years—a period just longer than their life spans. Like many modern businesses, the deer dine without considering the frequent, radical changes that are just outside their lived experience. The deer don't and can't know any better, but business leaders can and should.

WHY BUSINESS IS BROKEN

Modern business training rests on five great pillars that improve performance when the environment is stable:

1. **Scientific management:** the rationalization of business activity
2. **Game theory:** the quantification of the best realizable strategy
3. **Shareholder value:** the coordination of all business activities around profit
4. **Enterprise architecture:** the modularization and measurement of every business process
5. **Agile practices:** constant pivoting toward a broadly defined goal

While each pillar makes sense in theory, all are based on premises that are no longer true—if they ever were:

1. That reality is what you assume it to be
2. That the future will be like the recent past
3. That near-term value will inevitably create long-term value
4. That a captain can nimbly steer a ship that is too complex to understand
5. That it's a best practice to wait to adapt to systemic change after it occurs

While these modern business practices improve performance in calm waters, they put companies at grave risk in times of massive change. This is because they encourage an inward rather than an outward focus. They encourage small course corrections when sharp turns are necessary. The result is a generation of companies built to respond to the last storm but lacking the resilience to survive the next one.

Even if your investors aren't pushing you on these issues yet (which is inevitable), rogue waves will continue to hit harder, faster, and more frequently. You need better tools to forecast the storms that could hit in the next quarter or year.

Here are a few examples of the dangerous waves that are already beginning to build:

The end of globalization and US hegemony: Secular trends are driving a shift away from the Western-focused global harmonization that began in the 1980s. In the next decade, the United States will be the number two and eventually the number three economy in the world after China and India. The rapid growth of the Asian middle class will continue to accelerate innovation and resource competition. Even if your business doesn't trade in Asia or the United States, your supply chain and customers certainly do, so it'll impact you.

Technology-based differentiation: For most of the last century and the century before, the key drivers of growth were foundational, general-purpose innovations, like the internal combustion engine and transistors. Today, we are seeing more frequent but smaller technological innovations: recombinations of existing components, or incremental enhancements that drive tectonic shifts but often only short-term advantage.

Political volatility: Redefinitions of the social contract are occurring around the world as new great powers rise and the citizens of mature economies demand more from their governments in the face of rapid change and slower growth.

The storming of the US Capitol and Black Lives Matter demonstrations are dramatic domestic examples, but the issues move beyond civil rights and economic inequality. They can upend international trade, shift national security priorities on a dime, and damage global prestige.

National interests are fickle and can suddenly shift the flow of trade. For the past several decades this hasn't mattered much. In 2019 and 2020, it came to a head as the United States threatened to deny key technologies to China, causing a near heart attack of the country's telecom industry.

Then, as Covid hit, the United States suddenly discovered that it faced a critical shortage of equipment to protect its population. At first, the lack of simple items like protective masks caused politicians and public health officials to pretend they were unnecessary, though they knew full well the disease was airborne.[10] Then, lacking key resources, health officials recommended making masks out of T-shirts.[11]

We'll see more systemic crises in the coming decade as competition continues to accelerate around technology, labor, education, energy, and natural resources.

In this not-so-brave new world, strategy isn't just about the grand gestures that create sustained competitive advantage or build new markets. It's about how to ride out the inevitable disruptions that jolt the system while leveraging the opportunities they create. You can't do this by simply being more agile. You need to sharpen the senses that enable you to identify small shifts that can domino into outsized change. Only then can you navigate around them and turn them into massive opportunities, or, if they hit, make sure that you have the resilience and adaptability to surf even the biggest waves.

RESILIENCE IS YOUR NEW STRATEGY FOR GROWTH

Resilient organizations have redundancies that many Six Sigma aficionados find unacceptable—they're less efficient than they could be by their very nature. Yet resilience is the new strategy for growth. The life span of companies that have built themselves on Porteresque thinking is shrinking. The companies that have been the most aggressive about enterprise architecture, like GE, Motorola, and Xerox, are foundering. An armada of cutting-edge agile startups has already drowned because they couldn't hold their breath long enough to resurface when Covid hit.

Today's mandate is more than performance. It's also survival and recovery. Organizations have spent decades trying to build unsinkable ships or faster speedboats. Those strategies work in gentle seas, but not when nature unleashes her wrath upon you.

If you're in rough water, there are few better places to be than in a kayak—if you know how to control it. A high-performance kayak is closed-top and low to the water. You don't so much sit in it as wear it. It's also very unstable, as you know if you've ever tried to get into one the wrong way.

So why are kayaks so good at handling wild rivers and heavy arctic seas? Mainly because they're maneuverable enough to avoid the waves, and if you capsize, they can recover quickly. If you want to take a kayak into white water safely, you need to know how to roll. This is a tricky maneuver that starts with the kayak bottom side up—with you in the cockpit, inverted and under water. Move your paddle and shift your hips the right way, and your body and the boat will quickly flip over, putting you right side up. This is only possible because of the kayak's shape and low center of gravity, which are the same traits that make it easy to tip. Almost any other kind of boat is built to avoid tipping in the first place, which makes it much harder to right if it does. There's a reason you don't see a lot of cruise ships on Class IV rapids.

So, if a wave comes along that's big enough to capsize anything in its path, would you rather be on the *Titanic* or in a kayak? The trick to surviving and thriving in rough seas isn't being impervious to risk. It's being more agile and resilient. If you can flip your kayak faster—if you can recover and respond to new situations and your competition can't—then you win.

Navigating in the Dark of Night

The Inuit have accurately traversed arctic tundra and paddled their kayaks across open seas for millennia, without the benefit of maps, even in the dark of winter. The concept of navigation as Europeans understood it was absent from their language when they first made contact. But their ability to thrive in a hostile, highly dynamic environment isn't because of some sixth sense that you don't have. It's because they've studied the subtle contrasts that surround them and passed that knowledge down the generations.

They recognize the slight blue tint where the ocean's lip meets the horizon and the subtle shift in current pulling the tail of their vessel. They know how the changing wisp of a prevailing wind will impact the oncoming waves and what the pulsing shape of seaweed tells them about the undercurrents as their kayaks glide by.[12] They also know, in a very literal sense, how to flip their kayaks faster than anyone on earth.

Seemingly irrelevant changes can tell us a tremendous amount about what has happened, what will happen next, and how we can make the most of it. The Inuit sit at the apex of human resilience because when the wave crests, they know how to read its froth—the nearly imperceptible contrast of white on white.

The greatest thinkers, leaders, and companies all benefit from these same principles. They know that the future is unlikely to be a carbon copy of the recent past. They look to the breadth of human experience for wisdom, not just recent examples in business or in their industry. They use this knowledge to navigate around risks, to be more resilient, and to make better decisions. Most importantly, they practice processes for identifying big waves on the horizon, for having hard conversations about how to adjust before they arrive—and for being resilient after they hit. In short, they're comfortable with randomness because they understand how to control it and even profit from it.

There are two interrelated reasons that you can control and profit from randomness. The first is that what's unpredictable at one scale is often quite reliable at another. The second is that while random changes occur, they often self-organize into a reliable result.

For instance, if you randomly place sand or ball bearings on a table and vibrate them at different frequencies, their jumpy movements will gradually sort them into very specific patterns. If you shake a box of different sized potatoes, the large ones will rise to the top and the small ones will sink. The movement is unpredictable at the scale of the individual potato, but knowable at the scale of the system.

The Distribution of Randomness

Let's see how randomness plays out on a casino floor. Each of these interactions occurs every night between the clink of glasses, the smoking of cigars, and the shuffling of cards—and each is an example of what mathematicians call a random dynamical system.

- **The Cocktail Menu:** All the information you need to choose a martini or a Manhattan is in the open. In other words, a menu is what normal people would consider nonrandom.
- **Casino War:** The chances of winning this game are decided before the play starts. Everyone is dealt one card from a preshuffled deck, and the highest card wins.
- **Solitaire:** The possibility of success or failure is predetermined, but skill changes the outcome. The initial distribution of cards is random, and the deck isn't reshuffled when it runs out. The shuffle determines whether success is possible, but it's the players' skill and how they sequence their actions that determine whether they win or lose. While the possibility of winning is something like 80 percent, skilled players win less than half of the time.
- **The Roulette Table:** You have about a 1 in 32 chance of hitting the right number on the wheel. Because your chances reset every time, more spins of the wheel don't increase your probability of success.
- **Three Card Monte:** This is a grifter's game in which the dealer adds and subtracts cards from the deck. A good shyster can even drop new cards onto the table without you noticing, through sleight of hand. You might pick the ace of spades, but suddenly, it's something unexpected, like the 34 of elephants. You just don't know.

In each example, probability is distributed differently, sometimes at each turn, sometimes through the sequence of events. As a result, the way that you assess likelihood changes. People are aware of these differences on the casino floor, but when they leave Vegas, something strange happens. Much of the time—maybe even most of the time—they don't consider the game they are playing before choosing a strategy. They just use the one that worked before, even though they know full well that their poker face won't work at the roulette table.

A business that beats randomness looks less like a card table and more like a casino. It wins because it places controls around the unknown. Often, you don't even notice the controls because they occur at different times and places than the uncertainty. They're subtle changes, like which slot machines are open, the buy-in at the table, and who gets comped a hotel room or dinner.

Any reliable project, any business, any economy is a combination of games with different rules, different win rates, and different payouts. In a well-designed casino, the chips move around over the course of the day. No matter who wins any individual game, the house wins the night. You're playing a hand, but the casino is playing a thousand hands. While you're focused on blowing the dice and rolling snake eyes, the pit boss is making sure that no one shifts the flow of money too often. The result, much like the vibrating table, is that the casino controls the flow of information through the room.

This book will shift your thinking—and your strategies and tactics—from that of an individual player to that of a casino that always wins the night.

A PRACTITIONER AS YOUR GUIDE

For businesses and other large organizations, responding to uncertainty is the crucial task of the next decade. Doing it successfully requires more than just knowing that change is coming. You also need to create processes and instill habits that future-proof your operations, your products, and your go-to-market strategies. This requires every manager in your organization to know new methods of:

- Governance
- Need finding
- Value creation
- Performance measurement
- Risk-taking

This kind of transformation is hard, but it's not impossible. I know because I've been involved in making it happen. This book is my attempt to relay some of the lessons I've learned while working with companies that have succeeded and failed in the attempt. Certain patterns show up again and again, and many have historical precedent.

Unlike Michael Porter, I'm not on the faculty of a top business school and I don't have a PhD. I'm a practitioner who's become expert at observing what happens when systems collide. I've learned from hard knocks how to turn weaknesses into strengths at just these moments.

I'm also a study in contrasts. I spent much of my childhood in a hardscrabble fishing village in Maine. I've learned how to break-dance from gang members in East LA, been chased down the streets of Poipet, Cambodia, by a machete-wielding mob, and spent time with senators and a future president. I've worked in a cafeteria and developed menus with Michelin-starred chefs. I failed algebra not once but three times in high school, but I've collaborated with some of the top mathematical thinkers and elite engineers on the planet. I dropped out of high school, but I've guest-lectured at Harvard, Stanford, and MIT and taught at the graduate level.

I've been the CEO of failed startups and successful innovation firms. These companies have substantially improved the world, creating $27 billion for clients, conserving electricity on the scale of major cities, and helping educate tens of millions of people. I've made contributions in meaningful fields, like augmented reality. I also invented a machine that makes frozen coffee slushies.

As the senior global futurist at HP, I directed many of the Fortune 50 company's long-term consumer, economic, and technology research efforts and advised its leaders on the biggest decisions of their lives. The concepts in this book have been proven to be practical and scalable. I know you can do this because we did it at HP, and they worked when a takeover attempt, Covid, and market collapse combined to create a rogue wave.

Today, I help leaders make these changes as an executive advisor to startups and Global Fortune 500 companies and as a board member of Frost & Sullivan, one of the largest market intelligence firms in the world. I've also advised top leaders in the US government on the complex challenges facing the global food system.

We use these same techniques to invent new worlds at Territory Studio—the company that envisions future technologies for films, like Steven Spielberg's *Ready Player One*, Ridley Scott's *Prometheus* and *The Martian*, and other modern classics like *Blade Runner 2049* and *Ex Machina*—where I am the futurist-in-residence.

My point isn't that I'm special—it's just the opposite. I've experienced many more rounds in Neptune's dunk tank than most leaders. I've ridden rogue waves successfully. I've drowned in their wake. And I've helped my team flip its kayak to win the race.

The wealth, depth, and diversity of all these experiences inform this book. Many people have taught me. I've had more teachers than most because of the breadth of what I've done. There isn't a simple solution for making the hard decisions our future demands, but we can build on the knowledge and insights of those who have traversed the deep ocean. This book is my humble attempt to synthesize the wisdom of a thousand brilliant minds who've been kind enough to share their time and knowledge with me.

HOW THIS BOOK IS ORGANIZED

Rogue Waves isn't a map. It's a handbook for surviving and profiting from radical change. It presents a wide range of tools and techniques to simultaneously drive resilience and growth. You don't have to use all of them, and you don't have to use them in a particular order.

But, at some point, you will likely find all of them to be useful. The book is divided into three parts, covering the techniques and tools you need to survive and profit when the next wave hits.

I call them the ABCs of Resilient Growth: Awareness, Behavior Change, and Culture Change (Figure I.1, see next page).

In Part I: Awareness, we'll explore what rogue waves are, why they sink companies, and the 10 global undercurrents that will drive the next one. You'll learn how to spot them earlier and identify where you're vulnerable. You'll understand how to time your actions to maximize your ability to surf them and improve your resilience, if you fail to time them correctly.

In Part II: Behavior Change, you'll learn the techniques of systemic intuition—the thought processes that drive resilient growth strategy. You'll gain new tools to understand and manage risk so you can make bigger and better bets. You'll also learn how to train all levels of your organization to plan for, respond to, and exploit the unexpected. These are the tools that will help you prepare for the future that's likely to exist, instead of the future your organization wants to exist.

Finally, in Part III: Culture Change, you'll learn how to instill the habits and discipline your organization needs to manage risk, work more effectively as a team, and capture value from new developments.

Most good books on strategy focus on identifying the challenge to be addressed, yet most good managers are biased toward action. Much of this book is focused on pinpointing the places where small tweaks can create radical change, but the goal of analysis should always be to increase your impact. So, I want to highlight two important types of action that the sections on analysis build to: *impact amplifiers* and *nudges*.

Impact amplifiers are three basic strategies—timing, sequencing, and hedging—that can shift the fates in your favor (Figure I.2). They are the underlying rules that define a system. They have different names in different fields but are common in any process designed to benefit from uncertainty. You've already seen them play out in multiple ways in the casino example earlier.

Figure I.1 **The ABCs of Resilient Growth**

TECHNIQUES

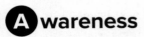

wareness

Know when and where radical change is likely to occur.

Horizon Scanning
Identify the social, economic, and technological trends that will drive radical change.

Impact Assessment
Understand the opportunities and threats for your organization.

Response Window
Assess the earliest and latest that makes sense to respond.

Indicators
Set up an early warning system.

ehavior
change

The ROGUE Method

Maximize resilience and growth when chaos occurs.

R	**Reality Test**	*Map your current situation.*
O	**Observe Your System**	*Test what would cause it to change.*
G	**Generate Possible Futures**	*Identify the range of possible futures.*
U	**Uncouple Your Threats & Opportunities**	*Manage to maximize your optionality and efficiency.*
E	**Experiment Through Portfolios**	*Deliver results on time by taking balanced risk.*

ulture
change

Amplify the quality and speed of experimentation on your teams.

Hard and Soft Incentives
Build the environment that drives optimal behavior.

Adaptive Leadership
Use the right tactics to minimize risk through intelligent risk-taking.

Context Awareness
Maximize knowledge of the situation so that you can adapt.

Agile Communication
Run faster, more actionable, more creative meetings.

Figure I.1 **The ABCs of Resilient Growth** (continued)

TOOLS

The Four FOES of Growth
Consider the major causes of value change, so that you can protect yourself and turn them into opportunity.

Rogue Wave Types
Position yourself for categories of waves, instead of specific changes.

The 10 Undercurrents
Identify the overlapping changes that are likely to cause the next rogue wave, time them, and position yourself to benefit.

The ROGUE Method:

REAL Framework
Gather information and develop theories in a structured way.

Confidence Marking
Ensure everyone on a team is discussing likelihood using similar terms.

Chess Tournament
Challenge assumptions and conclusions through oppositional comparison.

System Models
Map the dependencies in a system to reveal underlying the structure.

Causal Loop Diagrams
Map probabilistic systems.

Impact Amplifiers
Achitectural changes that shift the outcome of systems.

Tree of Possibility
Expand the range of possible outcomes.

Who Sank My Battleship?
Simulate future scenarios in order to find blind spots, vulnerabilities, and opportunities.

The 5Ds
Evaluate potential threats systematically, either to your own system or your competitor's.

VEGAS
Find a system's trigger points, where small efforts can have outsized impact.

Nudges
Tactics to change the reliability of systems.

Threat & Opportunity Dashboard
Track the progress of different risks over time, to take the politics out of decision-making.

Portfolio Balancing
Balance risk, reward and timing.

Designing Experiments
Planning experiments to maximize payoff.

The Dirty Dozen
Decrease your chances of misunderstanding the meaning of data using 12 rules of thumb.

Standard Operating Procedures
A set of procedures used by everyone in the organization to improve its capacity for innovation.

LEAD Messaging
A set of guidelines for communicating effectively with your team.

Innovation Culture Timeline
Phases of adoption, for tracking your organization's progress toward a culture of experimentation.

Download This Chart
jonathanbrill.com/rogue_waves

Figure I.2 **Impact Amplifiers**

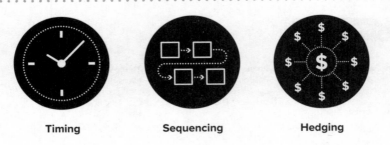

Timing   Sequencing   Hedging

The second type of action, which we'll explore in Chapter 6, encompasses the Five Nudges. When combined intelligently, these simple mechanisms can radically change the outcome of a situation (Figure I.3).

Figure I.3 **The Five Nudges**

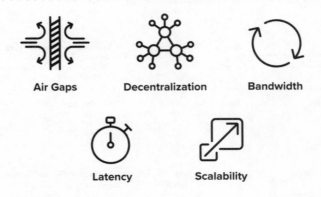

Air Gaps   Decentralization   Bandwidth

Latency   Scalability

The key to surviving and profiting from radical change is to pre-pare *before* the wave crests, not trying to outswim it *after* it wells up. If you want to make small tweaks that give you leverage when the rogue wave hits, you first need the knowledge and foresight to know where to focus your effort. So, let's cast off and start our adventure!

PART I

AWARENESS

*Do you know how the next rogue
wave will change your business?*

. . . .

Rogue waves, the radical changes that upend business, are hitting harder, faster, and more often. Your best option—your only real option—is to ride them and be resilient if you fail.

The collision of 10 rapidly moving economic, technological, and social undercurrents will cause many of this decade's rogue waves. While the scale of their impact is knowable, their energy is only now rising to the surface. If you want to create your own fate when they hit, you will need to:

- Learn how to spot and track them
- Have honest conversations about their implications for your business
- Position yourself to maximize your resilience and advantage

This increased awareness should inform both short- and long-term planning and the overall strategy at every level of your enterprise. It's not enough to know about these waves and figuratively brace yourself for their impact. You need to develop an action plan and a clear timeline for implementing it.

1

Transforming to Survive in Our Increasingly Volatile World

Are you capable of profiting from radical change or merely surviving?

I grew up in Five Islands, a small fishing village in Maine. It seemed unremarkable to me at the time. Everything in my childhood smelled of the ocean. There was a constant diesel thrum of boats humming in and out of our harbor. Several times a week, I'd walk to the pier and watch the ships roll in, heavy with cod, haddock, bluefish, or halibut, depending on the season.

The fishermen's steady pace reflected their assumption that the supply of fish was endless. When catches began to plummet in the 1980s, it was too late. Boats went out less frequently and came back half-empty, until they stopped going out altogether. People lost their jobs. Families moved away.

Eventually, Five Islands started to reinvent. First, it repackaged itself as a resort destination. People opened quaint B&Bs and stands selling chowder. Then, the seafood industry started back up, but in a dramatically different form. Instead of cod, it was lobster, and instead of a bunch of independent boats, it was a cooperative. That worked for about 20 years, until change came again and the warming waters sent the lobsters north.

On the surface, this is a straightforward story about overfishing and its effects. But if you dive beneath, there's much more going on.

The collapse of Maine's fishery was a catastrophic event, but it had many causes. One was the arrival of foreign "supertrawlers," just offshore, in international waters. Not only were they big and organized, they had better technology and were more motivated. Another was the US Department of Commerce's stubborn refusal to set significant limits on annual catches. Blame also lay with the competitive structure of the fishing fleet. Whatever you didn't catch, your neighbor did. So it was in everyone's interest to catch all they could. And of course, climate change and pollution had been depleting stocks for decades.

Any one of these trends would've been a problem, but none of them alone could have decimated the fish population so thoroughly. If the changes were spread out—if the fishermen had formed a self-regulating co-op before the supertrawlers arrived, for instance, the stocks might have replenished themselves. But they all happened together. Their individual impacts built on top of one another, compounding until the fishing stock simply disappeared, something that seemed impossible until, suddenly, it wasn't.

If you motor up the coast for about three hours, you'll pass through Gloucester, Massachusetts, another better-known fishing port. Gloucester's fame is due partly to being much bigger, but mostly to being the setting for *The Perfect Storm*. The book and movie tell the true story of the violent seas that sank several of its ships.

The poster for *The Perfect Storm* displays a terrifying image: a doomed fishing trawler climbing up the face of an enormous wave. The wave is so huge—at least a hundred feet high—that it defies belief, looking more like a geological formation than water. These rogue waves aren't Hollywood hyperbole. They're a regular feature of the deep sea.

CEOs FEEL LIKE THEY'RE OUT AT SEA

A rogue wave is not a regular wave, in the same way that the collapse of fishing stocks is not a regular event. What the two have in common is that they're caused by the compounding of several more normal-seeming phenomena. This might not appear like a profound insight on its face, but the idea that regular, predictable events can reinforce each other in unpredictable ways is one of the most important and least understood concepts in modern business.

I speak to a lot of CEOs, of big and small companies, in a wide range of industries. Almost without exception, our conversations turn to two subjects. The first is how much change is occurring in business and human society. The second is what organizations can do to thrive in the face of all this uncertainty.

More than once, executives have told me that it feels like we're in stormy seas and the waves are getting bigger. Some organizations know how to surf them; others are taking on water. But everyone, *everyone*, is getting hammered. Even so, I'm constantly amazed by how many executives—at startups, established companies, and Fortune 100 organizations—fail to appreciate how much bigger these waves will get.

You just need to look at the emerging technologies, social trends, demographic shifts, economic and public health events, and political and military conflicts that dominate the headlines. Artificial intelligence is one such trend. It's already in half of the digital tools we use, from search algorithms to image recognition. Trade tension between the United States and China is another. So are the dropping cost of consumer electronics and the growing threat of cybercrime.

Individually, these waves are disruptive. But when they converge, they produce sea changes that shock companies and governments.

- An attempt to shore up the British East India Company led to the Boston Tea Party, which dominoed into the American Revolution.

- An oil glut contributed to the fall of the Soviet Union.
- Covid–19 has decimated businesses that require physical contact.

Each sea change seemingly came out of "nowhere," but each was formed out of the interaction of several trackable undercurrents.

Fortunately, we know a lot more about rogue waves than we used to. But to take advantage of that knowledge, organizations need to abandon some deep-seated habits in the way they prepare for their future.

THE MATHEMATICS OF MONSTER WAVES

Until the 1990s, giant waves that appeared out of nowhere were considered sailor folklore, like mermaids, ghost ships, or the kraken of Greek mythology. But insurance executives suspected that something didn't quite add up. A hundred-foot-high wave was considered a once-in-10,000-years phenomenon, and yet hundreds of ships sank on the open ocean every year, many with no explanation.

Then in 1995, a North Sea oil drilling platform called Draupner E clearly recorded an 85-foot wave[1] that appeared suddenly and without warning. Researchers were flooded with calls from concerned marine insurance companies. Shortly after, a study of satellite imagery identified 30 rogue waves occurring in just a one-month period, in locations all over the world.[2] Today, ocean researchers estimate that rogue waves occur in the North Sea about every 10 hours during storms.[3]

By 2004, researchers and insurance companies had come to a new understanding, that many of the "unexplained" sinkings in open seas were due to rogue waves. But it wasn't until 2019 that we finally had a unified theory for predicting them—not on an individual basis, but as a field of probability. Rogue waves are still mysterious, but we are getting a clearer picture of what is necessary for one to appear.

In physical terms, waves aren't all that difficult to understand.[4] There's a concept in physics known as *constructive interference*, in which the peaks of two waves overlap each other, briefly producing a composite wave twice as large as the waves that produced it (Figure 1.1).

Figure 1.1 **Constructive Interference**

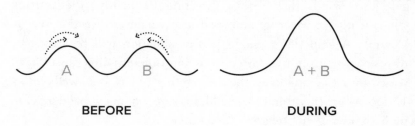

BEFORE   DURING

This is true for any kind of wave, whether we're talking about water, earthquakes, sound, or electromagnetic radiation like x-rays or visible light.[5] Constructive interference, for example, is why certain acoustic spaces have "live" and "dead" spots. The dead spots are where the peak of one wave intersects the trough of another, a phenomenon called *destructive interference*. If you've ever used noise-canceling headphones, you've benefited from its targeted use.

You can see constructive interference in water any place waves reflect off a solid surface, like the banks of a shipping canal. Imagine a buoy floating in the middle as a large barge goes by, trailing a long wake consisting of 8 or 10 waves. When the first wave hits the buoy, it bobs up and down, maybe a foot or so. Then the wave bounces off the hard bank of the canal, back toward the buoy, which is still bobbing, as more waves from the barge pass under it. If the waves from the wake have passed the buoy before the first reflected one returns, then it's just more of the same: bobbing up and down a foot or so, though this time, from a wave going in the opposite direction.

But what if the initial waves are still coming when the reflected one hits? If the peak of the reflected wave reaches the buoy at the same time as the trough of the initial wave, destructive interference occurs. They cancel each other out and the buoy hardly moves. But if the peaks of both waves hit simultaneously, the wave height doubles, launching the buoy up two feet and then crashing it down dramatically after they pass.

Now imagine the North Sea during a fierce winter storm, with gale-force winds that change direction frequently. The shifting winds whip the water up and send it in whatever direction they're blowing. A ship that's caught in this situation will be struck by waves coming from two, three, even four different directions. You'll see two waves crossing all the time, piling two 6-foot swells into a 12-footer—a scary thing to behold, for sure, but not a real danger to modern oceangoing freighters and tankers.

But what if three waves, traveling at 120 degrees to each other, overlap? What if the topography of the seabed or an oceanic cross-current channels a train of waves into a narrow slot, increasing their amplitude? All this happening at once is a rare occurrence. But the ocean is large and storms are frequent. Watch a stormy stretch of ocean long enough and eventually a bunch of big waves *will* intersect, spawning a 100-foot monster in seconds.

We can't predict a specific rogue wave more than a minute or two out, even in a laboratory setting. As one researcher explained, the best instrument for detecting a rogue wave is a window.[6]

But we do have an almost perfect understanding of the situations in which the sea can produce them and those in which she can't. New technologies allow us to create ever more precise maps, not of rogue waves themselves, but of the probability of a rogue wave occurring. We don't know when and where they'll occur, but we can know when and where they're possible and how likely they are.

Nazaré, the Covid-19 Pandemic, and the 2008 Financial Crisis

Big wave surfers know that the most consistent large waves in the world occur at Nazaré in Portugal. It's one of the few places on earth where 60- to 80-footers roll into shore on an average Tuesday. While oceanographers wouldn't technically refer to them as rogue waves, their dynamics are very similar, and because they grow so close to shore, they're highly documented.

If you drive half a mile on the coast north and south of Nazaré, the continental shelf drops off smoothly, diffusing wave energy evenly. But directly off Nazaré's beach is a kilometer-deep trench. It funnels the fury of Neptune across the continental shelf and into the unprotected bay as he seeks the path of least resistance. And then there are the currents. Nazaré is right where a cold water and a warm water current collide, forcing even more energy into the canyon.

These overlapping inputs turn Nazaré into a pressure relief valve for the Atlantic Ocean, though none of this is visible on the surface.

While Nazaré is an example of wave forces in the ocean, the same systemic issues can be seen in the Covid-19 pandemic. The increase in global travel, the push of China's rapidly expanding cities into the biome, rising urban density, and aging populations made the outcome nearly predictable.

The likelihood of an epidemic with an epicenter in central China was known. The only real question was *when* the outbreak would occur.

In business, you can look to the undercurrents of the 2008 financial crisis. We couldn't have known the day on which that dam would break, but the undercurrents were carving deeper and deeper canyons. It wasn't clear that this specific wave would well up in 2008. What we did know was that risk pressure was building and we were using new, unproven instruments to stave it off. Historically, we knew that debt crises tend to occur every 7 to 12 years. Given that the last great event had been in 2000, a catastrophe was likely to occur before much longer. When it did, we knew that a combination of market forces and deregulation made traditional risk management strategies less effective.

CONSTRUCTIVE INTERFERENCE IN HUMAN SOCIETY

The analogy of rogue waves is valuable for modern organizations. This is because the accelerating pace of change is increasing the frequency with which unexpected trends intersect.

The large-scale events that seemingly come out of nowhere to fell companies are rogue-like in their combination of power and unpredictability. A sea of six-footers is like the business landscape that many companies face every day. It's full of manageable challenges that can be addressed with a well-defined set of best practices. But when an upstart from a different industry with a new technology, like Craigslist or Google, comes along and crushes a 90-year-old company like YP, which publishes the Yellow Pages, in a couple of years, it's a challenge of an entirely different order.

Like rogue waves, the events that kill companies are often the result of several predictable trends that converge in unforeseen ways. For example, the window during which an innovation can be monetized is narrowing. This is changing the way businesses approach value creation. At the same time, some governments are constraining global competitors' access to technology and markets to protect their own industries. Rogue waves hit where these trends intersect, and a company like Google shelves its plans to reenter China, while Huawei, Xiaomi, and ZTE face the wrath of the US government.

Another similarity between oceangoing ships and businesses is that both are at increasing risk because of systemic changes in their surrounding environments. Climate change is increasing the severity of storms in areas that are already dense with shipping, leading to more frequent rogue waves. Climate change is one of many trends disrupting businesses—along with greater human mobility, and technologies that are changing the drivers of economic growth.

Consider that just 10 years ago China was a laggard in education and skilled labor, CRISPR gene editing was a research curiosity, and the whole planet's middle class amounted to about a billion people. Today we have gene-edited human embryos, and China's economy is larger than the United States' when measured by purchasing power parity.[7] If you look another 10 years into the future, the global middle class (earning the local equivalent of $35,000 per year or more) will have expanded by 2.1 billion people.[8] These changes challenge basic assumptions about the global order that have been in place since World War II.

A rogue wave is often a matter of perspective. What was a surprise for the fishermen was not a surprise for the fish. Fortunately, probabilistic analysis can help you to identify the threats and opportunities facing your business—much as it can help to manage fisheries. An explosion of what the tech industry calls "big data" is making our forecasting far more accurate and actionable. Satellite networks are monitoring the oceans. Mom-and-pop businesses are doing digital sentiment analysis of their customers. Massive sensor networks in factories are increasing their efficiency and flexibility. To take advantage of these technologies, you don't need to be a statistician, but you do need to know how probability works and how to work with it. The good news is that this isn't a math issue; it's a commonsense issue that even the most math incompetent, like myself, can master.

In a nutshell, probabilistic forecasting allows you to map the forest, even if you can only see the trees. Once you understand the bigger picture, you become like the fish in the previous analogy, who knew what the fishermen didn't. You don't need to be a data scientist or supercomputer programmer to take advantage of probability. I've made companies fortunes by doing most of what is described in this book on the back of a napkin.

Here are some examples of shocking events that wouldn't have been so shocking had leaders made back-of-the-napkin maps of the probabilities:

- The world was shocked when a tsunami inundated the Fukushima Daiichi nuclear reactor, but experts had long believed that an event of this sort was highly probable at one of the reactors that dot Japan's coast.[9]
- Recent AI "breakthroughs" that have caught businesses unprepared have been in development since the 1960s.[10]
- For years, epidemiologists have warned that China's wet markets, where wild game is sold for food,[11] or a lab outbreak could become ground zero of the next pandemic.[12]

THE FOUR FOES OF GROWTH

We talk a lot about risk in this book, so it's useful to have a simple taxonomy of the types of risk that are out there. Nearly all business risks can be sorted into one of four categories: financial, operational, external, and strategic. Browsing through the list in Figure 1.2, you can probably see the categories of risk that you touch.

Typically, senior managers are tasked with looking out for financial, external, and strategic risks—with good reason. In large organizations, these rogue risks accounted for major sustained losses in value (of over 20 percent) in 92 percent of occurrences over a 20-year period. (Figure 1.3).[13] Mid-level and junior managers are taught to focus myopically on operational risks, which are generally less threatening. This approach works well when you're sure you can see a wave building from the bridge. In a storm, waves come from all sides. You need to be aware of the whole system, which requires more than a pair of binoculars.

When change is rapid, what you really want is a risk radar. Everyone needs to be looking out at the ocean, providing you with a 360-degree view. Your junior people on the ground will often see

Figure 1.2 **The Four FOES of Growth**

F	O	E	S
Financial	**Operational**	**External**	**Strategic**
Financial Strategy	Efficiency	Input Costs	Demand Forecasts
Asset Losses	Costs	Political Shifts	Leadership Changes
Goodwill	IT Security	Government Regulation	Governance Priorities
Amortization	Accounting	Litigation	Pricing Issues
Liquidity	Capacity	Local Economics	Competition
Debt & Interest	Supply Chain	International Economics	Product Performance
	Fraud and Theft	Natural Disasters	Regulation
	Noncompliance	Pandemics	R&D
	Budgeting	Armed Conflict	Customer Satisfaction
	Financial Controls	Partner Losses	M&A Integration
	Supplier Availability	Credit Rating	Investor Guidance
	Workplace Safety	Industry Crisis	
	Systems Failures		

Figure 1.3 **Frequency of Catastrophic Risks by Category**

Financial	Operational	External	Strategic
17%	10%	37%	36%

an issue first, but not know what it means. You need to teach them what to look for and when to sound the Klaxon. What many leaders forget is that you also need to install mechanisms that ensure those warnings are heeded.

This matters for risk in general, but it matters much more when you're talking about rogue waves. We tend to think of them as edge cases, but as the world moves faster and becomes more connected, they impact us more often. Over the past century, external events of this magnitude—wars, financial crises, large natural disasters— affected large companies on average every seven years, from which it took several years to recover, if they ever did. Leaders of American organizations were responding to radical external change as much as 45 percent of the time.

While you can't prepare for every possible rogue wave, you can categorize them by the type of impact they will have on your customers, your competitors, and your vendors (Figure 1.4). This means that you can prepare to exploit entire categories, even if you don't know the precise wave that will hit.

Figure 1.4 **Rogue Wave Types**

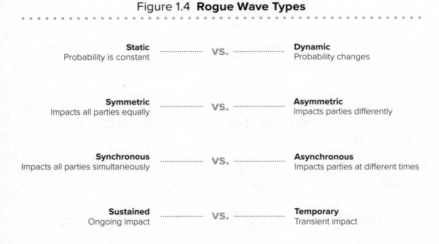

Static Probability is constant	vs.	**Dynamic** Probability changes
Symmetric Impacts all parties equally	vs.	**Asymmetric** Impacts parties differently
Synchronous Impacts all parties simultaneously	vs.	**Asynchronous** Impacts parties at different times
Sustained Ongoing impact	vs.	**Temporary** Transient impact

Rogue waves have one characteristic from each of these categories. For instance, Covid-19 was a dynamic, symmetrical, synchronous wave. In many ways, it was much like the impact of a world war on the European real estate market or the impact of a drought on almond growers in California's Central Valley. The probabilities change over time (dynamic), but they impact every company in the category (symmetric) within the same time frame (synchronous).

This is very different from a static, asymmetrical, asynchronous wave. For instance, thousands of focused cyberattacks occur each year (static). It could sink you but not touch your competitors (asymmetric). This happened to Mount Gox, the currency exchange that once managed 70 percent of global bitcoin trade. In 2014, they had to shut down days after it was discovered that a hacker had been syphoning off crypto for years (asynchronous).

Thinking through the impact of different rogue wave categories on the Four FOES is a great way to start building systemic intuition about the threats and opportunities they create. How would they impact you, and how could you create outsized value to others?

THE FUTURE IS NEITHER DETERMINISTIC NOR CHAOTIC

The idea that it's useful to forecast probabilities, even when we can't make specific predictions, should be self-evident. We have ever greater tools to make sense of systems that seem chaotic at first glance.

But medium and large companies and government agencies are typically run in heavily deterministic ways. Their forecasts are based on the extrapolation of current realities and outdated metrics. They make almost no acknowledgment of uncertainty beyond what has been experienced in the recent past, yet we know that rogue waves are becoming more and more likely.

A lot of this is just inertia, leftovers from the early days of modern companies, when change was relatively slow and knowledge of your inventory and customers was enough to keep you competitive. This is compounded by the demands of institutional shareholders who reassess their positions every few months. They are driven by quarterly results and are less impressed by portfolios of risk that can weather long-term uncertainty.

The result is that—while only a fool believes that the biggest wave he has seen is the biggest he'll see—fundamentally, large organizations incentivize an unhealthy discomfort with ambiguity. Their cultural identities are tied to their decisiveness. They like having a clear, single answer when the question is what's going to happen next.

Often, this preference is so strong that they'd rather be wrong than uncertain. Even more dangerously, they may answer the wrong questions because they rely on the data they have instead of considering the implications of the data they are missing. They often make decisions designed to reduce or prevent near-term uncertainties that ultimately leave the organization more vulnerable to volatility.

Recently, it has become fashionable to respond to uncertainty with cynicism. Many authors and pundits have effectively thrown up their hands, saying that if nothing can be predicted with complete certainty, why bother? Ideas like the butterfly effect (in which a tiny change in circumstances can have massive unanticipated consequences) and the black swan (unique, unpredictable events that swamp mitigation efforts) have led to a rash of pessimism: it's all chaos, so let's just do what we've always done and hope for the best.

The problem with this perspective is that it mistakes forecasting for certainty, massively discounting the value of knowing what's possible and what's likely.

One classic example that helps illustrate this is the assassination of Archduke Franz Ferdinand by a Slavic nationalist named Gavrilo Princip, the ostensible trigger of World War I. Many popular histories treat it as a black swan that set off a butterfly effect—a random event whose repercussions upended the entire world. But if the Great War was triggered by an unpredictable occurrence, the cascade of events that followed it was inevitable because of the conditions within the system in which they played out.

In his classic book *War By Time-Table*, A. J. P. Taylor recounts how the Archduke's chauffeur took a wrong turn, serendipitously delivering his passenger to the assassin. Here's how he tells it:

Potiorek called out: "Stop! You are going the wrong way." The driver stopped and began to back up into the quay. Princip was sitting in the cafe exactly at this corner. To his astonishment, he saw the Archduke immediately before him. He pulled out his revolver . . . [and] fired twice.[14]

If the driver hadn't erred, the Archduke would've stayed alive. But the war would not have been avoided; some other event would have set it off. If the Archduke's murder wasn't predictable, the breakdown of the political and power dynamics that had kept the European continent at peace for decades guaranteed that the peace would end. This is the knowable thing about systems. They break, and when they do, they unleash the forces they kept in check.

By 1914 it was already evident that a conflict between the United Kingdom and Germany was likely. English military leaders felt that the growth of German naval capabilities posed a direct threat and needed to be contained. This wouldn't be possible without coordination with France. Once the first shot was fired, the system of secret alliances, decades-old battle plans, and the logistical realities of war would necessarily drag the rest of Europe into the conflict. Blaming the assassination for the war that followed is a bit like blaming a forest fire on the discarded cigarette that ignited it, while ignoring the drought and mismanagement that made it inevitable.

As Edward Grey, Britain's secretary of state for foreign affairs, wrote, "There was little for me to do. Circumstances and events were compelling decision."[15]

Every management decision you make, every policy you install is based on a prediction of what will happen next. All policies will eventually fail because nothing stays static forever. This book isn't just about engineering yourself to benefit from or avoid a rogue wave. It's also about the more important lesson: how to build an organization that can patch its own hull when an oncoming wave inevitably cracks it.

In the next chapter, we'll take a closer look at the major trends that are reshaping our world, and their implications for you.

2

10 Undercurrents Will Cause the Next Rogue Wave

How many of your projects will fail or succeed due to radical change?

The daily stuff blinds us to the bigger trend.

—JUAN ENRIQUEZ

oday, the island of Ko Pha Ngan in the Gulf of Thailand is known for its world-famous Full Moon Parties, all-night raves, top DJs, fire dancers, shopping malls, and resorts. But 20 years ago, much of the island was still roadless, and the best beaches were only accessible by boat. I was working on the island with a real estate developer who wanted to speed its globalization along. We would hang out on Haad Rin beach, play guitar, and watch bioluminescent plankton glow as the moonlight hit the water. Sometimes a literal band of pirates operating off of the island would come and join us.

On the weekends, we would take a boat to the Sanctuary in Haad Tien cove, one of the few primitive backpacker resorts on the island. One day, as the sun was setting, a half-dozen of us were out in the water, bobbing up and down in the large, gentle waves. I closed my eyes and gave my body over to the sea.

When I finally looked up, everyone was gone. I started swimming to shore, but the harder I swam, the farther from land I was. Exhausted, I realized that the island's longtime residents knew something I didn't. Those large waves had been caused by constructive interference as the tide changed, pulling water from the beach back out to sea. The powerful riptide made it impossible for me to swim back to shore.

Eighty percent of lifeguard activity on beaches in the United States is due to riptides like the one that had captured me.[1] Thinking back to my own lifeguard training decades earlier, I recalled something counterintuitive: instead of swimming against a rip, the better strategy is to let it carry you farther out and then swim perpendicular to shore. After 500 feet, I was out of its grasp, and after floating for a few minutes to gather my strength, swam back to shore, landing just a short walk down from where I'd started. Exhausted, I went back to the boat to get an ice-cold beer.

Understanding what was going on underneath me literally spelled the difference between a beer on the beach at sunset and a tragic death at sea.

The Gulf of Thailand is a relatively calm body of water. For a more dramatic example of an undercurrent's power, let's look off the coast of South Africa. There, the waters of the Atlantic and Indian Oceans meet icy flows from the south to form the Agulhas Current (Figure 2.1), one of the most turbulent patches of water on earth. On a calm day, there's little to see on the ocean's surface, but down below, the waters transfer an enormous amount of energy, often forming eddies more than 500 miles in diameter.

Under the right circumstances, these eddies can push up against the continental shelf and form 100-foot-tall pyramids of water—rogue waves that the locals call Cape Rollers. These can appear from out of nowhere, even on sunny days. Though most of the action takes place underwater, the energy that feeds them starts on the surface.

Figure 2.1 **The Agulhas Current**

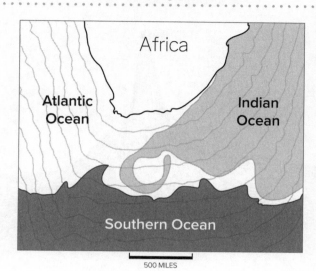

500 MILES

Often, they are caused by storms off the Antarctic coast, some 4,000 miles away. Most of the waves we experience at the beach or out on the ocean are driven by wind blowing consistently over long distances, known as the *fetch*. Wind adds energy to the system, while internal drag within the water depletes it, resulting in equilibrium. Even in stormy seas, these balanced forces place an upper limit on the size and power of waves. Cape Rollers are different. The wind energy combines with internal waves in currents deep below the surface. They amplify and reinforce one another (Figure 2.2). Much like in Nazaré, Portugal, the sea floor's topography focuses all of this energy. The result is a nonlinear wave that rises at a single point faster than gravity can pull it back down.[2]

This is why the area south of the Cape of Good Hope is one of the world's most dangerous places to sail. Nearly 3,000 ships have gone down in this patch of ocean, including the *Waratah* (aka "The Australian Titanic"), which sank without a trace, killing 211 people.[3]

Just as in the ocean, there are social, economic, and technological undercurrents that drive the movements of civilization. As the

Figure 2.2 **Simulated Rogue Wave**

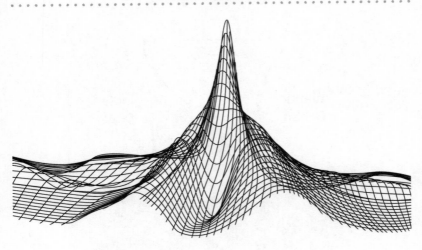

world becomes increasingly interconnected, those undercurrents get stronger, adding more and more energy into the system. New eddies form under the surface, just waiting for a storm to release their pent-up energy and shape it into the next rogue wave. Once-in-a-lifetime events are happening once a decade. And once-in-a-decade events are happening all the time, all over the world.

THE LOCAL IMPACT OF MACROTRENDS

We tend to think that what happens every decade, in fact, only happens every century, and, furthermore, that we know what's going on.

—NASSIM TALEB

When I started writing this book in 2019, I made a list of "moments in the future" that I had experienced that year. As I write these words, each of these trends has rippled from an oddity on the edge to a globally covered topic in the mass media. By the time you read this, they may be new ships riding in your sea lane. The point is that, no matter how fast you think the future is moving, it's moving faster.

- During a visit to Beijing's Tsinghua University in 2018, I made a casual joke to a Chinese colleague about drone technology. Sure, I said, autonomous drones are exciting, but when are we going to have one that can deliver a pizza?

  At first, he looked confused. Then a flash of recognition crossed his face. He told me that JD.com had been using autonomous vehicles to deliver goods to students for over a year.[4]

  I assumed it was some graduate student hack or a way of cutting labor costs. But no, he assured me, they were developing this technology because the labor simply wasn't available. In the world's most populous country and second largest economy, the demand for workers was so great that it was becoming impossible to fill once-common jobs like food delivery.

- At an energy company in India, an executive told me about their greatest challenge: the need to double their production capacity in the next few years. Never before in India's history had demand for electricity grown so rapidly.

  The reason? Air conditioning.[5] The Indian middle class is growing at a breakneck pace. And in the sweltering cities of the subcontinent, the first thing a family buys when they can afford it—before a car, computer, or flat screen TV—is an air conditioner.

- In Wisconsin, an ailing industrial town was gearing up for the arrival of a Chinese company that had recently decided to relocate some of its manufacturing. When I asked a Chinese executive what motivated the move, he explained that part of it was political and the need to put "Made in America" on its products. But the main reason was Wisconsin's abundant supply of skilled labor, which is increasingly hard to find in Shenzhen.

- In a small village in southwestern China that only got electricity a few years ago, a functionally illiterate woman named Wei Fu sells her traditional weaving online, using artificial intelligence to link her goods to likely buyers around the world. She's become so successful that she now runs a 25-woman cooperative.

Greater automation, the growing global middle class, and new technologies such as artificial intelligence are things we read about in articles. But they're also things that happen to real people in unexpected and often far-flung places. Unfortunately, it's very easy to ignore those macrotrends if we don't see specific and tangible examples of their impact.

For executives and managers, this often leads to skepticism about the value of following them at all. Sure, they might say, it's important to know what's happening with the climate, advances in AI, or growing energy demand in South Asia, but we need to focus on what's impacting the organization *now*, and what we can see happening in this quarter and the next.

A subset of the executives I talk with have a different take. The factors that will impact a business six months from now, they explain, are happening right now. As Jeff Bezos says, "Earnings this quarter were baked three years ago."[6]

A macrotrend is the sum of thousands of individual events, and some of those events can spell opportunity for a company—or ruin. A more connected, faster-moving market means that a local change can have global impacts within a few weeks, not a few months. As the saying goes, "There are decades where nothing happens, and there are weeks when decades happen." So any company dealing with an international market or supply chain, or that has vendors or clients who do—insert your organization here—should be paying attention to global macrotrends. The link between macro and micro is tighter than it's ever been.

Knowing which macrotrends to focus on can be difficult, though. As with the mixing waters of the Agulhas, huge amounts of energy are exchanged invisibly by these trends—and they don't seem like issues until they collide. As the world speeds up, these collisions will continue to become more frequent. This requires us to pay attention to the strongest macrotrends, even if they don't seem immediately relevant.

History doesn't repeat itself, but it does rhyme. So while last year's risk management techniques won't protect you from next year's challenges, they can provide insights into how they might evolve. It's also useful to examine how major economic, technological, and social undercurrents in past eras have changed the system in which they operate.

Things move far, far faster today, but the fifteenth century provides a slow-motion snapshot of the sea change that these undercurrents can bring.

The West began to transition from the Middle Ages to the modern era in the 1400s, giving birth to the Renaissance and the Age of Exploration, the fall of great empires (the Byzantine, the Golden Horde) and the rise of new ones (the Spanish and Ottoman). The undercurrents that influenced these outcomes were powerful and diverse. The Black Plague of the mid-1300s killed a third of Europe's population.[7]

The result was that power and wealth landed in new hands as local economies imploded. New patterns of growth needed to be invented. Labor shortages drove up wages, while demand for goods went down. As agriculture became more challenging, many farmers and small landholders moved to cities in the hope of improving their fortunes. This drove political upheavals, as new commercial centers like Florence and families like the Medici rose to power. Subsequent technological breakthroughs helped offset the high cost of labor, increasing the efficiency of trade but also consolidating wealth for the cities and merchants who benefited. Foreign trade imbalances and a century of military conflict collided with currency shortages caused by depleted silver and gold mines.[8]

At the beginning of the 1400s, the economy of Europe was effectively bankrupt; by the end, some of its nations were fabulously wealthy. The redistribution of wealth redefined the financial system, and a new globally connected civilization was beginning to coalesce.

There are echoes of those undercurrents in today's world, except now the globe is literally wired, and change is happening at the speed of the Internet. The onset of Covid-19, for example, brought about 10 years' worth of projected growth in online retail in the space of just three months.[9]

Being able to spot the next rogue wave before your competitor does requires three things:

1. Having at least a passing familiarity with today's major undercurrents
2. Paying special attention to events that cause two or more undercurrents to interact
3. Building awareness of those trends throughout your organization so that your entire team can scan the horizon for indicators of the next wave

There are hundreds of such trends, of course, but maintaining awareness requires focusing on the undercurrents that are most likely to drive change when they intermix. While it's not always possible, ideally, this means you have a project management office that coordinates this work across departments and specialties.

Figure 2.3 shows the 10 undercurrents that are most worth your attention.

ECONOMIC UNDERCURRENTS

Economics is the most human of the sciences, in that it studies what we value as a species—how we use our resources and the incentives that drive us to do so. As the field continues to become more quantitative, it gives us a window into where we can do better and where innovation can literally change the world.

Figure 2.3 **The 10 Undercurrents**

CURRENTS	UNDERCURRENTS	KEY ISSUES
Economic	Changing Demographics	Labor vs. Consumption
	The Data Economy	Value Creation vs. Value Extraction
	Automation	Labor Availability vs. Labor Cost
	The Rise of Asia	Market Access vs. Resource Availability
	Cheap Money	Growth vs. Profitability
Technological	Emerging Technologies	Efficiency vs. Social Impact
	The Closing Innovation Window	Faster R&D vs. Shorter Product Cycles
	Remixing and Convergence	Disruptive Innovation vs. Disruptive Integration
Social	Digital Trust	Public Goods vs. Private Goods
	New Social Contracts	Rights vs. Regulation

1. Changing Demographics

Demographics are the flywheel of the economy. They define the cost and availability of your most precious resources: your people and your customers. That's because consumer purchasing makes up more than half of the economy in many countries and 67 percent in the

United States.[10] In recent decades, the prime drivers of growth have been increased income due to global education and demand due to a growing population. This has been especially true in countries that possessed growing supplies of skilled labor. Consumers' influence on growth is changing.

Aging Populations

The average age of the population is rising in all of the 20 largest economies.[11] An aging population likely means lower interest rates,[12] slower growth,[13] and greater government debt.[14] In many countries, decreasing birth rates also mean significant shortages of college-educated workers.

In addition, while many older citizens no longer have steady incomes, a large fraction of them have significant assets, either in savings, property, or inheritance. This widens wealth gaps, on top of existing salary disparities between older and younger generations.[15]

Skilled Labor Shortage

As birth rates decline, especially in highly developed and educated countries, fewer young people enter the workforce, and the fraction of working-age people with advanced degrees falls. In California, for instance, by 2030, a one-million-person shortage of college graduates is projected.[16] The result is that, even in the age of tele-commuting, companies will need to place greater consideration on talent over tax advantages when making locational decisions.

By 2030, Korn Ferry projects that the only major country with a skilled worker surplus will be India—and its surplus will barely cover the projected shortfall in California alone.[17]

If borders are open or remote work options are viable, high-skilled labor will seek both onsite and remote work where demand is greatest. A disproportionate number of the workers and opportunities are likely to come from Asia. This suggests that Asian business culture will influence business norms throughout the world. The middle class that grows through this mobility will be globally aware. Their expectations for quality of life and business opportunities will be driven upward by exposure to established middle classes in Europe and the United States—but they will demand that their world revolves around them, instead of the West.

Accelerating Urbanization

Over the last few decades, and especially in recent years, the pace of urbanization has accelerated. More than half of the world's population now lives in cities (compared to just a third half a century ago), and the proportion is growing.

There are good economic reasons for this. Studies by Geoffrey West of the Santa Fe Institute suggest that every time a city doubles its population, its average income increases by 10 to 15 percent. The greater densities of larger cities tend to improve their efficiency, and their larger knowledge bases make them more innovative.[18]

The global economy will continue to pivot from agriculture and manufacturing to services and technology. Productivity and wealth growth will continue to pool around a relative handful of great cities. These cities will have more in common with each other than with the countries in which they are located. Globalization, to the extent it continues, will be city-to-city rather than country-to-country, as urban powerhouses like Singapore, Beijing, Mumbai, Tokyo, London, and New York increasingly look to each other for people, trade, and ideas.[19]

These cities will be constrained by the natural and human resources that are close by. For instance, Los Angeles has famously grappled for decades with its limited water supply.[20] Similarly, the Chinese government recently put an official growth cap on Beijing, citing limitations in the supply of water[21] and (perhaps surprisingly) unskilled labor.

What This Means for You

Perhaps more than anything, these shifts are changing the global distribution of wealth and growth. As global wealth grows, so will carbon emission, and the polluters won't just be energy companies. Transportation, heating, and cooling make up less than a quarter of current emissions. The growing challenges will include agriculture, which is responsible for 19 percent of emissions, and steel and concrete for construction.[22] To give a sense of scale, China uses as much concrete every two years as the United States did in the entire twentieth century.[23] This will only be amplified as the growing middle class in India, Southeast Asia, and Africa increase their consumption. As the global economy evolves, companies will need to consider the simultaneous impact of rising labor costs, changing consumer expectations, and new margin constraints, like regulation.

- **Investor demands:** As the investor class ages, the financial institutions that service them will increasingly seek near-term profit over long-term growth.
- **Government revenue:** Tax pressures on corporations will increase as larger, lower-income, older populations contribute less and cost more.
- **New service expectations:** Greater density, wealth, and age will continue to change expectations around product, convenience, and price.
- **Market shift:** The rise of South Asia as the center of growth and development will move it from a follower market to a leader market for innovative products and companies.
- **Multigenerational workforce:** Companies will face cultural challenges as they attempt to retain older workers while meeting the expectations of AI-native youth.
- **Political tensions:** The continued consolidation of wealth among educated city-dwellers will widen the schisms between rich and poor, old and young, urban and rural.

2. The Data Economy

As the world becomes increasingly connected, more data is generated about the interactions between machines, people, and their environments. In just the next 3 years, we'll produce more data than we did in the last 30.[24] "Big data" will yield incredible insights into every aspect of our lives as its patterns are discerned and parsed by high-speed computers.

This data explosion makes it possible to digitize real-world processes, and to track and manage them in real time. Having virtual models of nearly any good or service and digital twins of any factory or process lowers the cost of optimizing them to nearly zero. It also makes it faster and cheaper to explore alternate processes. This, in turn, accelerates new innovations and new solutions.

Data is poised to become the world's most valuable commodity. Maybe you've heard the phrase "data is the new oil," but this isn't quite right. Data's not a finite resource to be extracted and sold. It's something we generate every day, in growing quantities, and use in increasingly sophisticated ways. It also has qualities that are unlike other commodities. While the cost of oil might drop 20 percent on a bad day, it inevitably rebounds. In applications like high-frequency trading, the value of data can drop from billions of dollars to worthless in a fraction of a second.

Data is more like the new electricity—something that's constantly generated. Like electricity, it powers an incredible range of processes that make people more effective and more efficient. All of this is part and parcel of a larger global shift in business, away from goods (which are expensive to move across borders) and services (which are a bit easier to move) to data (which moves cheaply, unless constrained by regulation). An actionable market insight, a piece of software, a 3D printer file, or a technique for making a new polymer is often far more valuable than a shipment of physical goods. Anyone with an internet connection and the skills to produce useful data can participate in the global economy. If you want to buy some data—whether it's an article, a movie, a marketing list, or the genomic codes that are needed to produce cutting-edge pharmaceuticals—it hardly matters where on earth it's coming from.

Value Creation Versus Value Extraction

One feature of digital business models is that they often increase efficiency faster than they create new financial value. Data can increase asset utilization without growing the profit pool.

Increasingly, data and consumers are being aggregated in marketplaces, whether those are retailers like JD.com or Amazon, or peer-to-peer networks like Uber or Airbnb, or a marketplace for your DNA code like Nebula Genomics.[25] These businesses have highly monopolistic characteristics, so it's important to understand how and for whom they deliver value.

Uber is an example of a company that, while often maligned, has unlocked transportation capacity while increasing total worker wages and tax revenues. Conversely, a data broker like Airbnb works with a very constrained resource—housing—that was already heavily utilized. While it offers a useful service, it hasn't substantially increased tourism or spurred replacement of the low-cost apartments it takes off the housing market. Overall, Airbnb has extracted far more value from the market than it's created. Much of it has been transferred from hotels that governments depended on for tax revenue.

What This Means for You

As companies digitally transform, they'll need to be clear about who they create value for versus the who they extract value from. This balance will define which initiatives are profitable in the long run. It will also be central to the relationship that companies have with governments. Digital business models that are able to generate better services while increasing tax revenue will thrive. Businesses that don't will find themselves edged out by local competitors and hampered by regulation.

- **Increased utilization:** New opportunities will arise for using data to extract value.
- **Co–option of resources:** Businesses will need to find new ways to co-opt resources using data and to protect resources from being co-opted.
- **Data protection:** The explosion in the production and movement of confidential information will lead to growing data theft and demands for greater data protection.
- **Government policy:** Uncoordinated government policies will regulate data trade to protect consumers and domestic companies and to maximize tax revenue. The lack of harmonization will also create new burdens for foreign organizations.

3. Automation

For all the hysteria about AI and automation threatening jobs, its impact isn't likely to be as catastrophic as feared. A recent PwC report estimates that roughly 5 percent of global jobs are currently at risk from automation, rising to around 30 percent by the mid-2030s.[26] Most will be jobs that primarily consist of repetitive tasks, especially in areas like construction, manufacturing, and transportation. While many of those jobs could be replaced by automation, it's actually unlikely that they will be, either because the cost of automating them is too high, or the tasks performed are too diverse. For example, self-driving trucks may become the norm on long-haul routes someday, but it will take much more than a new vehicle to fully replace the activities of a delivery person in a city. Entirely new systems would need to be developed to unload items from the truck, stock shelves, protect cargo, and maintain relationships with shopkeepers.

Beyond safety and public relations concerns, there are also significant economic hurdles to clear when introducing automation. Robots are expensive, presenting a significant up-front cost. Programming, reprogramming, and field maintenance are even more expensive. While robots and AI can increasingly be trained on the job, they are often more difficult to repurpose than people. Unless this is resolved, it will limit adoption.

The best use of automation, now and in the near future, is to make human workers more efficient. This is particularly true for high-skilled workers: people with at least a bachelor's degree or equivalent. On average, the cost of this labor is projected to rise by 16 percent over the next decade. In some countries, like Singapore, the costs are projected to grow by 27 percent on top of cost-of-living increases.[27] Worker productivity will need to increase dramatically to offset these costs.

In chess, we've long known that a "centaur"—a skilled human player working with computer assistance—can reliably beat just about any non-centaur opponent, whether man or machine.[28] Something similar happens on the factory floor or the open highway. Combine the flexibility and perception of a human with the precision and speed of a machine, and the benefits are often greater than automating completely.

The most likely scenarios will bring increasing numbers of digital assistants into the workplace to collaborate with expensive high-skilled workers. Automation will reshape the job market dramatically, but not primarily through cost reduction. Its most significant benefit will come from improving quality and consistency.

What This Means for You

As companies digitally transform, they'll need to look at labor availability versus labor cost. Straightforward economic decisions about location, outsourcing, and offshoring become more complex when you add new variables. For instance, the changing cost of labor and the availability of skills to take advantage of automation.

- **Linking IT and location strategy:** Companies will need to consider location strategy and technology to take maximum advantage of high-skilled labor.
- **Tax incentives:** Companies will need to consider long-term labor costs and skills availability against tax incentives.
- **Linking HR and IT strategy:** Companies will need to calculate both labor cost and availability against automation priorities.

4. The Rise of Asia

The system of international trade and political power that has existed since the early twentieth century is now dead.[29] In this old system, "global trade" meant transactions between a handful of economies, mostly in Europe and North America, joined more recently by Japan and industrializing Asia. It assumed a sharp divide between the developed and developing world, with the former possessing nearly all the capital and political power, and the latter a source of resources and the game board on which the great powers vied for influence.

While many Americans and Europeans have not yet noticed, reality has changed. In 2019, 121 companies in the Global Fortune 500 were from the United States and 129 from China, including 10 from Taiwan.[30] Not only has China's rise redrawn the map of global competition, it has also brought about a dramatic expansion of wealth among Chinese citizens and across Asia as a whole. While the typical income in India and in Southeast Asia still lags behind that in China, it is catching up quickly. By 2035, 2.1 billion new people will be earning the local equivalent of $35,000 per year,[31] and 87 percent of the growth will be in Asia, based on pre-Covid models.[32]

Wealth, production, and power are reorganizing—not just in Asia, but all over the planet. Trade among a few countries is becoming trade among dozens of countries. This is driving geopolitical tensions around the distribution of power and resources.

A doubling middle class doesn't double resource consumption; it causes a step change. An American lifestyle requires 32 times the resource consumption of an impoverished person in a rural, developing economy.[33] As the world gets more affluent, more consumers will purchase more cars and air conditioners. They will fly, eat more meat, use more devices, and demand more services. All of this will drive a massive increase in demand for water, energy, agricultural land, and data.[34]

China and India are already skirmishing over the headwaters of the Himalayas, and India is holding naval exercises in the South China Sea. The Chinese government is reshaping policies in Southeast Asia through commerce, while investing in regional infrastructure and exerting control over water resources.[35] The growing Chinese naval presence across the Gulf of Thailand, South China Sea, and Indian Ocean[36] is shifting the balance of power with the United States.

The positive and negative impacts of these trends are enormous. The global rise out of poverty is perhaps the great accomplishment of human history. On the flip side, countries with significant ethnic divides often experience unequal growth. This stokes tensions. For instance, India is home to some 172 million Muslims.[37] That's half the population of the United States. If they do not see the same gains as the Hindu majority, strife is likely to worsen.

What This Means for You

The world will be challenged as a rising middle class demands far greater resource access. The opportunity will be driven as much by demographics as by the growth of business in Asia. These new companies will serve their local customers, but also seek global expansion, creating new sources of competition.

Multinational corporations will likely face growing pro-tectionism as governments try to defend their markets, resources, and the spoils of growth for their people. To do so, they will redraw many of the trade and security agreements that Westerners have taken for granted since World War II.

- **Resource competition:** Companies will need to ramp up their government relations as they protect their supply chains and avoid getting pulled into geopolitical brinksmanship.
- **Asia–first products:** Companies will need to see the Asian market as both an opportunity and a threat. It has new cus-tomers, but also regional competitors with global ambitions.
- **Asian business cultures:** Foreign companies will need to take on local business customs to attract talent who can work for equivalent local companies.
- **Local government cooperation:** Maintaining strong regional government relations will become increasingly important to sustained local access.
- **Home country government relations:** Organizations will need to be more proactive in educating their govern-ments about how trade tensions may impact them.
- **Local labor:** Historically low-cost labor markets will require a rethink as they become innovation exporters and major consumer markets.

5. Cheap Money

We are moving into a world of slowing structural growth, increasing government and private debt. These interacting forces will drive a trend toward low-cost money.

A Rise in Stimulative Spending

In countries with aging populations, slowing non-healthcare consumption will be a drag on economic growth.[38] Legislators and central bankers will use loose monetary and fiscal policy to stimulate growth and offset revenue shortfalls caused by the increasing needs of aging citizens and a smaller working population. This creates a feedback loop in which governments, particularly those without reserve currencies, must keep interest rates low in order to manage their growing debt burdens. Many—most recently Venezuela and Turkey—are failing to walk the tightrope between debt service and growth. Currency crises are the inevitable result.

Higher Savings Rates

Beyond the government-driven explosion of money printing,[39] aging populations will be moving their assets into investments that produce steady retirement income, further lowering interest rates.[40]

Rapid Automation

Excess productive capacity is deflationary.[41] As automation takes hold over the next decade, the ability to be more productive, to deliver higher quality, often at lower cost, will put checks on inflation.[42] This may make it harder for central banks to tighten up lending by raising interest rates.

Private Currencies, Securities, and Digital Money

An explosion of private digital currencies like Tenpay and Alipay, the mobile payment services of the internet giants Tencent and Alibaba, are rapidly changing the global financial landscape. Chinese consumers prefer to do transactions via services like these, instead of with cash or credit or debit cards issued by banks.[43] In the face of Covid-19, zombie airlines have been attempting to securitize their frequent flier miles.[44] These private means of exchange are moving the control of money further away from central banks and nation states. Though governments are doing their best to slow down the future with regulations, the dikes likely won't hold. Over the next decade, they'll need to either collaborate with or deliver low-friction alternatives to the upstarts. The Chinese government's digital Yuan is the first example.[45] If it is successful, it could rapidly erode American power by moving international trade away from the dollar and US banking standards. However this plays out, the powerful financiers who have spent a century defining global monetary policy are likely to find themselves competing with a whole new set of players who suddenly have a seat at the table.

Together, these trends create a structural tendency toward low interest rates for a long time to come.

What This Means for You

The worldwide focus on growth over profitability will continue to put performance-driven organizations at a disadvantage. It will also impact the growing pantheon of unicorn companies who don't get to profitability fast enough and see their investors flit to the next overvalued company. What once looked like a bubble is becoming the norm. A once tightly managed financial market will become a three-ring circus as Chinese, EU, and US regulators vie for control.

- **More inorganic growth:** Aging investor demographics will shift board priorities toward profitability earlier in corporate life cycles. In a world of cheap money, this means more M&A activity.
- **Joint ventures:** Corporate debt load and geopolitics will encourage an increase in co-investments.
- **Currency crises:** Debt-driven regional currency crises will continue to pop up as countries have trouble balancing foreign trade, debt, and growth.
- **Startups at scale:** Startups will continue to develop and scale, particularly those that deliver low-cost platforms that compete with existing infrastructure.

- **Radical outsourcing:** More "as a service" business models will allow debt-laden organizations to outsource expenditures on capital assets.
- **Aggressive taxation:** Populism, combined with the rising cost of social welfare, will encourage more aggressive corporate tax policies, especially in slow-growth countries.
- **Margin pressures:** Larger organizations, particularly sellers of critical products and services, will face growing pressure to decrease pricing while simultaneously paying higher taxes.

TECHNOLOGICAL UNDERCURRENTS

The fifteenth century was full of overlapping innovations. Between its invention in 1440 and the end of the century, printing presses, like the Gutenberg, rolled off over 5 million manuscripts, distributing new discoveries and newly recovered ancient wisdom.[46] New printing technologies also resulted in a proliferation of new maps across Europe.[47] The caravel, a revolutionary lateen-sailed ship that could tack against the wind, drove the Portuguese exploration of Africa and its eventual claim to the route from Europe, around the Cape of Good Hope, to India. Better marine technologies, such as improved compasses and astrolabes, made it possible for them to navigate more accurately and record their routes in repeatable fashion. In response, the Spanish were forced to attempt to find an unlikely western route to Asia, sending dozens of ships into the Atlantic, where they famously stumbled across the "New" World. At the same time, the dual ledger accounting system made long-distance direct trade easier and allowed for more complex financial arrangements.

None of these technologies on their own would have driven the reinvigoration of Europe, but as they integrated into new business models, they defined the world for the next three centuries. Their overlap increased the rate of knowledge production and the number of trading partners within Europe and around the globe.

Today, we may be on the verge of a similar reordering of human affairs. The role of technology is growing more quickly, but like the telegraph and the radio, the telephone and the internet, these new inventions will require both new infrastructure and tight integration before they can achieve their full potential. Much as in the fifteenth century, the outcomes will depend on how well governments and businesses are able to coordinate their efforts and agree on standards.

6. Emerging Technologies

Of the dozens of fascinating technologies making their way into the mainstream, four are worth special attention: connected devices (IoT), artificial intelligence (AI), distributed ledgers (blockchain), and next generation wireless networks (5G and satellite).

All four are buzzwords right now, but their names will likely change before they hit scale. And it's unlikely that any one of them will change the world on its own. But together, they comprise the technological foundation that will drive growth in any field you can think of, not just traditionally high-tech ones.

The internet has digitized and streamlined much of the physical world over the past decade. These technologies will accelerate the trend by automating tasks and transactions, providing real-time information, and making sense of it. Businesses that could not be digitized or automated during the first internet age will succumb to the second. Organizations structured to take full advantage of these technologies will experience leaps in efficiency. Those that don't will founder.

Connected Devices (IoT)

Connected devices reduce friction by automating tracking and sensing tasks, giving accurate location, status, and identity information, and storing data locally at very low cost. Better contextual information is making manufacturing and delivery far more flexible and efficient. When combined with a distributed ledger system and embedded artificial intelligence, these devices make it possible for systems to coordinate tasks dynamically, without human intervention.

Artificial Intelligence (AI)

AI isn't what we see in the movies. It's simply a suite of statistical methods that computers use to assess large data sets. You can actually do many of the tasks that AI does yourself in Excel, if you have enough time. Unlike traditional computing, which relies on a series of yes/no answers to come to an absolute conclusion, most AI calculates likelihoods.

AI is already widespread in a variety of forms, powering recommendation engines, searches, fraud detection, medical diagnosis, self-driving cars, and hundreds of other applications that depend on advanced pattern-spotting capabilities. In most of these cases, AI enhances human cognition by adding diligence and precision, as well as the capacity to analyze enormous data sets quickly.

More than any other technology, AI has the ability to dramatically increase human productivity, since so much high-value work depends on the type of analysis it can perform. When paired with IoT, its potential is vast, from optimizing traffic and distribution networks, to spotting epidemics before they happen, to radically increasing the efficiency of factories.

Distributed Ledgers (Blockchain)

A distributed ledger is a database that makes it possible to log transaction records reliably and without the need for constant access to a central controlling entity. Cryptocurrency (think Bitcoin) is its most famous use case at the moment, but long-term applications for blockchain-like technologies reach much further. Personal identity, corporate bookkeeping, and even contracts could be tracked, verified, and stored without a central authority, eliminating huge amounts of clerical and security overhead. When combined with AI, blockchain enables the creation of tailor-made "smart contracts." Teams can be created, data can be shared, and commerce can be securely conducted with complete strangers, almost instantly and at trivial cost.

For connected IoT devices to act autonomously, they'll need to be able to make decisions and trade data in places where connectivity is spotty or where the cost of transmitting all of the data is too high. To act autonomously, they'll need to be able to keep a distributed ledger of their interactions.

Next Generation Wireless Networks (5G and Satellite)

5G promises orders of magnitude speed improvements over older tech. But more importantly, it offers far greater efficiency. A 4G tower can support about 4,000 devices per square kilometer, whereas 5G supports around one million, and uses one-tenth the energy.[48]

5G's near-term impact is overhyped, however. The new infrastructure needed to realize these gains at scale will take years to install, largely because of the price tag (as much as $500 billion to cover the entire United States).[49] Instead, the real near-term impact of 5G is likely to be local: within factories, hospitals, office buildings, and commercial environments. Think of 5G as an enabling technology that amplifies the impact of other technologies (especially IoT) by speeding communication between devices.

Perhaps the more important technology breakthrough, if it works, is satellite internet, which will bring broadband communications to the oceans, deserts, and rural lands that have been denied low-cost access to the internet revolution.

Other Technologies to Watch

At least two other foundational technologies are likely to evolve significantly over the next decade, but their path to productization before 2030 is less clear. They are still worth tracking because if they commercialize faster than expected, they have the potential to change the way we think about economics.

Quantum technologies: Much is being made of quantum computing, which may or may not scale in this decade. If it does, it could radically accelerate information technology, allowing far faster and potentially more efficient computation. But it is one of those ideas that has been supposed to happen in the next decade for decades. Other quantum technologies, related to far more precise sensing and security, are advancing as well. The former may radically accelerate the rate of data production and breakthroughs. The latter may be ready to move into the industrial pipeline in the next several years, solving security issues that would otherwise slow the rollout of new technology.[50]

New energy: Perhaps the most important technology breakthrough of the first half of the twenty-first century will be fusion reactors and small modular fission reactors (SMRs). At the end of the day, much of the cost of producing any good or service is the cost of the energy that is embedded into it.

For instance, the device or book you're reading combines resources that were extracted from the earth, refined, and organized into a specific shape. Beyond that, you and your teachers likely commuted every day for years to a school where you learned to read. This all required a massive amount of carbon-emitting energy to build the machines to do the work and the facilities to make this happen.

But if a globally scalable, low-cost clean energy source becomes available, it will transform how we think about work and the value of goods. Physicists generally agree that nuclear technologies, not solar and wind, are the best long-term candidates to upend energy economics.[51] While practical fusion may be proven this decade, it probably won't scale within it. When it does, it has the potential to shatter many of the limitations of energy economics. For instance, critical climate engineering technologies, like water desalination and carbon sequestration, which aren't economical today may become far more feasible.

What This Means for You

Together, these technologies will improve quality of life around the world while improving resource efficiency. We may even see living standards go up as resource consumption goes down, even in the face of slowing growth. On the flip side, these technologies will have massive social impact as they expand the ability of organizations and governments to surveil, control, and manipulate people. This will demand dramatically different social contracts (discussed in undercurrents 9 and 10).

- **Increased IT budgets:** As these new capabilities become table stakes, technology investment will grow.
- **Closer partnerships with IT consultants:** The increasing complexity of IT systems will require greater reliance on specialist vendors.
- **Tighter linking of IT and other business functions:** IT will play a growing role in organizational strategy, as the ability to analyze metadata about company activities becomes more vital to performance.
- **Devolved control through the organization:** The ability to provide closer to real-time 360-degree awareness allows more strategic decisions to be made lower in the organization.

7. The Closing Innovation Window

Global economic expansion has been driven by a combination of population growth and relentless innovation over the past 250 years, first in agriculture, energy, and manufacturing, and then in communications and information technology. If you had a genuinely useful, innovative idea, you could patent it, build a company around it, and prosper for years, even decades, before your competitors caught up.

Today, for many industries, that "years or decades" has shrunk to weeks or months. The innovation window—the time between when a new idea becomes viable and when it gets disrupted by a cheaper, better, faster competitor—is closing.[52] This is inevitable in a globalized economy in which competitors can see what everyone is doing in real time and approach each other's customers directly. It's easier than ever for an agile fast follower to piggyback on someone else's innovation.

What's new is the rate at which the last century's innovation importers are becoming this century's innovators.[53] While patent production has remained about even since 2010, the proportion that comes from emerging economies is growing.

China, in particular, is worth watching. While many of its patents are for domestic use only, its high-quality triadic patents (those that are protectable under all three major global patent systems) sextupled between 2007 and 2017.[54] Chinese triadic patent production is already in line with Germany's. If the trend continues, China could be producing twice as many as the United States by 2030. Citations of Chinese academic papers in the World Science Database have been growing steadily as well,[55] further suggesting that the center of gravity of global innovation is shifting toward China.

Perhaps more importantly, the global production of science, technology, and engineering PhDs has increased 58 percent since 2000. China is churning out domestic PhDs almost as rapidly as the United States.[56] The quality of Chinese research citations has been going up at a steady clip as well.[57]

India, with its massive youth population and growing IT sector, is likely to follow.[58] If China's Alibaba, JD.com, ByteDance, Baidu, iFLYTEK, and Tencent were the first serious competitors to US software dominance, India's Reliance Jio and Indonesia's Gojek are showing that the rest of Asia is gearing up its knowledge industry, too.

What This Means for You

More innovation from more places means faster product cycles. This reduces the time that companies can extract rents from it. Once a profit engine, innovation is becoming a table stake.

For larger companies, this means restructuring to accommodate new processes and business models to compete with upstarts that scale faster. To stay ahead of the curve, companies will need to increase their intelligence and investment efforts, not just in their markets, but in other industries around the world.

- **Structural innovation:** Given shorter product cycles, sustained differentiation will come from innovation of *processes* and *business models*. When linked to *product* innovation, they are more defensible than any of the three on its own.
- **More R&D at lower cost:** Companies will continue to be more dependent on contract R&D and licensing. They'll also need to invest more in internal process innovation.
- **Deep innovation:** The organizations that use internal R&D as a strategic pillar will need to focus on longer-term, higher-risk, and difficult-to-duplicate investments.
- **Local R&D centers:** The combination of more demanding global customers and geo-dispersed innovation will require greater investment in satellite R&D, venture, and market research.

8. Remixing and Convergence

Though the pace of technological change may feel overwhelming, there have actually been far fewer profound innovations recently than there were 50 or 100 years ago. The internal combustion engine, electricity distribution, powered flight, synthetic fertilizer, the transistor, and the silicon chip reshaped the world just by their introduction. No single innovation has had a comparable impact in the last few decades.[59]

Instead, existing technologies are being incrementally improved and then combined and optimized. Information technology innovations, for instance, are powering simultaneous breakthroughs in manufacturing, biotech, and business processes. They aren't due to an individual breakthrough. They are the result of suites of technology being integrated into a larger ecosystem.[60]

Bioconvergence

Biology research is still largely conducted by armies of pipette-wielding graduate students in basement labs. But as sensors get cheaper, it becomes cost-effective to make them extremely task-specific, and sensitive enough to offer reliable experimental data at scale. Robotic control is becoming more precise, to the point where microfluidic devices can drop an individual cell into an assay—something even the most meticulous grad student can't do.

AI-driven analysis also has a lot to offer the field. Major breakthroughs still require human insight, but machine learning lets us plow through mountains of data, making those insights easier to derive, with less drudgery.

Automated experiments already allow agriculture companies to create hundreds of variants of new crop strains simultaneously, and then rapidly test them for features like pest resistance or yield. This empowers small teams of researchers to compress what might have been a decades-long breeding process into a single season.

In the pharmaceutical industry, the combination of AI and blockchain is streamlining new drug discoveries. Researchers can focus their investigations by analyzing data sets from past trials to spot promising compound interactions and potential hazards. This is much more time-effective than the old "pipette and pray" approach.

Improving the efficiency of biological research also makes it possible to expand its reach into unlikely places. The field of biomimetic design—using unique features and processes from living things to improve manufactured goods—has been around for years, but mostly as a curiosity. The difficulty has always been that evolution is slow, and it's hard to replicate its genius in the lab.

But with the rapid, massively parallel research techniques described above, biomimetics is starting to yield real benefits. We already have anti-graffiti paint inspired by the microscopic structure of lotus leaves,[61] but now we're developing stuff that comes straight out of sci-fi. DNA extracted from spiders is being used to spin thread that's stronger for its weight than steel cable. Neural cells are being used to detect bombs.[62] Microbes are being modified to consume toxic waste; biologists are even experimenting with artificial bugs that can do the same.

Next Generation Manufacturing

Robotic assembly and computer numeric control (CNC) machining have been improving the capabilities of factories and lowering their costs for decades. The newer a factory is, the more automated it's likely to be, and this has steadily lifted productivity across categories.

As 3D printing and related methods become cheaper and more powerful, customized parts and products will become more accessible to a wide range of industries. Nike can already custom-build Flyknit shoes in thousands of unique sizes and color patterns, essentially replacing an entire factory with a single machine.[63] What happens when a single machine can print a motor, a transmission, or a steering wheel? Or even all three in rapid succession?

AI is uniquely suited to processing the information produced by an IoT sensor–laden factory, and making small adjustments that improve efficiency. In "digital twinning," an entire process—like a factory, organization, or distribution system—is digitally modeled at high precision. This allows humans working with AI assistants to explore alternative processes quickly and cheaply. A digital twin can take real-time sensor data as input, and then simulate the elements that are being modified. In effect, data from the real world can be experimented on within a video game. A process developed this way can be implemented quickly and with minimal interruption, yielding more predictable results than real-world tinkering.

Beyond Human

Just as IoT, AI, and blockchain are working to push computing to the edges of the commercial network, they're also pushing it to the edge of the human network. This means computing on and even within the human body.

Consider how people with type 1 diabetes manage their disease. In the 1950s and 1960s, a patient might have had to make regular visits to a clinic for sugar monitoring and insulin injections. By the 1970s, she could self-administer both. Then came digital meters that completed blood sugar tests in just a few seconds, so they could be taken multiple times a day. Today's state of the art is an integrated meter and insulin pump, continuously monitoring blood sugar and administering insulin to maintain ideal levels with little conscious input from the user.[64]

This approach to human–computer interaction has broader applications. Any health, wellness, or performance goal that involves measurement and feedback can be made less intrusive and more effective by integrating it more closely with the body. A cheap, safe, smart blood meter could monitor metabolic rates, helping athletes optimize their training and diet, or guiding people as they try to lose weight. There's hardly any aspect of human wellness that couldn't benefit from direct monitoring, from minimizing stress to improving sleep to reducing cholesterol.

The digital world is merging with our minds as well as our bodies, bringing the promise of truly effective cognitive augmentation. This includes voice assistants that offload mental tasks, AR glasses, and electronics that "read" our thoughts.[65] We already have social networks that track the interests of projects across a company and feedback devices that help us focus on the right things. While many of these projects are still in the laboratory stage, they are rapidly becoming commercial realities and starting to integrate into useful systems.

As companies seek to optimize productivity in the face of shrinking workforces and rising competition, being able to track and improve employees' focus and well-being offers a genuine competitive advantage. In undercurrents 9 and 10, we'll discuss the inevitable ethical and legal considerations.

Frictionless Business

Using technology to make business processes more efficient is the convergence trend with the broadest application. Reducing paperwork and improving bandwidth might not sound as revolutionary as robots doing biotech research, but it could ultimately be far more important. High-skilled workers are the biggest fixed cost for many businesses, and this trend makes them far more efficient.

Today, when employees return from a business trip, they might spend hours reviewing receipts and preparing expense reports. Now imagine a machine learning algorithm, trained on thousands of business trips, that can monitor the employees' spending while they travel. By comparing it with an established model, the algorithm could flag any unexpected expenditures and automatically approve the rest. This leaves the manager with just an occasional anomaly to review, and it allows employees' expense checks to be direct-deposited before their return flights touch down. Extend this example to the thousands of other mundane tasks that eat up half of any knowledge worker's day—resource requests, time sheets, scheduling, sales sheets, and so on—and the efficiency gains add up quickly.

In the longer term, these more flexible controls can empower frontline workers to take more risks and make more autonomous decisions. The line-and-staff model of management, which dates to nineteenth-century railroads and factories, relies on armies of middle managers to direct employees, in an expensive but necessary process of meetings, memos, and more meetings.

Much of the middle manager's role, though, is straightforward logistics: assigning tasks, disseminating information, approving requests, processing paperwork. Today's artificial intelligence is already sophisticated enough to handle much of this. In the near future, it will also offer decision support, helping employees test ideas through simulation, spotting potential problems, and offering the kinds of insights that currently require whole departments of data analysts.

This doesn't spell the end of middle management, but it does shrink its job description. There will be fewer managers in tomorrow's organizations, overseeing larger groups of people, and acting more as specialist problem-solvers than constant hand-holders. A streamlined management structure, coupled with better data filtering and visibility, also means that crucial information can travel much more rapidly from the front line to the executive level.

What This Means for You

This remixing and convergence of technology, biology, psychology, and business represents a great opportunity for us as a civilization—it allows us to reinvent ourselves faster than the changes that pursue us. As foundational innovation slows, faster integration can make our economy more efficient in the face of resource and demographic challenges.

- **Investment timing:** In a world where smooth integration is critical to success, engaging with technology too early or too late can change your organization's fate.
- **Moving from capital expenditures to operational expenditures:** In a debt-laden, performance-focused environment, companies and consumers will turn to pay-as-you-go services that update frequently, rather than owning assets that could be underutilized or quickly become obsolete.
- **Labor productivity:** Companies will need to balance employee well-being with productivity, often looking to technology to solve the dilemma.

- **New products:** Many more products and services will rely on collaboration in larger platform ecosystems and markets to survive.
- **Labor reskilling:** Organizations will need to increase the time and effort that goes into improving decision-making and analysis skills—like the ones covered in this book—so that employees can take advantage of frictionless technologies.
- **Agility:** Production-oriented companies will need to rethink their processes to become more agile and deliver continuously.

SOCIAL UNDERCURRENTS

In the fifteenth century, a succession of cash-poor popes went out, hats in hand, to secure the funds and the armies they needed to protect their interests. In return, they granted favors, such as trade rights and pronouncements on who would control the New World. A changing economic and technological environment spawned large regional governments, with strong national identities to match, and shifted the center of power to the Iberian Peninsula. Portugal took control of trade with Africa and India, importing gold and slaves, while Spain began trading westward.

All of these changes happened simultaneously, causing radically new relationships between business, the elites, and the masses. The merchant class began its rise, as the Renaissance diffused through-out Europe and the persecution of religious groups increased.

We can see similar eddies forming today, as economics and technology shift the global political landscape. In the process, they'll challenge a century of assumptions about the distribution of power, rights, and wealth.

9. Digital Trust

Digital tracking has already reinvented sports and fitness, and it has begun to raise worker productivity as well. In addition to tracking email and locations, we can now capture more intimate data, like facial expressions, heart rates, and blood sugar, leading to some incredible possibilities. Imagine if your office computer told you to take a break and go home because you won't be able to focus anymore today? It could potentially improve your quality of life at no cost to your company.

But this also brings enormous ethical and legal challenges. The laws governing data privacy are fractured and inconsistent. It's nearly impossible to fully comply with both the EU's General Data Protection Regulation (GDPR) and US Cloud regulations, and 21 US states are considering (or have already passed) their own data privacy laws, which will inevitably conflict.[66] The challenge becomes even greater if companies are unable to both comply with the law and generate maximum social benefit.

Regulation can also be used as a political or economic cudgel. The restrictions on TikTok and Huawei are recent US examples of using or threatening the use of regulation to shape the data economy. So is the EU's protectionist GDPR and the growing political pressure on companies like Facebook, Twitter, and Parler to restrict free speech in the aftermath of the storming of the US Capitol on January 6, 2021.

As data becomes more valuable and useful, it's increasingly urgent to figure out what is a public good and what is a private good; in other words, which data is "yours" and which is "ours." What if your personal genetic information is vital to saving other people's lives? And what if that information is linked to your identity? Is using it a violation? When should you be compensated for its use?

What This Means for You

The public discussion about data value and ownership will only grow, and different regions will develop different standards about who owns it. Leaders will need to structure products, organizations, and technology to be flexible in the face of shifting regulation.

- **Managing for changing regulations:** Companies will need a dedicated department to manage compliance, and invest in educating legislators on these issues.
- **Locating R&D based on privacy laws:** Data-driven innovation will want to move to regions with lower liability for misuse of personal data. At the same time, countries will use export controls to slow the drain of intellectual property.
- **Customized targeting to grow profitability:** Complex predictive models of individual behavior will be used to target and customize products. But each market will have different rules about what data can be used to do so.
- **After-the-fact changes in data rights:** Changing privacy laws will result in liability for data usage, long after it has been incorporated into projects and products.
- **Employee monitoring:** Local laws about employee privacy will limit the ability to improve the efficiency of internationally distributed teams.

10. New Social Contracts

Companies and governments will need to rethink their relationships with individuals and with each other as debt, productivity, and inequality increase. This will prompt deep shifts in what we expect from social contracts. We can already see this happening in movements that resulted in the assault on the US Capitol, Brexit,

Black Lives Matter, and Hong Kong's Umbrella Movement. In each case, populations left behind by globalization are making their voices heard.

As elites invest in new technologies and business models, they'll also consolidate wealth and resources. The wider and more pervasive the inequalities, the more likely a backlash becomes.

Governments will be forced to change the way they deliver social services, especially as populations age and expectations rise. If technology fails to significantly decrease the cost of services and administration, governments in developed economies like the United States will be forced to find new sources of revenue or further weaken their social safety nets.

For decades, tech companies and governments have been growing apart in the West. As geostrategic tensions ratchet up, governments will discover that they no longer have the technology prowess or the budgets to build their own tools. The result for tech companies will be growing pressure to support the security interests of governments in areas like surveillance, propaganda, military robotics, space weapons, and bio- and cybersecurity.

What This Means for You

The balance between who benefits and who pays will shape nearly every election in the developed world for the next decade. This may lead to a long period of populist governments, and your company could face shifting regulations because of this. Direct government relationships will become more important to most businesses. Positive emotional bonds with customers and employees will help insulate organizations from the worst effects.

- **Fractured regulation:** Governments will use populism as an excuse to regulate markets in order to increase tax revenue.

- **Nationalization:** Governments will threaten to co-opt the value chains of platform businesses, especially of foreign companies that are perceived as monopoly or security threats.
- **Employee relationships:** Companies that address employee and customer issues ahead of regulation and public sentiment will be able to use government relations to shape the conversation. Those that don't will fall victim to the fickle politics of perception.

IF THE FUTURE'S SO OBVIOUS, WHY DO COMPANIES KEEP GETTING HIT BY ROGUE WAVES?

When a rogue wave hits, a blame-finding investigation usually follows. Most discover that:

- Someone knew something bad was going to happen.
- Their warnings were ignored.
- The communication breakdown was systemic; the right hand didn't talk to the left.

The problem is obvious in hindsight, in ways that weren't obvious at the time. Depending on the politics, a scapegoat is found, or if the investigators themselves were culpable, it gets chalked up to fate.

The reality is that most of the time, the cause wasn't a person, but a process. People generally don't try to do a bad job or make decisions that they think are crazy; but they do tend to perform the tasks that the system incentivizes. When we recognize this, it's possible to develop better ways to anticipate and head off disasters and seize opportunities.

When a well-run organization is capsized by a predictable catastrophe, the failure can usually be described by one or more of the analogies listed in Figure 2.4.

Figure 2.4 **Avoidable Causes of Failure**

Using Binoculars Instead of a Radar	Coming to the wrong conclusion because you only analyzed part of the data
The Elephant Problem	Looking at the parts instead of the whole
Fighting the Last War	Assuming the future will look like the past
Packing for the Wrong Trip	Preparing for a future that won't occur
Surrendering to Reality	Failing to change probability through innovation

You see these same failures again and again, whether in the annals of history, case studies in the *Harvard Business Review*, or on the latest episode of *The Simpsons*. The twists in most jokes turn on them, and they are the central theme in many a cautionary tale.

In nearly every case, the lesson is the constant: While most problems are similar, we create unnecessary risk by assuming that they are all the same. We ignore this lesson at our peril because, in a world of rogue waves, the chance that they aren't the same is growing.

SUMMARY

Assess Your Threats and Opportunities

1. **Scan your horizon.**
   - Identify the economic, technological, and social undercurrents that will impact your business.
   - List the high-impact changes in politics, markets, and consumer behavior that they would cause.

2. **List the implications of radical change on your Four FOES.**
   - Imagine the impact of changes in the external environment on your finance, operations, and strategy.
   - Expand the list by making sure that you are considering all six characteristics of rogue waves (see Figure 1.4).
   - List an equal number of threats and opportunities they would create for you, your customers, your competitors, and your vendors.

3. **Identify your response window.**
   - When is the earliest the changes would become relevant to you, and when is the latest you could course correct?

4. **Build a dashboard of indicators to watch.**
   - Set up a dashboard to track the threats and opportunities.

Creating this written assessment is the first step to building a resilient organization that's able to survive and profit in stormy seas.

Today's To-Dos for Tomorrow

- **Complete a threat and opportunity assessment.** Access tools at jonathanbrill.com/roguewaves.

- **Evaluate your strategic team.** Do you already have dedicated resources for monitoring rogue waves and a mechanism for identifying high-risk, high-ambiguity scenarios? If not, consider assembling a cross-functional "Future Unit" that does not have P&L pressures and reports to the executive committee. Ideally, this unit should consist of both internal and external members.

- **Understand what you're measuring.** Identify changes in governance, measurement, and incentives that could increase your organization's willingness to spot and respond to less likely, external events before they happen.

- **Find the low-hanging fruit.** Identify the immediately actionable, budget-neutral steps you can take to position yourself for knowable changes in the future.

- **Designate a sponsor.** Which leader in your organization is ready to facilitate a shift in mindset? Assign an executive sponsor, and, ideally, have a skilled third party develop a train-the-trainer program to scale up rogue thinking in your organization.

- **Establish a reporting cadence.** Review your Four FOES dashboard on a quarterly basis and do an in-depth assessment every 12 to 24 months.

- **Teach your team.** Have a conversation with your team about the exercises above and share your ideas with your organization.

PART II

BEHAVIOR CHANGE

Are all levels of your organization capable of planning for, responding to, and exploiting the unexpected?

The only reason history remembers Captain John Edward Smith is because of what he did (and failed to do) one night in 1912—just weeks before his planned retirement—after his ship sailed at full speed into an iceberg in the North Atlantic. Smith went down with his ship, but he was strongly criticized in the investigations after the fact. Ninety minutes into the disaster, much of the *Titanic*'s crew still had not been told what was happening. Even if they had, they had not been trained in what to do. The result was that sailors were standing idle at their stations, awaiting orders, instead of saving lives as the ship went down.

Smith believed that better training and communication protocols weren't necessary because the *Titanic* was unsinkable. The result of his hubris was that, though there weren't enough lifeboats for all the passengers, the ones that were launched were only partly filled, and many more weren't launched at all. Two-thirds of the passengers and crew perished. The iceberg caused the tragedy in the same sense that Gavrilo Princip, Archduke's Ferdinand's assassin, caused World War I or a tossed cigarette causes a forest fire—it was the precipitating event, but the factors that made it catastrophic were baked into the processes and the culture that Captain Smith presided over.

Your career will be defined by moments of crisis, not by years of smooth sailing. The next rogue wave that hits your company might be a natural disaster, a war, a data breach, or a financial implosion. Whatever it is, *you will be in charge*, and it will be the processes that you have installed, not your individual performance, that will drive results.

A ship that is constructed for resilience in heavy seas is built differently than a pleasure craft that hugs the shore. Today's companies are built for performance because investors are primarily concerned with profits. Since Covid-19 put its brakes on the worldwide economy, the conversation has shifted to survival and resilience. In the coming years, your investors, your board, and your C-suite will demand profits *and* resilience. They may or may not be saying it yet, but they are thinking: are you, the profitable pleasure boat captain, the right person to refit their ship for stormy seas?

This puts leaders like you in a tough spot. Resilience requires inherently inefficient processes, so how do you drive quarterly performance while improving resilience. More importantly, how will you do it when stimulus money dries up revealing the true tide—structural slow growth and rising competition? The only answer is to pursue resilience in ways that drive growth by removing inefficiencies and by training yourself and your team to think longer term. You don't need to hire rocket scientists to future-proof your company. You just need to fully understand your operating context, know how to deconstruct problems into solvable parts, and be able to ask "what if?" While it takes some effort to embed this type of thinking in your organization, new digital training tools make it testable and scalable.

When organizational thinking and behaviors are realigned in the ways that I describe, you can have confidence that your people will spot both the weak point in your hull and the coming wave before it's too late. If you've installed the right command, control, and communication processes, they'll already have patched it and put the ship on a better course by the time you hear about it.

Analysts had pointed out the danger of operating like the *Titanic* did. Captain Smith and the White Star Line were neither the first nor the last to turn a blind eye to an imminent threat. Whether it's Kodak or Blockbuster, Enron or AIG, there are any number of cautionary tales about companies that were brought low because of impending disasters that they should have seen coming. In each case, the issue was not the disaster. It was the refusal to discuss and prepare for the inevitable iceberg that would stop their way of work.

The past 40 years of business culture have encouraged managers to prize agility, nimbleness, and efficiency over sustainability.

Investors have become obsessed with short-term risk, the measure of investment uncertainty, and boards have responded by prioritizing growth through M&As and incentivizing hitting quarters over investing in the future. The perverse impact is that the value of shares has become more important than shareholder value.

All of these trends serve to silence the people who spot potential problems first. They are often in the engine room, not on the bridge. They don't speak up because they fear the political fallout. More importantly, they haven't been trained to describe an apparition they can feel but not yet see. The result is that leaders don't learn about the hidden players that founder their flotillas.

You don't want to be the captain who only learns of the iceberg when it goes bump in the night. If you want to be prepared, you need to provide your team the space and the training they need to look out for the unknown, the processes that will give them the confidence to speak up, and the assurance that they'll be heard.

THE ROGUE METHOD

In the next five chapters, you'll learn the ROGUE Method (Figure II.1)—the tools you will need to see the subtle fissures in reality and shape them to your purpose.

People with different educational backgrounds will find some of these chapters familiar and others new. For instance, the next chapter, on reality testing, tends to be very comfortable for lawyers, while the chapter on experimenting may be novel. Programmers and economists breeze through the chapter on observing your system, but it's often a breakthrough for English majors, one of whom used it to reorganize the strategic priorities of a major research and development lab a few weeks after reading it.

Early in my career, as a specialist, I used only some of these tools. I was less efficient, creative, and successful than I could have been because I wasn't even aware that there was a whole toolshed to choose from. I encourage you to spend time with any sections that

Figure II.1 **The ROGUE Method**

R	**Reality Test**	Determine your present state and the systems that got you there—to avoid making decisions on the wrong information.
O	**Organize Your Forces**	Model the forces that keep your current system stable to determine what would cause it to change and what would cause it to break.
G	**Generate Possible Futures**	Build scenarios that explore the full range of likely futures—not just the future you want.
U	**Unbundle Your Risks**	Work backward from your potential futures to identify and exploit key decision and trigger points.
E	**Experiment**	Build a portfolio of experiments that maximize the benefits of success and minimize the impact of failure.

are a struggle. As my English major colleague discovered, having a new mental tool—even if you haven't mastered it—can change your business because you suddenly discover that you can speak the language of a computer scientist who uses it regularly.

The point is that the ROGUE Method is a broad set of mental models that balances out thinking across an organization. You don't need to master all of them, but someone on your team should have strengths in each one, and all should share a common language for discussing them. Knowing where your team members' natural strengths and weaknesses lie will help your organization develop better responses to threats and opportunities and be more resilient to the rogue waves on the horizon. As Pope Francis said, "By ourselves, we risk seeing mirages, things that are not there. Dreams, on the other hand, are built together."

3

R: Reality Test

Determine your present state and the systems that got you there—to avoid making decisions on the wrong information.

Rogue waves are becoming more likely each day. Every organization should expect to get hit by one at some point. But radical change doesn't mean your company is going to fail, any more than sailing through the North Sea in winter means your boat is going to sink. There is a crucial difference between the companies that thrive and the companies that don't. It's how clearly their leaders understand the changing sea and how well they prepare their crews. When you understand what is causing the change, you have a better sense of how it is likely to affect you. You might even be able to stake your future on it.

Most organizations put great effort into collecting data about the past and forecasting the future, but far less into understanding the present. You may have reams of data about last quarter, but when the system is changing, it can't tell you what will happen next. If your model of the present is wrong, your model of the future will likely be wrong as well, with potentially catastrophic results.

Earlier, I referred to the butterfly effect. Mathematician and systems dynamicist Edward Lorenz proposed the idea when he was trying to improve weather forecasts. His insight was that tiny changes in atmospheric start conditions can have disproportionate impacts on end states.[1] As we have improved our baseline measurements and our understanding of complex systems, our weather forecasts have gotten more accurate. The science of system dynamics applies to business forecasts as well.

Anaïs Nin once said, "We don't see things as they are, we see them as we are." It's human nature to focus on what we know, instead of what we can know. This is especially true in times of peril. Often, our inaccurate models of reality work fine. But when the unexpected occurs, these models break down and we need tools that allow us to investigate reality as it really is. We were taught many of these tools in school, but they mostly sit unused in the back of our minds, along with forgotten homework assignments. Few people learn to put them together to truly test reality. Those who do are the ones who change the world. Leaders like Steve Jobs, Elon Musk, and Jeff Bezos make such good bets on the future because they see the present with such clarity. You can do that, too. The processes for turning information into insight are well established, and they work—even when the information you have is very limited.

INVESTIGATION: THE ART OF SEEING THE INVISIBLE

In science class, you probably learned that science is based on *deductive* reasoning: start with a hypothesis, test it under controlled conditions, and either prove or disprove it. You might have also learned about *inductive* reasoning: how to draw general conclusions from specific data, a technique that is used in the social sciences where limited studies are often designed to form broader conclusions. The scientific method works well in the academy, but in the real world, real leaders rarely have time to apply, much less test, theories. They know that something just happened, and they want to find out why as quickly as possible so they can respond. One consequence of this is that we often mistake coincidence for causation. As mathematician John Allen Paulos wrote, "The most astonishing coincidence of all would be the complete absence of all coincidences."

In 1887, Scottish author Arthur Conan Doyle introduced the character Sherlock Holmes. Over the course of four novels and 56 short stories by Conan Doyle (and countless more by latter-day adapters), Holmes became the most famous fictional detective of all time. If you read a Sherlock Holmes mystery carefully, you'll notice that the great detective never actually begins with a hypothesis, and he rarely uses induction. Instead, he relies on a different technique, called *abductive* reasoning (Figure 3.1). Holmes's strategy, explained many times in the stories, was straightforward.

Figure 3.1 **The Sherlock Holmes Method**

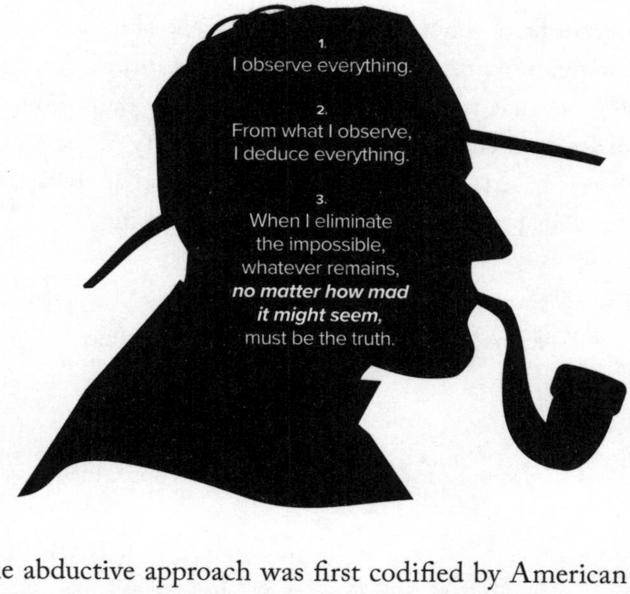

1.
I observe everything.

2.
From what I observe,
I deduce everything.

3.
When I eliminate
the impossible,
whatever remains,
*no matter how mad
it might seem,*
must be the truth.

The abductive approach was first codified by American philosopher Charles Sanders Pierce, around the time that Conan Doyle was writing his stories. Pierce was interested in the early stages of ideas, how they lead to breakthroughs and how they have occurred throughout history. He believed the thought process went something like this: *The surprising fact, B, is observed. But if A were true, B would be a matter of course. Hence, there is reason to suspect that A is true.*

Abductive reasoning begins with an incomplete set of observations and proceeds to the likeliest possible explanation for them. An insight achieved through this process is easy to dismiss at first; it won't get past a hard-boiled executive who demands conclusions based on data and proof. But as any child who has mastered the game of 20 Questions can tell you, a few carefully chosen queries can lead to better questions, which can lead you to the right answer—even if you don't have all the facts.

Abduction underlies many breakthroughs of the past 50 years, from the Bayesian networks that underpin Google's search engine to the AI-powered image recognition technology that will make self-driving cars possible. Abduction is also how companies like Amazon make bets.

But to be useful, this approach requires you to discover as many relevant facts about a problem as possible (Figure 3.2). In our faster-moving, more uncertain and ambiguous future, you have less knowledge of what you're looking at, almost by definition. So the quality of your conclusions depends on the quality of the arguments on which it is based. This makes fact-finding and analysis the most important skills for improving your decision-making.

Figure 3.2 **The Three Types of Reasoning**

1.

Deductive
Determining causality based on widely accepted truths

2.

Inductive
Inferring causality based on observation

3.

Abductive
Assessing likelihood by examining what is known and unknown

THE REAL FRAMEWORK

The difficulty lies not in the new ideas,
but in escaping the old ones.

—JOHN MAYNARD KEYNES

The only subjects Silicon Valley talks more about than the latest IPOs and gadgets are food and wine. Twitter cofounder Jack Dorsey invested in Saison, one of San Francisco's most exclusive restaurants. The Napa and Sonoma wine country runneth over with startup founders turned winetrepreneurs. The reason for their interest is more than aesthetic; it's also financial. Grapes are one of the most valuable crops on earth, and contrary to its mom-and-pop reputation, winemaking is a rapidly growing, $300-billion industry. There are 27,000 winemakers in France alone.[2]

At storied joints like The French Laundry, the wine library can be worth more than the restaurant. Restaurateurs who invest wisely can see certain wines grow in value by 25 percent a year, generating more profit than if they were sold to customers. This kind of money attracts criminals. As a result, counterfeit wines have also become a major industry.

Top restaurants need someone to advise them and protect them from counterfeits, which is the job of a master sommelier. A well-trained, experienced "somm" can identify any wine, its place of origin, its vintage, and its method of production in about four and a half minutes, simply by looking at, smelling, and possibly tasting it.

The incredibly precise way that somms go about investigating and describing wines offers broadly relevant lessons in how to gather and analyze information. Every step in the wine-making process leaves a distinct chemical signature, from the grape variety, to the soil and weather, to fermentation and aging. These signatures are nearly impossible to fake. And wine experts use a highly specialized vocabulary to describe them.

Wine tasting isn't the only field in which people have to make high-stakes decisions based on a large number of probabilistic observations. Forensic accountants, supply chain managers, financial forecasters, and product managers all do this, too. The value of looking at the sommelier's approach is that it's so codified: wine tasting is a standardized process that's performed by a single person, with a very clear right-or-wrong outcome. While it might not be the most business-focused example of reality testing and decision-making we could examine, I chose it because it's unusually explicit. The relationship of impression to chemical signature are all laid bare for anyone to examine, and many of them are written down (in *Fenaroli's Handbook of Flavor Ingredients*, for example).

Abduction is at the heart of what sommeliers do. They start with limited information about a specific wine and link it to their vast knowledge about wine in general. Then they gradually refine their analysis and gather more information (through sight, smell, taste, and texture) until they are down to one wine, from one year, from one location, that could be a patch of soil the size of a tennis court or a football field.

How do they do it? The romantic answer is a golden tongue, combined with a lifetime of industry experience, five years of continuous study, and a qualifying test with a 3 percent pass rate. The practical answer is far more relevant to your organization's decision-making.

All effective reality testing is the result of a process that delineates evidence collection from analysis. Its four-step framework spells REAL (Figure 3.3).

The first skill that an investigator must master is separating the facts of the case from the theory of the case. We must be careful, in other words, about coming to conclusions before we make sure we have all of the available evidence. A court case involving the death penalty undergoes perhaps the most rigorous reality testing imaginable. But even after spending years and millions of dollars on investigations, trials, and appeals, it's estimated that more than 4 percent of the inmates on death row in the United States are, in fact, innocent.[3] The problem is that there are a lot of facts and a lot of

Figure 3.3 **The REAL Framework**

R   Reconnaissance Method

E   Evidence Collection

A   Alternative Analysis

L   Likely Realities

assumptions to be found in any situation. Investigators, prosecutors, judges, and juries all have a natural desire to focus on the facts that support their biases.

The way we structure our search for facts, then, can have a huge impact on our ability to find the correct ones, and thus our ability to make good decisions.

Reconnaissance Method

Are we not more likely to hit the mark if we have a target?

—ARISTOTLE

Leaders often avoid research, thinking it's a wasteful effort that rarely results in a better decision. This can be true, and I've certainly ended up in that situation. But usually, the issue isn't the research itself; it's that the wrong methodology was used. It's not that people spent too much time smelling the roses; it's that they smelled the wrong roses.

When reconnaissance fails, it's often because we haven't defined what success looks like in a clear, attainable way. That leaves us without appropriate search boundaries. The nearly inevitable result is that we fail to identify the strategic features we were sent off to find. So the first step in planning reconnaissance is deciding what decisions you need to make, how much proof you'll need to make them, and the size of the universe you need to search. A manufacturer developing an operating plan, for example, might need to know:

- That production will generate $1–$2 million of profit
- From a certain demographic
- That would buy from a known channel
- In a specific region
- Over the next 12 months
- With an 80 percent likelihood

Getting to this kind of clarity can be surprisingly difficult. But like many business problems, there's a process that makes it easier. It starts with understanding the limits of what we can actually know.

What Is Known, and What Is Knowable?

Figure 3.4 shows a helpful chart of knowns and unknowns.

One of the most powerful planning and organizing tools you can use—even today, with a million software packages to choose

Figure 3.4 **Knowns and Unknowns**

Known Knowns	**Known Unknowns**
What we are aware of and **do** understand	What we are aware of but **don't** understand
Unknown Knowns	**Unknown Unknowns**
What we understand but are **not** aware of	What we are **neither aware of nor** understand

Figure 3.5 **The 5Ws and 1H**

Who	**W**here
What	**W**hy
When	**H**ow

from—is a simple list. And one of the most useful lists you can make starts with what you know and what you don't know about the 5Ws and 1H of the situation (Figure 3.5). For example, if you're doing reconnaissance to decide whether to invest in a company, you'll probably want to find out things like its past performance and the competitive landscape in which it's operating. This may sound obvious or trivial, but it can help clarify the picture tremendously, as long as you're rigorous and brutally honest.

In any reconnaissance process, there are things you already know and things that you know you want to find out. That gets you halfway to a complete list. But there are two other two kinds of information worth considering. The first is the Unknown Knowns: information you have that you haven't explicitly acknowledged, such as biases. I'll address these later in the chapter.

The second is Unknown Unknowns: information that cannot be known (often because you don't know to look for it). Writing these down in a list is a creative exercise that can potentially change your decision. One common technique is considering counterfactuals, or what-ifs. An Unknown Unknown could be a new technology or form of competition that doesn't yet exist (or isn't widespread enough to matter). This isn't something you can effectively research, but listing it helps you expand your definition of the problem. It can also make you more sensitive to useful information that comes to light as you search. All of this helps you assess threats and identify priorities against your metrics of success.

These terms have been around for some time, but they were thrust into public awareness by former US Defense Secretary Donald Rumsfeld when he famously used them in a DoD news briefing in 2002.[4] He was castigated by the media, not because the approach was wrong, but because he had misused it to make his case about weapons of mass destruction in Iraq. By pointing out that there was information we didn't know to look for, he implied grave hidden dangers, which justified military action on flimsy evidence.

Rumsfeld was right, however, that it's crucial to understand what you don't know—unexpected risk usually comes from zombie assumptions. The iconic investor Warren Buffett put it best: "What counts for most people in investing is not how much they know, but rather how realistically they define what they don't know."

Mysteries Versus Enigmas: Is the Problem Solvable?

> *How can the prisoner reach outside except*
> *by thrusting through the wall?*

—CAPTAIN AHAB, *MOBY DICK*

In international espionage, there's a useful concept of "mysteries" versus "enigmas." Both are unknown, but a mystery is something that can be found out. An enigma cannot, and no amount of reconnaissance will deliver an answer. The underlying issue about WMDs in Iraq was that Saddam Hussein needed to simultaneously convince the international community that he didn't have WMDs, and suggest to his hostile neighbor Iran that he might. The result was an enigma: contradictory signals that could never be fully resolved.

Timing is everything in business, and more than one company has been overtaken because it failed to prioritize mysteries over enigmas. That's why Dion Weisler, the former CEO of HP, referred to the process of trying to solve enigmas as "chasing ghosts."

The Search Tree

> *There are two questions you ask yourself as you look at the*
> *decision you'll make. (A) Is it knowable? (B) Is it important?*

—CHARLIE MUNGER

For master sommeliers, the unknowns are clear: the vintage, the grapes, the place of origin. To avoid bias, they're not allowed to look at the bottle. Instead, they gather evidence by looking at, smelling, and tasting the wine. An individual datum might not say much, but a network of supporting evidence speaks volumes.

Simply gathering information at random and then hoping to make sense of it afterward might work when there are only a few dozen possible solutions. But what if there are hundreds of thousands or millions? This is the challenge that somms face, and it's why they approach information gathering in such a structured way.

They look, smell, and taste in a particular order, gradually narrowing down their options as they move forward.

The best analogy for this approach is something Elon Musk describes as a "semantic tree," where the most consequential and provable truths form the trunk and then branch out into more nuanced and uncertain ones. That's why Musk suggests, "Make sure you understand the fundamental principles, i.e., the trunk and big branches, before you get into the leaves/details or there is nothing for them to hang on to."[5]

Constructing the trunk of the tree starts with identifying those fundamentals. Much like a grown-up game of 20 Questions, a well-designed search tree reduces the range of answers as quickly and cheaply as possible. The way to do this is by asking questions that, if correctly answered, will define the boundaries of the search area most effectively. You could ask: What country? What state? What city? What neighborhood? Or you could just ask: What zip code? A significant experiment can require billions of dollars and a Large Hadron Collider. But for many business decisions, a good experiment can be constructed simply by thinking in a careful, structured way.

In 1986, the space shuttle *Challenger* exploded while my entire class watched it live on national television. This was my first experience of catastrophic systems failure. Richard Feynman, the Nobel Prize–winning physicist and educator, was part of the blue-ribbon commission that investigated it. He suspected that an O-ring, used to create a gastight seal between sections of the solid fuel booster, may have been responsible. While others were doing a sprawling investigation, he cut right to the chase. He bought a $3 C-clamp and an O-ring from the hardware store, tightened the clamp against the O-ring, and dropped both in a glass of ice water. What he demonstrated was that the unusually cold temperatures on the morning of the *Challenger*'s launch were enough to reduce the O-ring's flexibility so that it no longer made a good seal. This simple experiment—which he repeated on live TV—possibly stopped a government cover-up.[6]

When master sommeliers approach the one-in-a-million problem of identifying a wine,[7] they think in a similar way as Feynman:

What one detail, if it was known, would narrow the search space the most?

In the case of wine, a simple direct observation cuts the search space at least in half: is it red or white? But to get all the way to an acceptable proof, you also need to make inferences from indirect observation—what fact or network of facts can tell you about the probability of something being true (see Figure 3.6).

Figure 3.6 **Wine Tasting**

A master sommelier uses four visible qualities to narrow the search area of a wine by 75 percent:

Clarity
A clear wine means filtration, which suggests that it was not made in a European style.

Color
The purity and gradient of the wine's color helps classify its age. A vibrant gold, for example, suggests a younger wine. An ochre hue often suggests an older one.

Lip
This refers to the meniscus, the slight curve that forms where the wine meets the glass. As light refracts through the meniscus, it changes color, indicating the presence of certain compounds. A green tint, for example, indicates compounds that are common in Riesling.

Legs
Legs are the little streams that run down the side of a wineglass after its contents are swirled. Their thickness and the rate at which they fall depends on the sugar and alcohol content. Thin legs suggest the wine is not from sunny regions, such as Chile or California, or was less ripe when harvested, like a champagne.

You will hear somms use terms like "probably" and "suggests" when investigating a wine. Most reconnaissance isn't deduction. It's inference and abduction, so it's probabilistic. A somm creates the network of suggestions that reduce the search area by combining these probabilities.

The next round of information comes from smelling the wine, often for up to a minute. Humans can sense far more aromas than tastes—over 10,000 of them[8]—and these indicate different fermentation and aging techniques in addition to information about the grape. There are a number of ways to categorize this data, but one of the most common is:

- **Fruit** The combination of fruit aromas suggests the variety of grape, and the complexity suggests growing climate. In sauvignon blanc, for example, a lime flavor suggests less ripeness, while a peach flavor implies more.
- **Nonfruit** Compounds such as alkylpyrazines, which smell like asparagus, are particularly common when sauvignon blanc is grown in wet climates.
- **Earth** Imparted by soil chemistry and local yeasts. The coastal wines of France are known to have an iodine note, like salt.
- **Wood** Tells you how the wine was aged. If it was aged in steel or concrete, it won't have this aroma.

None of these observations can identify a wine on its own, of course. To do that, somms need to combine the data in a systematic way.

Evidence Collection

When making an argument, one of the most common mistakes is to conflate what may be true with what *is* true (politicians and lawyers do this all the time). One reason the law and police investigations are so complex is that everyone needs to know how reliable the evidence must be before passing judgment—and how to ascertain when that level is reached. This is called a *standard of proof.* It's why, for example, someone can be acquitted of a criminal assault charge but be found liable for violating someone else's civil rights for the same act. They're different kinds of charges, so they have different standards of proof.

The process of determining whether something is sufficiently true is a whole field of study called *epistemology*. If you've ever taken a formal logic class or if you remember the agony of writing out high school geometry proofs, it might sound familiar. Start from point A (known information) and move steadily toward point B (logical conclusion) in a series of concrete intermediate steps, each supported by a single, clear reason. If your experience was like mine, this process was presented in the abstract, and you haven't done a proof or word problem since. But epistemology gives us the ability to objectively separate what's true from what's not, and this has been the foundation of nearly every major discovery since the Enlightenment. We won't get into all the details here, but there are a few key insights from the field of formal logic that are worth reviewing.

The first is that you don't need to have all of the information in order to make a decision. In fact, knowing exactly what you don't know is useful information too. In some cases, it's easier to build an argument around what you don't know than around what you do. Astronomers have come to understand a huge amount about the universe and its evolution, for example, by realizing that much of its mass is undetectable. If you've read an article about dark matter, this is what they're referring to: a substance that can't be detected but must be present in order for the math to work.[9]

Similarly, if you're doing competitive reconnaissance on a product or service, a lack of information about a potential customer segment might indicate that you're looking at an underserved market. When REI, a major retailer of outdoor gear in the United States, started researching millennials' attitudes toward wilderness recreation and equipment, they were surprised by how little information was available. This ultimately drove them to create a new sub-brand to fill what they suspected was a gap in the market, and they suddenly had a new, mostly untapped consumer group on their hands.

Formal logic lays out all the different ways of making a valid argument. In case you're curious, logicians call these *syllogisms* and there are 19 of them. Much more useful to our purposes are the faulty forms of argument, what are called *Logical Fallacies*. This list is a lot longer. When people make bad decisions, it's often because they reached a conclusion based one of them. Just a few of these are responsible for most poor decisions. If you can learn to spot just five Logical Fallacies (Figure 3.7), you're on a better footing than most.

The standard of proof for master sommeliers isn't as high as it is in a criminal court, and yet their success rates are considerably higher. Even a mediocre sommelier can decrease the search area for a wine by 99.5 percent in less than two minutes by using a combination of logic and probabilistic observations. The trick is that the reconnaissance method for evaluating a wine is optimized for combining many probabilistic observations into a reliable conclusion.

So how do you do it? To understand it precisely, you'd probably need to dedicate several years of your life to sommelier training. But the general explanation is that the process they're using has been evolved and refined over decades and millions of individual tastings. When thousands of people make the same kind of decision—which wine is this?—over and over, they're able to learn through trial and error how best to make that decision, and then codify it. This is why the tasting process is such a strict, and sometimes bizarre-looking, ritual. It forces the sommelier to observe, smell, and taste in a particular order, use a specific vocabulary, and apply a defined standard of proof at each step.

If I pick up a glass of white wine and gather five data points (clarity, color, lip, legs, and aroma), I can say that it's almost certainly a sauvignon blanc from the Marlborough Coast of New Zealand—even though none of those observations is certain. And I'm definitely not a master sommelier, just someone who took a weekend course at the CIA. I don't mention this in order to show

Figure 3.7 **Five Most Common Logical Fallacies**

Circular Arguments	A causes B because B causes A. *For example:* "You must obey the law because it's illegal to break the law" relies on itself to prove itself.
Overgeneralizing	Just because A causes B does not mean that A always causes B or is the only cause of B. *For example:* "A butterfly flapping its wings could cause a hurricane." This doesn't mean that butterflies are the sole or most likely cause of hurricanes.
Confusing Correlation and Causation	Just because A and B occur at the same time, or in proportion to each other, doesn't mean one causes the other. Often they're both caused by a third event, C. *For example:* Increased ice cream sales don't cause violent crime, but they both rise during warmer weather. Sometimes, it's just coincidence.
Order of Argument	Just because A causes B does not mean that B causes A. *For example:* The fact that "sugar causes cavities" does not mean that "cavities cause sugar."
Equivocation	A term that has multiple meanings can often lead (intentionally or accidentally) to faulty conclusions. *For example:* The term "innovation" means "something different" to some users and "something world-changing" to others.

off, but to show that precise observation isn't the unique province of a special few. Nearly everyone in that CIA course was able to do the same thing (that's the Culinary Institute of America, by the way, not the Central Intelligence Agency, which we'll get to later).

What Additional Data Might Be Worth the Effort to Collect?

While 99.5 percent certainty is a fine standard of proof for an amateur like myself, a sommelier might be assessing a $20,000 bottle of wine. The last 0.5 percent is where the real work begins.

The somm's experience is the crucial differentiator: after the above observations, you or I could narrow our search down to 500 possible labels, but a master sommelier would be homing in on 10 or less, based on their knowledge of the region, how its wines are distributed, and the year-to-year growing conditions.

When we have a clear idea of what information we can gather and what answers we're looking for, we can build a robust approach that rapidly narrows the field. Doing this in the right order (as in the wine example) is crucial. But without a standard of proof, it's easy to spend time and money going around in circles and making false arguments.

This kind of process is important when you're talking about an expensive bottle of wine, but what if you're talking about enormous million-dollar kites with thousand-foot tethers that generate electricity through wind power? The stakes here are much, much higher, in terms of investment, potential payoff, and danger if something goes wrong. You might expect a team that's building kites like this to be exceptionally rigorous about validating their hypotheses—and you'd be right. I was lucky enough to observe this firsthand in 2006 as a client, Squid Labs, prepared to spin out Makani Power.

Squid had found a need that intersected with all four FOES of Growth (see Figure 1.2) for a broad swath of companies. Their first step was to look at the potential market. Their novel technology solved the challenges of a future market, not an existing one. So they researched how global trends were likely to change demand

and cost (essentially, they looked at the 10 undercurrents in Chapter 2, Figure 2.3). Here are some of their findings:

- The growing data economy and changing demographics were driving up the demand for energy.
- Solar and terrestrial wind, the leading renewable technologies at the time, were far from a sure bet. Access to natural gas was limited and the rate at which it could expand was unclear.
- A social trend toward interest in climate change and green energy was starting to shift the regulatory and political dynamics of extractive energy production.

If all three undercurrents continued to overlap, they would create a massive opportunity for a new source of clean energy.

Generating power using huge tethered kites involved a number of subsystems, and each had its own level of risk and required a technology with a different level of maturity. The evaluators on the team wanted to see a proof of concept for each, but they set various levels of proof for different elements:

1. **Cable retraction:** Motors and motor controls were a well understood technology, so the team only built a rough, scaled-down model to prove it was appropriate.
2. **Cable safety:** Makani was justifiably concerned about a 1,000-foot-long cable falling from the sky, so the startup's engineers built a fully functioning prototype and ran it through rigorous tests.
3. **Aerial kite control system:** Collision avoidance and maneuvering of autonomous kites was a new and significant challenge. Before investment, the team built an initial proof of concept and then focused on mastering the technology between initial funding and later stage investments.
4. **Buoys:** While custom engineering would be necessary here, a proof of concept wasn't required because the core technology was well understood.

We'll discover what happened with these superkites soon enough. If I've learned anything from Sherlock Holmes stories, it's that you need to build suspense. So first, let's have another glass of wine and take a brief trip to China.

Evaluating Information Sources

Sommeliers can gather direct data about a wine by observing, tasting, and smelling it. But for most business problems, our noses aren't of much use. We don't have direct experience with much of the data we review, so we rely on sources like newspapers, trade journals, or industry analysts. While these may be useful starting points, high-risk decisions deserve a deeper dive.

False information is a persistent obstacle to accurate prediction, whether due to error, mistaken understanding, or intentional fabrication. Before we even begin to analyze information, we need to ask ourselves fundamental questions about its sources:

- What are the goals and interests of the party that generated or communicated it?
- Where is that party's attention focused, and could this create blind spots?
- Are there likely to be omissions or inaccuracies because of bias, technical challenges, or simple incompetence?

The highest quality information tends to come from academic writing and direct analysis of source data. This information is typically more reliable, impartial, and balanced than general reports from professional services like Gartner, or publications like *Wired* or the *New York Times*. The issue isn't with the quality of the organizations. They have different goals and differing standards of proof.

An example from a recent research project I worked on helps illustrate why it's crucial to choose your information sources according to your project's goals and standards of proof. Our research team had to create a report about China's aging population and its impact on the go-to-market prospects of a large technology firm.

The mainstream press has published frequently on the "graying of China" in reported articles, blog posts, and opinion pieces. In January 2019, for example, the *New York Times* ran an article titled "China's Looming Crisis: A Shrinking Population."[10] Featuring numerous charts and citing data from a variety of credible sources, it argued that China's falling fertility rate spelled doom for its economy and social structure.

The Center for Strategic and International Studies' non-peer-reviewed *China Power* took a less alarmist view in an article conservatively titled "Does China Have an Aging Problem?"[11] Like the *Times*, it noted China's labor market and tax base would be negatively impacted by the lingering effects of its one-child policy. But it also discussed how those effects could be managed, looking at steps that countries like Japan and Germany, which are further along the aging continuum than China, have already taken.

A juried academic symposium published by the Hoover Institution provided an even more complex and nuanced assessment. Entitled "China's Demographic Prospects to 2040: Opportunities, Constraints, Potential Policy Responses,"[12] its authors considered fertility decline and an aging population alongside other demographic issues, like internal migration and the uneven geographic distribution of age among its population. They also looked at Chinese government policies already in place, such as the hukou system (which defines to whom and where social services are delivered), mass education, and social credit systems. These tools and many others are successfully driving youth toward major cities, where most economic productivity occurs, and moving the elderly to rural areas, where they are less expensive to support.

Two major conclusions emerged:

- The Chinese government is putting long-term mitigation strategies in place, and while they might not be to Human Rights Watch's taste, they've been quite effective so far.
- Long-term fertility trends, the basis of concern, are difficult to forecast.

It's important to note that all three of these sources—the *New York Times*, Center for Strategic and International Studies, and the Hoover Institution—have high standards and provide reliable information. But that doesn't mean the insight they provide is equally useful.

Information scientists often talk about the *structure* of an information set, which is different from size or accuracy. All of the information in the *Times* article was accurate and came from large, reliable data sets. But it wasn't structured in a way that was useful for our team's purposes. Determining whether an information source has the right structure for a problem depends on three factors:

1. **Focus:** Does the data measure something that's well defined and constrained to the problem we're examining? If we want to know about traffic patterns in Houston, for example, then data for the United States as a whole won't do us much good.
2. **Givenness:** Is the information nonobvious enough that it will shed new light on the problem? A study proving that most drivers in Houston are over 18 may be rigorous and accurate, but it's still useless.
3. **Relevance:** Is the information relevant to the problem in a way that will generate new insights? Even if we have a high-quality study about driving habits in Houston, it might be focused on commuting behavior, while we're interested in how people drive when they go shopping. Same city, same demographic, same activity, but still not relevant.

In the case of "Graying China," we saw a lot of low-focus information (about China as a whole), a lot of given information (declining fertility), and a lot of nonobvious information that wasn't relevant to the size of the addressable market for our client's products.

In fact, the demographic trends within major cities—where the client company sells most of its products—are different from China's overall. This suggested that the research team would actually do better to narrow its focus. After five minutes of our own recon, based on Oxford Economics and Haver Analytics data, we discovered something nearly the opposite of what we would've concluded from the *New York Times* article. In economically productive cities, the number of households with the local equivalent of a $35,000–$100,000 USD income is projected to rise. Contrary to what one might conclude from general reporting, demand indicators suggest explosive growth for the client's products in their markets.

Beyond that, China's Belt and Road Initiative seeks to actively import labor from other Asian countries. If this policy is effective, it could grow the market for the client's product categories even more.

The three sources we mentioned have different motivations and circumstances. The academic papers were written and edited by China experts for policy makers. The better ones were peer reviewed or jury selected. The *New York Times* article was based on a single study that was published the week before. It was written by a correspondent who was new to the China beat and charged with covering the whole country in 1,000 words for a general audience half a world away.

By digging deeper, we gained a much better understanding of the issue at hand. Thinking critically about information sources may come naturally to some, but truth finding is not an innate skill. Much like the standard of proof, it helps if you clearly establish your criteria for focus, givenness, and relevance before you start.

Forming Theories of Reality

Unlike Sherlock Holmes, businesses don't routinely put a lot of effort into figuring out "whodunit." When we do reconnaissance for clients, it's to figure out what to do next, not what happened last. This often prompts decision-makers to jump straight to the future, looking at trends and forecasts, rather than seeking out a thorough understanding of what's happening now.

This is a problem for a few reasons. One is that knowing what's happening today is often all you need to make a good decision. Many of the great innovation stories in modern history begin with an insight about current possibilities. When Fred Smith founded FedEx in 1971 (it opened for business on April 17, 1973), for instance, it was because he realized overnight air shipping could already work at scale with the right hub-and-spoke model. Many other companies could have done this, but they didn't understand the current situation as thoroughly as he did.

Understanding the differences between the past and the present is also powerful because it puts trends into context. The impact of a future change is clearer when you know how things have progressed up to this point. For instance, it might be interesting to know that transistor density and processor speeds are increasing at a slow, less steady rate. This knowledge becomes much more significant when you're aware that Moore's Law suggests this should occur much faster. Transistor density has historically doubled every 18 to 24 months. The Chinese mainland is investing heavily in semiconductor technology because Chinese companies believe that this trend presents them with an opportunity to catch up to the industry's present leaders, TSMC and Intel.[13] If they can create new standards that use their own applications onto their own chips, they'll gain a competitive advantage.

Perhaps the greatest value of figuring out "whodunit" is that it's a powerful differentiator. Yet, few organizations take the time to do it properly when making decisions. This brings us to the next step in the process of reality testing, in which we take the information we've gathered and begin to form a theory of reality.

A theory of reality is just a succinct, accurate way of describing your current situation, that can then be used to inform decisions: What do we know about the 5Ws and 1H, and what does that tell us about what happens next?

When we form a faulty theory of reality, the scientific method isn't what's at fault. More times than not, it's that we carried out its steps in the wrong order (Figure 3.8). We built our hypothesis without gathering all the relevant information. We speculated in the face of uncertainty. We gave supporting evidence too much weight and falsifying evidence too little.

Our imagination is our greatest strength, because it allows us to envision things that haven't happened, but it becomes a weakness when we envision emotionally reassuring things, and then believe them. This leads to unconscious cognitive biases, which produce all of the problems above. There's only one way to overcome that tendency: systems that are properly sequenced.

Figure 3.8 Testing Reality in the Right Order

Boundaries	Define the boundaries of your search area.
Standard of Proof	Identify your criteria for evidence collection and a baseline for validity.
Search Tree	Design a search process that will shrink your search area in the most useful way.
Reasoning	Consider where inductive, deductive, and abductive methods are most appropriate.
Direct vs. Indirect	Collect evidence through a combination of direct and indirect investigation.
Reliability	Evaluate your sources and collect your data before you analyze it.
Investigate Before Judgement	Analyze your data before you weigh it.
Additional Information	Identify what additional data might be worth the effort to collect to either verify or falsify the information you aleady have.

Alternative Analysis

Much like a politician, I make persuasive arguments for a living. Every word in the presentations I give is chosen to lead people toward a predetermined conclusion. It's a great way to focus audiences, persuade juries, win reelection, or sell to customers, but it's the opposite of a disinterested search for truth. To understand the realities of the present, you must approach it with an open mind. The evidence you're relying on could be incomplete or inaccurate. That's why, in ambiguous and complex situations, your first conclusion probably isn't the right one. The best way to deal with this uncertainty is to systematically consider alternatives.

Most people think of this as considering both sides of the coin. In their bestselling book *Decisive*, Chip and Dan Heath mention a study of a German firm. Whenever it considered two or more alternatives, they wrote, "it made six times as many 'very good' decisions."[14]

Overcome Your Cognitive Biases by Developing Alternatives

A master sommelier's most critical skill isn't data collection. It's the ability to use process to avoid bias. There are a lot of people with highly developed taste buds and good noses. Many read *Wine Spectator* magazine and go on learning tours in Beaune. Yet studies suggest that many of those wine geeks can't tell the difference between a red and a white wine in a blind test.[15] As much as they may enjoy a good bottle of wine, their sense of quality is based on indicators other than its taste. Indicators that can be faked: the logo, the bottle, the color, and the price tag.

Much like Sherlock Holmes, sommeliers collect information before analyzing it and coming to conclusions. They only consider which theories are supported by the data after they've finished collecting. In both cases, separating collection from analysis reduces the influence of bias—and bias is the enemy of every business decision-maker.

Psychologist Daniel Kahneman has spent a lifetime investigating these types of biases and how they occur. *Thinking, Fast and Slow*, the masterwork he produced with Amos Tversky, his late collaborator, is perhaps the best summary out there of the syllogisms and logical fallacies we use to make decisions. In addition to defining the valid ones, Kahneman also identifies 12 cognitive biases that make us especially susceptible to fallacies. Of these dozen cognitive illusions, several occur quite frequently. Fortunately, there are strategies to help resolve them.

Availability Bias

Availability bias is a mental shortcut that humans use to decide which information to put their faith in. From an evolutionary perspective, this makes a lot of sense. For our hunter-gatherer ancestors, seeing a lot of deer tracks was a good indication that there were deer nearby. In the modern world, where our main challenge is no longer too little information but too much, the availability bias leads us to believe things that are probably false.

During World War II, British statistician Abraham Wald was asked to recommend design upgrades for aircraft that had been damaged in combat. He shocked the generals with his seemingly absurd answer. He suggested adding armor to the areas that *hadn't* been hit by enemy fire in the aircraft he examined. He recognized something that no one else had: the officers were only seeing the aircraft that had survived, not the ones that had been shot down.

Wald realized that just because he was seeing a lot of airplanes with holes in them didn't mean that most airplanes were getting shot in those places. He was self-aware enough to consider the key information that wasn't being presented to him because it wasn't available. What you don't know can often tell you more than what you do know.

There's a similar dynamic in Arthur Conan Doyle's *Silver Blaze*:

Inspector Gregory: "Is there any point to which you would wish to draw my attention?"

Sherlock Holmes: "To the curious incident of the dog in the night-time."

Inspector Gregory: "The dog did nothing in the night-time."

Sherlock Holmes: "That was the curious incident."

In both cases, a similar technique to countering the availability bias was used. The practitioners stepped back from the high-priority evidence and asked:

1. What is the larger set being evaluated? (The bodies of all the planes, not just those that survived.)
2. What is knowable vs. what is known about that set? (Knowable: the places bullets did and did not hit the planes that survived. Unknowable: where the bullets hit the planes that did not survive.)
3. Are the full range of options being considered? (The bullets only hit planes that survived in these places vs. the bullets only hit planes in those places.)

Here are a few techniques to ensure you're considering all of the information:

- **Question assumptions:** Take a mental step or two back and make sure that your current assumptions hold.
- **Enforce a beginner's mindset:** Make sure your list of unknowns is as complete as your list of knowns.
- **Consider what you don't know:** Make a list of hypotheticals that, however unlikely, would change your analysis, if they were true.

Representativeness Bias

It's human nature to think in terms of emotions and stories instead of math and probabilities. Marketers and politicians take advantage of this by manipulating your tendency to believe that an example of a phenomenon is representative of the whole phenomenon. But the fact that a thing is similar to something that belongs to a category doesn't always mean that it belongs to that category. For example, "nine out of ten dentists" might agree on something, but are those 10 dentists actually representative of the set of 200,000 dentists in the United States? If cats have four legs, and another animal—say, a dog—has four legs, does that make it a cat?

The way to overcome this cognitive illusion is to ask:

1. Am I certain that I am assessing the right set (four-legged things vs. four-legged things that say "meow")?
2. How large is the set (cats and dogs vs. all four-legged things)?
3. Do the sets nest within each other (omnivores and carnivores, for example, are not nesting sets)?
4. Why is the example representative of the whole set (cats)?

One advantage sommeliers have over amateurs like myself is their understanding of the markets. Knowing how much white versus red wine is produced in a region, how much chardonnay versus sauvignon blanc, and how much chardonnay is grown in New Zealand versus Australia allows them to eliminate or add some probabilities to the balance.

It allows them to consider the whole equation, working with the denominator as well as the numerator. They consider every set a wine might nest in and the likelihood of its existing within the context of each set. Balancing evidence against likelihood is the key to making decisions under uncertainty.

Confirmation Bias

It's in our nature to confirm what we already believe. Sherlock Holmes makes this point with tremendous clarity in the 1891 story "Scandal in Bohemia," in which he says, "It is a capital mistake to theorize before one has data. Insensibly one begins to twist facts to suit theories, instead of theories to suit facts." All of human affairs, including business, are bathed in confirmation bias. Decision scientists have found it to be particularly pernicious.[16] Falsifying our own deeply held beliefs is an unnatural act, and few of us have the discipline to even try. Somms taste blind to avoid prejudicing themselves. But as billionaire investor Warren Buffett puts it, "What the human being is best at doing is interpreting all new information so that their prior conclusions remain intact."

Even if we want to root out and eliminate our prejudices, we might not know what they are. A better approach is to build multiple competing hypotheses and then seek to disprove them one by one.

When somms evaluate a wine, they say things like, "It may be this . . . it may be that. It's in this range. My initial conclusion is . . . My final conclusion is . . ." They do this out loud, not in their head. It's quite bizarre the first time you see it happen, but you quickly realize that it's very intentional, and more or less universal among professional sommeliers.

The act of intentional *waffling* allows them to avoid many of the common traps decision-makers fall into. It forces them to remain fully aware of the whole range of possibilities and the exact level of their uncertainty about each variable.

Many of the most decisive-seeming entrepreneurs also use this approach. As Jeff Bezos puts it, "Wandering is an essential counterbalance to efficiency. You need to employ both. The outsized discoveries—the 'non-linear' ones—are highly likely to require wandering."

Master sommeliers wander widely as they move from sensing to analysis, testing their logic to make sure it holds together.

Inviting Criticism

The unknown can be a dark place, and it's easy to get lost if you're alone. If there is only one thing you do to improve your decision in uncertain situations, vow to work in small groups that hold themselves to rigorous checklists. This is one of the best ways to ensure you keep an open mind.

Elon Musk suggests: "Really pay attention to negative feedback and solicit it, particularly from friends . . . hardly anyone does that, and it's incredibly helpful."[17] We only know what we know. It's always good to get a second set of eyes on a complex problem.

Research in a variety of fields, from aeronautics to critical wine tasting, proves this.[18] Serious somms study for the master sommelier test in peer groups that are both highly supportive and highly critical, challenging each other's assumptions to sharpen their investigative instincts. Similarly, working in pairs can significantly increase the accuracy and decisiveness of decision-making if the critique is rigorous and tests for specific issues.

The Chess Tournament

Ted Selker is one of the most prolific inventors in the United States. Since we met 20 years ago at the MIT Media Lab, we have used a reality testing approach that we call the Chess Tournament. It has improved the quality of our investigations in everything from medical diagnostics, personal computers, and HVAC systems to office furniture, construction systems, and election security.

When approaching a new problem, we'll identify four competing hypotheses, which we call Chess Boards, and spend 15 minutes collaboratively attempting to confirm each. In the second hour, one of us will spend 15 minutes attempting to demonstrate why each solution won't work, while the other attempts to defend it. When one potential solution fails, we add a new one to the tournament, so that we are never emotionally engaged in just one solution and there are always more options at play than we can fully remember.

While this approach works for the two of us, other approaches may work well for you. The key is to develop a process that offsets the likelihood of succumbing to bias. If you want to develop your own technique, here are the reasons why the Chess Tournament works:

- The structured brainstorming that we use counters availability bias by *expanding the range of possible options* beyond what we can hold in our heads. This forces us to take notes, second-guess our conclusions, and double-check our assumptions. Testing a range of hypotheses leads to a more objective understanding of what is always true, what is sometimes true, and what cannot be proven based on the evidence.
- It uses *adversarial testing* to put a check on representativeness bias. This forces a rigorous interrogation of assumptions about the size of the set and its range.

- It counters confirmation bias by having us *argue both pro and con*. This limits our emotional attachment to a single point of view. It forces us to constantly test new options, broadening our thinking.

Likely Realities

If you don't know where you are going,
any road will get you there.

—LEWIS CARROLL

Some of our assumptions about the past and future can be held to a high standard of proof: if we have video of someone committing a crime, we can usually assume that they did it. If we know how fast a train is moving when it departs from Chicago and that it doesn't change speed, we can accurately predict when it will get to Duluth. But when situations get more complex and multivariate, we need to think probabilistically. We have to weigh the likelihood that this or that will happen and place our bets accordingly. We need to separate the plausible from the probable.

Confidence Marking: Developing a Language of Likelihood

We all know how to express likelihood, by writing it down or assigning a number to it. *This thing is highly likely; I rate its chances as a 9 out of 10.* But it's much harder to do this when you're working in groups. People may use the same words to mean different things, or the meanings of the words may shift over time. Having a common vocabulary to describe perceptions of probability helps to identify where our perceptions diverge. Writing down the group consensus is also important when tracking whether perceptions have changed over time. Humans have a powerful capability to reinvent history when it suits them. As Charlie Munger put it, "You tend to forget your own mistakes when your reputation is threatened by remembering."

This process of assessing probability based on what is known is called *confidence marking*. It's critical when considering ambiguous situations because consensus views are often more trustworthy than individual ones. For example, group averages are bizarrely accurate when guessing how many pennies are in a jar.

Confidence marking, particularly when done through secret polls, provides a reference and a range in situations where more data is likely to become available over time. It is often useful to know whether your range of confidence is increasing or decreasing.

If you listen carefully to the news, you'll hear the precise and measured language security officials and police investigators use when they speculate about outcomes. The CIA (the Central Intelligence Agency this time) has published a ranked list of common terms used to indicate likelihood within the US Intelligence apparatus (Figure 3.9).[19] The lesson here is that, if you are in the business of unraveling mysteries and assessing enigmas, you need a common language for probabilities . . . and we're all in that business.

Figure 3.9 **Confidence Markers**

Confidence Markers	Likelihood
Are, Will	90–100%
Almost Certainly, Undoubtedly	80–100%
Highly Probable, Highly Likely	75–95%
Probably, Will	70–90%
Probably, Good Chance, Likely, Seems Likely	60–80%
Better Than Even Chance	50–70%
May	40–60%
Probably Not, Unlikely	10–30%
Some Slight Chance	0–20%

It's crucial to ensure you're using the same scale and terminology when discussing the likelihood of an event occurring or estimating how successful something will be with your team. In many company cultures, it's extremely common to have a roomful of people all nodding in agreement and saying things like "I think we're on the same page here," when, in fact, each of them has a different idea of what's on that page. One of the easiest ways to avoid catastrophic misunderstandings is to be explicit about what terms mean and to ask team members to give a concrete description of what they think is going to happen. It's even more critical to have a baseline when making decisions based on likelihood, particularly when the likelihood will change over time.

What Experts Can and Cannot Tell You About the Future

Confidence marking is particularly useful when working with domain experts. They are generally quite accurate off the cuff when assessing historical baselines or categories of events that might cause change to occur. They can help you to better understand what forces will cause your current reality to remain as it is and what in your system's 5Ws and 1H (who, what, when, where, why, and how) could cause change to accelerate, decelerate, or stop.

But domain experts are notoriously bad at predicting the future in the abstract. They can't tell you how the world as a whole is likely to look in 2070. They are also terrible at predicting the timing of high-impact, low-probability events. This is because their expertise is typically a mile deep in just one area. But, as we have seen, rogue waves typically rise up when multiple undercurrents interact.

If you're looking to find out the average number of paid K-pop songs that Japanese teenagers will stream wirelessly five years from now, you might start off with an expert opinion from an A&R executive at Sony music. They know Japanese tastes inside and out, so their insight is somewhat better than a coin flip. But you'll get much more useful information if you add some knowable baseline context that A&R executives might not have at their fingertips, say:

- The free time of Japanese teenagers
- Their spending power
- The total number of songs streamed in Japan
- The mix of songs streamed by teenagers worldwide
- The cost of bandwidth for wireless streaming in five years

Synthesizing information across domains leads to much more accurate models of the future.

Assessing the Likelihood of the Inevitable

There are many major causes of business disruption that leaders assume won't impact them. One is violent conflict, whether it is spontaneous protests, like the Arab Spring; insurrection at the US Capitol Building; international terrorism, like the September 11 attacks; or state violence.

On Thursday, July 23, 1914, the front page of the *New York Times* featured the following:

- The murder trial of Madame Caillaux, a magazine editor and wife of the French prime minister
- A royal wedding
- A domestic tiff in Ireland

Its financial coverage of continental Europe amounted to four sentences, noting that the bourses in Paris and Berlin were doing fine, but with a bit of softening in late trading.[20]

On Saturday, July 25, 1914, the *British Army & Navy Gazette*, the weekly publication of the British military reserve, devoted its entire front page to marksmanship competitions.[21]

On Monday, July 27, the London bourse had its biggest fall in a generation after the Paris and Berlin markets crashed. And then on Tuesday, July 28, World War I broke out.

All of the information was known. All of the causal relationships were out in the open. A balance of power had secured peace, but the data, viewed through a cold calculus, suggested that the likelihood of war was actually going up because technology and geopolitics had reduced the power of trade as a disincentive. The question was not if, but when.

A general could look at the network of diplomatic alliances among the European powers that had held for the past 40 years and see that the house of cards would collapse if fighting threatened the borders of any of the major powers. Railroad executives might not have been able to predict that a world war would occur in 1914, but they could have told you that European generals were terrified about the speed at which other countries could now rally for war. A politician would only have had to open the 1913 edition of *Jane's Fighting Ships* to see that Germany's naval buildup was a growing concern to the United Kingdom. Everyone knew that if a great war occurred, it would pit Germany against Great Britain, two of the major powers in the region. Jean de Bloch, the military theorist, had predicted, with terrifying accuracy, the protracted battle on the Western Front.[22]

But business, military, and political leaders didn't see the signals, nor did the markets, because they were preoccupied with their lived experience instead of the current situation: what was, instead of what is and what's next. They hadn't done any true reality testing, which blinded them to a perfectly plausible scenario in which a final straw would break the camel's back.

Why was everyone so out of step with reality? Because they succumbed to all three biases. They assumed that what was true in their field, whether domestic politics, diplomacy, or defense, was what was true throughout Europe (availability bias). They assumed that peace was the norm, contrary to centuries of history (representativeness bias), because they had not experienced a major Continental war in over a generation. And they assumed that the system that had benefited them until then would continue to benefit them in the future (confirmation bias).

They also failed to ask the three most important questions about causality, probability, and completeness. The completeness issue is probably the most significant: they hadn't sought out other, possibly conflicting points of view. The generals didn't talk to the diplomats, and the politicians didn't talk to the generals. If they had simply asked each other one question, the course of history might have changed: What sort of critical data, that remains stubbornly unknown, would cause a great war?

You can avoid many catastrophic outcomes by considering:

- **Causality:** Are there clear causal relationships at play?
- **Probability:** Have I considered the probabilities in the context of the right-sized set?
- **Completeness:** What additional categories of data and options might be worth the time and cost to analyze?

For a business, there's a similar question that's worth asking: what are your foundational assumptions, and what would upend them? The Makani Power team was quite good at asking this question. This is clearly demonstrated by the way they dealt with the kite-based power system described earlier. Faced with a unique energy technology, they held off on making any quick judgments. Instead, they went through a systematic process to inform their decision-making and ensure they weren't misled by bias. Observing this process in real time, in fact, was part of what inspired me to codify the REAL framework that you're currently reading about:

- **Reconnaissance:** From a product viewpoint, the Makani team looked for the most likely reason the program might fail. It turned out to be the flight control system. By focusing on the riskiest component first, they were able to shrink their search universe quickly and move on to lower risk issues.
- **Evidence:** Projects like Makani typically receive investment in stages, starting with a seed stake that lets them create prototypes for evaluation. This gave Makani's investors time to gather more evidence around both the market and the system's strengths and weaknesses before purchasing greater

equity. The project was eventually fully acquired by Google (now Alphabet).

- **Alternatives:** Analysts and engineers working on the project took multiple approaches to the system's technical challenges, and tracked alternative solutions the entire time.
- **Likelihood:** One of the painful realities of maintaining alternatives is that you eventually have to make up your mind. In 2020, when Alphabet reviewed its portfolio of investments, Makani didn't make the cut—despite the project's proven technology. Alphabet continuously tracked the project's performance against other technologies and the market. Then, they took quick action when they realized that the future had changed, making other investments were more appealing.

If all this research, verification, staged investment, and waffling sounds timid, consider that Makani was trying to do something radical: revolutionize the way the world generates electricity by launching massive kites, of a type and size that had never been tried before.

Being systematic about decision-making is what makes it possible to tackle such high-risk projects in the first place. If Makani had simply let their early decisions go unchallenged and unchecked, they would never have survived long enough to create something so phenomenal.

The Key to Effective Reality
Testing Is a Checklist

One of the most powerful ways to validate assumptions is with a checklist. Successful investigators, whether they are spies, scientists, entrepreneurs, or investors, have learned to use checklists effectively. Sommeliers walk through theirs out loud repeatedly, forcing themselves to test and retest their assumptions.

Evidence supporting the use of checklists in fields like medicine and aviation is overwhelming. Their introduction after fatal plane crashes in the 1970s dramatically improved air safety, while the proper use of checklists in hospitals has been shown to cut patient mortality in half.[23]

Charlie Munger put it this way:

> Generally thinking, I think you need mental models—and what I call checklist procedures—where you take a worthwhile list of models and run right down them: "Is this here? Is that here?" and so on and so on . . . Now if there are two or three items that are very important that aren't on your checklist—well, if you're an airline pilot, you can crash. Likewise, if you're trying to analyze a company without using an adequate checklist, you can make a very bad investment.

In a world of accelerating economic, technological, and social change, leaders who take the time to assess what is actually happening will have a massive strategic advantage over those who assume things aren't changing.

Here is a checklist you can use to ensure that you're basing your decisions on the world as it is, instead of how you would like it to be.

SUMMARY

Test Your Present Reality

1. **Decide how you will do reconnaissance.**
   - List what you know, what you don't know, and what you can't know.
   - Identify the search tree that will most efficiently reduce the number of important unknowns.
   - Assess the branches that are best explored through inductive, deductive, and abductive reasoning.

2. **Evaluate the usefulness of your data.**
   - Decide on a standard of proof before you start collecting any evidence.
   - Set criteria for knowing whether the information you collect is accurate.

3. **Develop multiple theories and test their validity.**
   - Identify findings that would invalidate your theory if true, no matter how improbable.
   - Establish what the impact would be if your theory was invalid.
   - Understand the most common biases—especially availability, representation, and confirmation—and create processes for minimizing their influence.
   - If certain key evidence can't be found, consider what its unavailability means.

4. **Ensure you've explored the full range of options, given the level of proof that you have.**
   - Consider whether the unknowns you're investigating can actually be forecast.
   - Confirm that you have subjected all possible theories to the same level of logical scrutiny.
   - Make an honest assessment of how confident you are in your conclusions and rank them.

Today's To-Dos for Tomorrow

- **Teach your team.** Have a conversation with your team about the importance of reality testing and the process you use to analyze ambiguous information.

- **Use reality testing to reassess your assumptions on a regular basis.** Identify and reinforce your organization's mechanisms for identifying and challenging beliefs. Make sure to do so on a regular tempo.

- **Budget to increase vital knowledge.** What portion of your research and consulting budget supports directed investigation of blind spots and terra incognita?

- **Teach reality testing in your training program.** Verify that your learning and development, training, and recruitment initiatives focus on foundational investigation skills as well as role-specific competencies. Assign a senior sponsor to champion these skills.

- **Prioritize training the teams that could benefit most from reality testing.** Assess where poor investigative hygiene is impacting your decisions.

4

O: Observe Your System

Model the forces that keep your current system stable to determine what would cause it to change and what would cause it to break.

On April 10, 2020, Marguerite McDonald was one of the first people in the United States to die of Covid-19. Like many of the pandemic's victims in its early months, she lived in a nursing home.

In many ways, the setting where she lived should have been among the safer places on earth in a pandemic. A nursing home is a nearly self-contained environment, with excellent hygiene, on-site medical services, and residents who rarely leave. Covid-19 originated on the other side of the planet, and its existence and dangers had been known for months. The United States is the world leader in medical research, and the Centers for Disease Control is the world's most respected institution of public health.

Yet opportunity after opportunity to protect Marguerite and her fellow residents was missed. These failures doomed tens of thousands of people in her age group. One failure was a shortage of personal protective equipment (PPE). Critical gear like N95 masks was in such short supply that residents and even some staff went without. Another was a lack of adequate testing. Contact tracing, which played a crucial role in controlling infection in many Asian countries, collapsed in the United States almost as soon as it began. Respirators were also hard to come by. So were qualified staff to operate them.

Each of these failures had a few clear immediate causes. PPE and respirators hadn't been stockpiled, and contact tracing efforts were scaled up too slowly to keep up with spiraling infection rates. Researchers had developed effective Covid tests early on, but poor communication and regulatory bungles had kept them out of the hands of most doctors and public health entities.

But the real failures happened much earlier. Prestige Ameritech, the leading US manufacturer of medical masks, made the decision to shutter four unprofitable US production lines, letting more cost-efficient offshore factories take up the slack. Local medical supply distributors decided to minimize overhead costs by keeping their inventory lean. The testing debacle was predetermined by years of underfunding of local health departments and an increasingly centralized, politicized chain of decision-making within the CDC. This made it impossible for universities and hospitals to scale up and distribute their own tests. Contact tracing was essentially DOA, mowed down by years of decaying public trust in government institutions and growing privacy concerns.

Everyone knew about the danger of pandemics: the nursing home, Prestige Ameritech, local public health departments, and especially the CDC. So did the White House. By January 22, 2020, the outbreak in Wuhan was already underway when Robert Kadlec, the Department of Health and Human Services' Assistant Secretary for Preparedness and Response, appears to have decided that they would not stockpile medical masks.[1] The nursing home had some protective equipment on hand but assumed they could order more when they needed it. It wasn't as if they had ever run out before.

We depend on increasingly complex, interconnected systems to deliver our goods and services. Most of the time when they fail, it's an inconvenience. But sometimes, people die. What killed

Marguerite wasn't a missing mask, respirator, or test, and it wasn't a pandemic. It was a series of small overlapping decisions that seemed inconsequential, even beneficial when they were made, because no one was looking at the larger system.

Marguerite was my mother-in-law and my friend, and she was a victim of a system in which everyone mistook their job for *the* job. None of them had the courage to scream that the sky was falling, even when it was. None of them were prepared for a future that was different from the past they already knew.

THE THING ABOUT THE FUTURE

The thing about the future is that there isn't just one. There's always a range of possible futures, and a range of timelines over which they can appear.

The default practice for anticipating tomorrow is to extrapolate from the past, but this presents a problem. Linear extrapolation rarely foresees the big shifts that pose the greatest dangers and opportunities. The fact that the stock market has been a good investment over the past 70 years is no guarantee that it will be next year. In fact, if you had invested in a portfolio of major stocks in 1930, you would have had 15 years of good growth. If you had invested in 1928, it would have taken until the end of World War II to recover after 1929's financial crash.[2]

The key to preparing for what happens next is to figure out what is *possible,* and then what is *likely,* based on what is happening *now.* Even if specific futures can't be seen, many of the underlying forces that will determine them are obvious and reliable. One of the most reliable is entropy, or disorder: all systems in the universe are in the process of decay. Sometimes the disorder accelerates abruptly, as happened to social and economic systems in the wake of Covid-19. Sometimes it moves slowly, like the death of a star over millions of years. But the natural progress of any closed system is toward greater disorder. That's the second law of thermodynamics.

External organizing forces can keep the chaos in check, however, and there are many such forces. The predictable growth of consumer demand based on demographics is one. So is a stable regulatory framework. Any process that drives reliable supply or demand brings order. The 10 undercurrents described in Chapter 2 reliably indicate the future because they are organized and maintained by millions of people and systems that are dedicated to their continuation.

Entropy, Inertia, and Control

In any dynamic system, two tendencies are in opposition:

- **Entropy:** Growing disorder
- **Inertia:** Resistance to change

Entropy will eventually win if no external work is done on the system, though how quickly depends a lot on how strong its forces are. Friction is a powerful entropic effect that turns orderly, directed motion into disorderly heat. This is why brake pads get hot after extended use.

In a stable system, entropy is further offset by some kind of external effort, like a jet engine fighting air friction. This is how an airplane flies. Lift, gravity, thrust, and drag are all balanced to keep it in the air.

A system becomes unstable when there is a change in force. For instance, a sudden loss of thrust can cause a jet to fall from the sky.

The same equilibrium and the same exceptions apply to markets. Regulations that drive home ownership cause reliable trends in demand, and investors tend to assume that homes are safe investments. But when a recession hits, many new homeowners default, and the system falls out of balance. Before the 2008 crisis, derivative risk portfolios made up of seemingly safe investments, like mortgages and the insurance policies on them, became unbalanced. A few months later, the global financial system was in tatters. That was a rogue wave: unpredictable in its specifics, but ultimately inevitable.

In his book *The Black Swan: The Impact of the Highly Improbable*, Nassim Taleb writes about the surprise Europeans feel when they see black swans in Australia, where they're fairly common. It's a great book, but it has led to a decade of nonsensical discussions in conferences and board rooms, where "black swan" has become a shorthand for an event that isn't predictable. This ignores one of Taleb's cardinal points: that most "black swans"—including the literal ones in Australia—are knowable if you understand the broader situation. The real surprise isn't the black swan. It's that so few people bother to consider the bigger picture.

Second-Order Effects

In 2006 and 2007, my girlfriend at the time was brokering home mortgages for companies like Countrywide. It was clear to her that the run-up in real estate prices was out of line with income growth. McMansions were being sold to people who had no realistic ability to pay for them in a financial downturn. The market was frothy. Insiders knew this but kept feeding the beast.

Most investors chose not to look under the covers, and they got fleeced. They assumed that the market would keep doing better, simply because it had been doing better. They assumed that more debt would inevitably drive more growth. This is first-order thinking: A causes B, and no need to look any further than that.

But in any complex system, A is going to indirectly cause a lot more than just B. These second-order impacts are less apparent, but because they're often ignored until it's too late, they can be more significant. Debt can drive growth, but in the long term, it can also drive more bankruptcies and lower investment.

It's counterintuitive to think about second-order impacts, but it's easier to do so if you consider your first principles and ask "what if?" questions like, "What would happen if that debt wasn't backed by an ability and incentive to pay?" The investors who profited from the Great Recession asked that specific question. One of them was Ray Dalio, the founder of Bridgewater Associates and the author of *Big Debt Crises*, a foundational text on the subject. Dalio's underlying principle (similar to the one Sherlock Holmes advocates) is that every outcome has a cause.

You can often identify the red flags by mapping the process of failure in reverse. When you have slow growth and zero interest rates, for example, central banks have to print money to backfill government debt and stimulate the economy. This causes a growing wealth gap[3] as investors buy up depreciated assets with debt, and the working class, with less access to capital, gets relatively poorer. Eventually, debt service grows past the point where even the wealthy can keep up, and the bubble deflates. Not only are such causes and effects predictable, they've occurred numerous times throughout history.

Ray Dalio didn't have insider knowledge. He studied history—not to extrapolate the future, but to learn the warning signs of inevitable events that he hadn't experienced personally. Then he followed the same logic laid out by Bernard Baruch, who profitably shorted the 1929 crash, in his memoir *My Own Story*:

1. Make a periodic reappraisal of all your investments to see whether changing developments have altered their prospects.
2. Always keep a good part of your capital in a cash reserve. Never invest all your funds.

Unlike most investors, Dalio looked under the covers. Then he assessed the changing developments, mapped their likely first- and second-order impacts, and changed his investment portfolios accordingly.

The best analogy for the 2008 financial crisis isn't a black swan. It's another proverbial animal, an ostrich with its head in the sand.

MAKING SENSE OF YOUR SYSTEM

In the mid-1800s, before Darwin published *On the Origin of Species*, Gregor Mendel[4] was busy figuring out the basics of hereditary genetics.[5] He did it long before anyone knew anything about genes—never mind DNA—using nothing more than a pencil, a sheet of paper, and a patch of peas.

The details of his experiments and observations are often taught in grade school biology. But looking at them now, from the perspective of modern forecasting and pattern-spotting, his insights seem almost magical.

Mendel's experiment began with a plot of pea plants, which he classified using seven characteristics: flower color, flower position, seed color, seed shape, pod shape, pod color, and stem length. He didn't know what was going on inside the plants, but he was able to make inductive assessments by cross-breeding them in specific ways and observing the outcomes in terms of those seven characteristics.

After many years of breeding and meticulously recording the results, he'd compiled a list of over 29,000 hybrids. Careful review revealed distinct patterns, which eventually became the laws that bear his name:

- Mendel's *law of segregation* defines how traits are distributed from parents to immediate offspring.
- Mendel's *law of dominance* predicts how dominant and recessive traits are distributed in successive generations.
- Mendel's *law of independent assortment* states that inheriting one trait has no effect on how another is inherited.

Mendel didn't understand any of the inner workings of genetics, yet he was able to come up with a precise and highly developed model of inheritance that's used by scientists to this day.

For those of us dealing with uncertainty in the business world, Mendel's example offers hope. It's possible to understand how a system works by paying close attention to the links between its elements—even if you don't know *why* it works. This makes it possible to create reliable forecasts, even if there's a lot of randomness in the data.

To do this, though, you need to be meticulous about what you observe and how you build your model. You also need a keen sense of abductive reasoning. Otherwise, you can easily end up with 29,000 experiments worth of data and not know how to separate the peas from the pods.

Building Models to Understand Systems

At its most basic, systems modeling simply means linking causes and effects. You shake an apple loose from a tree, and gravity makes it fall to the ground. An organization spends more than it earns, and its cash reserves get depleted. These are straightforward, deterministic, first-order effects, and they're predictable within a well-defined system with little randomness.

Linking cause and effect becomes more complex once you start adding multiple causes and effects, variability, or randomness (which are unavoidable in human systems). Unlike Mendel's pea plants, the traits of an organization, a market, or a financial system aren't usually independent. They affect each other. Inflation and fluctuating interest rates, for example, have large enough impacts on cash flow that they have to be accounted for, along with direct costs and revenues.

As these complexities stack up, people and organizations tend to do one of two things. They might use first-order thinking, hoping that the less predictable components don't impact the outcomes too much. They might also throw up their hands and insist, "If it's too complex for me to model, it's too complex for everyone else, so why bother?"

It's almost always possible to develop a model that's better than nothing—and failing to create any kind of model leaves you vulnerable to others who do. That's why resilient organizations tend to be keen modelers. Can you guess who recruits more PhD economists than any other private company in the United States? The answer is Amazon, and the economists are almost entirely focused on modeling possible futures.

Systems models show up in many different areas, from finance to manufacturing to traffic management. And while they use different terminologies, they all contain more or less the same elements. For our purposes, we'll call these: nodes, links, inputs, outputs, rates, and frequencies (Figure 4.1).

Figure 4.1 **Elements of a System Model**

Nodes	Locations within a system that can be connected to each other, and where inventory or potential can be stored. To use the analogy of a road system: *Where are the cars parked?*
Links	The system's capacity to move inventory from one node to another. *Is this a dirt road or a superhighway?*
Inputs	How much potential is added to the system? *How often do people buy new cars?*
Outputs	How often is potential subtracted from the system? *How often do they scrap their old car?*
Rates	The speeds at which inventory moves from one node to another. *How long does it take to get from home to work?*
Frequencies	How often does inventory move from nodes into links and vice versa? *Do you drive into the office every day or only on Mondays and Thursdays?*

To use another analogy, the human circulatory system has:

- A heart (node)
- That pumps blood through vessels (links)
- At a pace of 60 beats/minute (frequency)
- Every minute, it moves five pints of blood around the system (rate)
- To other organs (additional nodes)

The circulatory system also has an additional characteristic that is often important—direction:

- The blood flow travels from the heart to the lungs, where it picks up oxygen that feeds the organs, before returning to the heart (direction).

Progressively smaller subsystems nest within these nodes. For instance, the heart has a left ventricle and a right ventricle. Each has smaller subsystems nested within it, like muscle groups and nerves, which are themselves made up of cells.

A wide variety of control systems are designed using this approach, especially in business. A distribution chain is one familiar example:

- A factory puts new products into the chain (inputs).
- Multiple warehouses at different points in the chain stock inventory (nodes).
- Vehicles move products along supply lines (links).
- Appropriate transport, whether plane, train, or boat, is used depending on the rate and frequency required.
- The seller is paid when the product gets to the final destination (output).

The power of this approach, which we'll call a *system model*, isn't necessarily its predictive ability, but its clarity. You can list out the elements in a notebook or spreadsheet, and draw the model on a napkin. Many decisions still need to be made about what kinds of controls to put into place. But laying out the variables in this structure can help you focus on the small changes that will have the greatest impact.

System models show up almost anywhere that complexity needs to be made clear. It's how scientists model climate change, how intelligence analysts identified the location of Bin Laden's compound, and how Elon Musk decided he could make a profit building rocket ships.

These models work when all the inputs are known. They also work when a range of theoretical inputs are fed into the system. When statisticians want to understand the range of possible outcomes, they'll feed every possible combination of variables into their model (a Monte Carlo simulation).

As systems become more complex, however, this approach can become time and computationally intensive, and end up with a bad result. One particularly egregious example occurs in Douglas Adams's fictional *The Hitchhiker's Guide to the Galaxy*. In this case, a supercomputer named Deep Thought spends 7.5 million years calculating the Answer to Life, the Universe and Everything, which turns out to be 42.

So while the underlying structure of a system model is extremely useful, it also has some real limitations. And as we'll see in the next section, the familiar conflict between "visionary" and "practical" mindsets often comes down to the visionary's ability to create a useful and comprehensible model despite those limitations.

GETTING COMFORTABLE WITH UNCERTAINTY

It's human nature to look for simple, linear models: because A, therefore B. We tend to think of organizations as org charts and projects as critical path diagrams, and we stick with them because they're familiar and predictable. But many business decisions are recursive: they don't just change the outcome; they change the process itself. This is why we need more advanced models to make sense of them.

As the data economy continues to grow, more decisions will be made using more information, some of which will be conflicting. The result is that critical decisions will become even more probabilistic and less deterministic. A no longer leads to B, and everything impacts everything else, making it complicated and difficult to map. This comes into conflict with the culture of many organizations. The natural tendency of businesses is to try to force things into linear relationships.

So, how do you make sense of questions with a range of answers? Or cyclical problems in which the answer changes the question? What if it's not the chicken or the egg, but the chicken *and* the egg?

The good news is that there are better ways to plan and make sense of complex, recursive systems. Researchers who deal with complexity, in fields like biology, intelligence, finance, and AI, all use conceptually similar tools to model systems. AI experts use what they call *finite state machines* to predict what is likely to happen next. Financial analysts have *stock-flow models* on their workstations. Biologists use a similar technique called a *causal loop diagram* to explore entire ecosystems, like the Amazon basin, on whiteboards.

The truly wicked problem with the future isn't that it's totally unpredictable. It's that we typically only know the answers to *some* of our questions (the 5Ws and 1H) or only for a given time or only under certain circumstances.

The Spreadsheet That Launched a Hundred Rockets

Jim Cantrell is one of the most skilled, successful mechanical engineers on the planet, and he cofounded SpaceX in 2001. But he quit the company a year later, believing there was no way it could be successful. He describes his decision like this:

> I sat there and looked around at our merry band of misfit engineers and designers, all of us refugees from Corporate America, none of us dressed better than the average beach-goer, and thought to myself, "and we are going to revolutionize the space transportation business ???" I could not conceive of success at that point. . . . I soon came to realize that the only reason that I might stay was to make money and I frankly could not see us succeeding technically nor financially. So I left.[6]

Cantrell was trying to deconstruct the problem instead of modifying the system. Thinking deductively, he cataloged the parts without seeing how they worked as a whole and how that could change. Elon Musk, on the other hand, was using an abductive process that let him see the whole system, *including* the parts that he didn't know or only knew imprecisely. This allowed him to estimate the probability of success and identify what needed to change to improve it.

According to Ashlee Vance's book *Elon Musk*, this is what happened:

> "We're thinking, 'Yeah, you and whose fucking army,'" Cantrell said "But, Elon says, 'No, I'm serious. I have this spreadsheet.'" Musk passed his laptop over to Griffin and Cantrell, and they were dumbfounded. The document detailed the costs of the materials needed to build, assemble, and launch a rocket.
>
> According to Musk's calculations, he could undercut existing launch companies by building a modest-sized rocket that would cater to a part of the market that specialized in carrying smaller satellites and research payloads to space. The spreadsheet also laid out the hypothetical performance characteristics of the rocket in fairly impressive detail.[7]

Musk's approach hinged on the question of what would *probably* happen in the future versus what *might* happen. *Humanity will eventually move toward sustainable energy; otherwise, we'll run out or make our cities uninhabitable. The colonization of space, on the other hand, isn't inevitable.* Then he worked backward from his end goal, creating a branching tree of probabilities in the process. He used the tree to identify actions he could take to make a desired branch more likely, by either accelerating or slowing down certain trends.

Originally, SpaceX started off as a bizarre fascination. As a freshly minted Silicon Valley zillionaire, Musk wanted to do something new. He loved rockets and he loved sci-fi. He was talking to various space geeks like Cantrell and reading rocket science textbooks at night. Reportedly, his initial plan was to send mice on a one-way trip to Mars using surplus Russian ICBMs.

But while he was hatching this completely loony plan, he had a number of insights about rockets and the space industry. Here's how he explained his thought process during a 2013 conversation at the Khan Academy:

How hard is it really to make a rocket? Historically, all rockets have been expensive, therefore all rockets will be expensive. Actually, that's not true. If you say "what is a rocket made of?" and say "ok, it's made of aluminum, titanium, some copper, carbon fiber if you want to go that way." And you break it down and say "what is the raw material cost of all these components?" And if you had them stacked on the floor and could wave a magic wand to rearrange all of the atoms, then what would the cost of the rocket be? I did that and discovered that it's really small. It's like 2 percent of what a rocket costs. So we have to figure out how can we get the atoms in the right shape much more efficiently.

I had a series of meetings on Saturdays with people—some of whom were still working at the big aerospace companies—just to try to figure out, is there some catch here that I'm not appreciating? There didn't seem to be any catch, so I started SpaceX.

. . . [we were able to make our first] rockets for one quarter [the cost] of existing rockets . . . If we make it reusable, we can make it two orders of magnitude cheaper [one percent of the price].

. . . Our Falcon 9 Rocket costs about $60 million dollars, but the propellant cost, which is mostly oxygen (two-thirds oxygen, one-third fuel) is only about $200,000 . . . it costs about as much to refuel our rocket as it does to refuel a 747.[8]

Through this process, Musk had discovered something extraordinary: rockets could be commoditized. If they were made reusable, their cost would drop even further, opening up space to entirely new markets.

While Musk would never admit it, sending mice to Mars was likely a ploy to extract information. How could you not take a call from a Silicon Valley star with such a madcap idea? In fact, while Musk was openly calling the Russian military to price ICBMs, he was also building a model of the rocket industry, to disrupt it.

It's possible (though not certain) that Musk was explicitly using a system model to do this. But it's easy to demonstrate his reasoning using this kind of structure. Here's how the elements of his rocket business would break down:

- The *nodes* are the major suppliers of rockets. In this case, there are only a handful of private manufacturers in the United States and Europe, plus the governments of a few other countries (notably Russia).
- The *links* were largely between governments and military contractors. There were plenty of private companies that wanted to launch satellites, but only governments were big enough and incentivized to fund the development of new launch platforms.

- The *rate* was how long it took to develop and build a new launch platform, which was about a decade.
- The *frequency* was how many launches there were per year. Rocket launches had dropped by half since the end of the Cold War, so there wasn't enough demand to justify a systematic approach to improving it.
- The *inputs* were what it took to actually make the rocket: labor, fuel, and materials.
- The *outputs* were the number of pounds of payload launched into orbit.

Each of these pieces of information by itself wasn't that remarkable, just as any pea plant in Mendel's garden was just a pea plant. But certain insights started to emerge by linking them together.

One of the biggest was that the cost of materials and fuel was just a tiny fraction of the cost of a rocket launch. Another was that the market for launches could potentially be much larger, if the cost could be brought down. The entire market was built on single-use heavy-lift spacecraft that were going up less and less often after the Cold War ended, sending costs and defense contractors' interest in the wrong direction. Musk realized he could build a company around agile Silicon Valley–style methodologies and more frequent launch schedules.

A third insight was that innovation was almost nonexistent in the industry because demand for launches was so low. The only major competitors were US government suppliers and the Russian military. Neither had the desire to employ agile methodologies, even though they had the technical skill to make good rockets. Musk could disrupt the supply network by either insourcing or recruiting suppliers from outside the industry. These three connections formed a kind of catch-22. Nobody was innovating because the demand wasn't there, and demand was low because costs were too high. Yet innovation could bring the cost down. Musk used these insights to develop the idea for SpaceX, recruit a team, and eventually sell the concept to investors.

KNOWING THE PATTERN WITHOUT KNOWING ALL THE DATA

As the world's systems get more complex, more decisions have uncertain outcomes. One of the crucial skills that great decision-makers of the past 30 years have shared—from Jobs to Dalio to Musk—is a willingness to make bold bets. That's because they're very good at understanding probabilities and shaping circumstances to make those bets likely to pan out.

Hurricanes, Terrorists, and Other Unpredictable Threats

Even the most complex dynamic systems, like hurricanes, can be predicted within a range of probability, if you have the right tools. Unlike in the past, we have more data than can be computed. But a lot of seemingly important data doesn't, in fact, have predictive value. So we need to know what information to pay attention to. It's not intuitive. In many cases, rates, flows, and frequencies are just as important as the structure of the system being observed. In fact, what goes on across the links can often tell us more than what goes on in the nodes.

For example, El Niño (the climate event) is a periodic trend that's announced by changes in ocean temperature data. But its existence and effect on global weather was not discovered by looking at specific temperature measurements. Instead, a correlation was found between the rate at which certain weather events occurred and the rate at which certain ocean temperature readings changed. Spotting El Niño depended on seeing a recurring large-scale pattern, not a connection between a specific temperature reading and a specific storm.

Technologies from companies like Palantir have successfully forecast terrorist actions by spotting patterns in data production. It's very easy for terrorists to avoid making phone calls in which they say things like "I have the bomb." But it's much harder to mask a pattern of mobile phone data showing calls between certain locations, made by people fitting certain age, gender, and income ranges, recurring at certain times of the day or night. Changes in pattern can be enough to raise a credible alarm if they are sufficiently rare, specific, and correlated to a past event—even without knowing the contents of the calls.

These techniques were initially developed in military intelligence to separate signals from noise. Today, they are used in any number of fields. Companies like Facebook and Google apply them to huge data sets to target advertising. The FBI uses them to trace money laundering. Until recently, the technology needed to gather this volume of data and spot patterns within it was limited to governments, universities, and a few very sophisticated companies. It's rapidly moving downstream, and the potential applications are vast.

More Data Does Not Mean More Insight

As the volume of collected data grows, so does the amount of noise. The result is that most data isn't useful for directing decisions, but recent improvements in analytical tools, AI-powered and otherwise, make it far easier to distinguish signal from noise. Automated analysis is only practical when we know what a useful signal looks like—whether a set of information is *explanatory*. Does it allow us to build a model that can be used to assess current behaviors and forecast the likelihood of future ones.

In the real world, most datasets are incomplete. For instance, there's no way to predict the weather perfectly because we can't create a complete model. We can't know the exact temperature of every bit of air and water on the planet or the velocity of every gust of wind. We can't model the movement of every molecule in the atmosphere. Instead, we use incomplete data sets to produce imperfect predictions. As the data improves, so do the predictions. But the same is true of predictive models: a better model (i.e., set of rules) can produce more accurate insight, even using the same set of incomplete data.

Fluid dynamics models, for example, are based on general observations of billions of molecules bumping into each other. We could never model the complete system. But we can find recurring patterns if we observe enough fluids in enough situations. Our knowledge of these patterns can help us build models that work well with low-resolution data. In meteorology, granular observations are often generalized to larger contexts. For example, the movement of air in a wind tunnel can tell us a lot about how air moves over a mountain range.

Such inductive models are *probabilistic*, meaning that they are used to forecast a range of potential outcomes. They are useful when you don't know the rules of the system, or you're looking for patterns in the noise. They give their outputs in terms of probabilities because they assume that randomness within the system and in its inputs will cause variability.

Probabilistic models can be used to determine:

- **Relative frequency:** What is the likelihood of the next card in a deck being an ace?
- **Equal probability of an outcome:** What is the likelihood of winning at the roulette table?

Paradoxically, this increased ability to predict likelihood can lead to poor decision-making. More and better information can decrease human bias, but it can also kick it into overdrive. This is particularly true of a probabilistic measurement called static risk. Increasingly sensitive tests for breast and prostate cancers have given people advance notice of risks, but they have also led to an increase in unnecessary invasive surgeries. Sometimes the certain danger of a surgery outweighs the risk of the disease. For many older patients, the slow progression of these diseases means that they often die of other causes. Just because more information is available, doesn't mean you are in greater danger. You need to ask about dynamic risk, how probability changes over time. If you don't understand the type of wave that's coming at you (see Figure 1.4), you end up chasing ghosts.

SEARCHING FOR HIGHER-ORDER EFFECTS

Future-proofing your business means developing strategies to identify and take advantage of second- and third-order effects that will change your industry. As Carl Sagan once said, "When the car was invented, it was easy to predict the highway. It was much harder to predict Walmart."

In the next hour, someone in the United States will die in a drunk driving accident.[9] Such tragedies occur when multiple systems that aren't normally coupled overlap. A bartender is incentivized to serve one too many drinks. Someone makes a poor decision to drive and their friend doesn't stop them. A cop notices that the car is weaving but doesn't bother to pull it over. Two cars are on the same late night stretch of road at the same time. Any one of these events creates a first-order impact that's trivial. But when several of these trivial impacts intersect, the result is a preventable catastrophe.

Usually, the culprit isn't where you think it is. In the case of the car accident, the most effective place to put the air gap (a term that IT people use when they isolate an insecure computer from a vulnerable network) is at the bar. Maybe you need to eliminate tipping to change the bartender's incentive to serve too many drinks.

The system breakdown often occurs long before the system breaks down. PPE, testing, and contact tracing might have protected my mother-in-law from Covid-19. In the case of a heart attack, the culprit might be a long-term buildup of cholesterol due to lifestyle choices or genetics. The highest-leverage, most cost-effective intervention isn't a stent, a defibrillator, or triple bypass surgery. It's diet and exercise and maybe a prescription for statins. By the time you're in the hospital, it's expensive and often too late.

The threat to keep your eye on isn't the rogue wave. It will already be on top of you by the time it forms. What you want to watch out for are the second- and third-order effects that compound to form it.

There are three archetypal systems to keep on your radar: tightly coupled, loosely coupled, and uncoupled (Figure 4.2).

Figure 4.2 **System Coupling**

Tightly Coupled	A system where there is no mechanism to offset the impact of a change.
	For example: The drunk driver, whose extra cocktail cascades into a catastrophe.
Loosely Coupled	A system where changes are offset by reliefs or reservoirs. The probability of an outcome can shift when changes overwhelm the system.
	For example: A heart attack, caused by a large number of small factors that add up over time.
Uncoupled	A system where changes within it don't impact the outcome.
	For example: Your poker face doesn't work at the roulette table because they act independently of each other.

You can identify opportunities by figuring out how to shift your industry from one archetype to another. In the case of the iPhone, it took competitors years to duplicate Apple's tightly coupled system of sensor technologies, wireless standards, and its app store.

When it started, Netflix physically shipped movies to customers, serving markets that its bricks-and-mortar competitor Blockbuster didn't want. What Blockbuster didn't notice was the impact of Netflix decoupling video rentals from retail locations. When internet video streaming became possible, Netflix moved from serving niche customers to serving Blockbuster's core audience.[10] It decoupled Blockbuster's value proposition—same-night movies—from the retail store. And it did it with a superior customer experience and cost structure.

Netflix became the Walmart of video, using the information superhighway to stream movies to 195 million subscribers.[11] Blockbuster went bankrupt.

CAUSAL LOOP DIAGRAMS

As useful as complex, detailed system models are, they require a high level of certainty and completeness. Otherwise, you can't fill out all of the nodes and links, known and unknown inputs, deterministic and probabilistic relationships, and second- and third-order effects. The causal loop diagram is a visual tool that is flexible enough to yield insights from much less information and certainty. Deceptively simple on the surface, causal loops predict second- and third-order effects and accommodate both deterministic and probabilistic relationships. To build one, you simply write down the different nodes in a system and then draw arrows indicating the direction of links.

For a very limited system that only goes in one direction, like a bicycle pump, the diagram is minimal. It looks something like Figure 4.3.

Figure 4.3 **Air Pump Sequence Diagram**

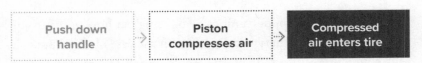

This diagram is simple because the causality is clear—we know what caused what. It's also simple because each event has only one cause, and causation only occurs in one direction: the piston compressing the air does not cause you to push down the handle.

Of course, this diagram skips a lot of steps. An engineer might point out that the force from your hands must be transferred through the pump shaft to the piston head before it can compress the air. A physicist might point out that there is, in fact, a reverse causation: as the pressure in the tire goes up, so does the pressure in the pump. And we've also left out the hose and valve that connect the pump cylinder to the tire (and so on). Although the diagram doesn't list every element of the system, it does show enough detail for each step to make sense.

A causal loop diagram is good for expressing what we do know, so that we can start to understand what we don't know. If we know nothing about the design of air pumps, for example, then the compression of the air is a "black box": something consistently happens when we act on it in a certain way, but we're not sure why.

The more complex the system, the more necessary it is to plot it out explicitly. Where causal loops really come into their own is when the causal relationship is less certain or reliable. An increased training budget for sales staff, for example, might increase revenue, or it might not. We can still map this out in a diagram, but we'll need to be clear that certain causal relationships aren't automatic outputs. They're just probabilities. In the case of sales staff training, there are several steps between spending the money and measuring the change in revenue (Figure 4.4).

Figure 4.4 **Training Investment Sequence Diagram**

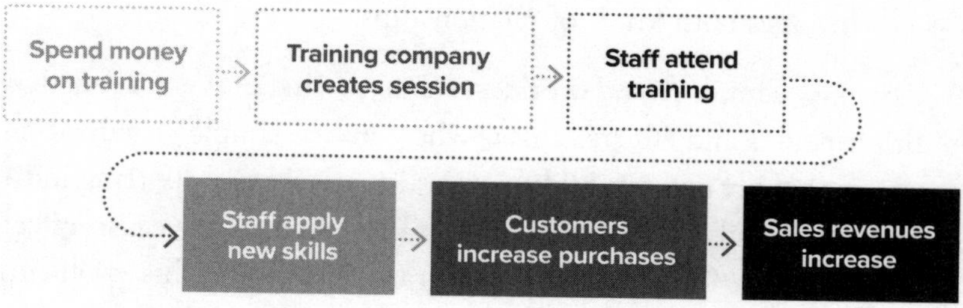

Looking closely, y u might recognize that there are two kinds of relationships here. The first two arrows are deterministic (rules-based): you can assume that staff will attend training if you pay for it (if not, you've just identified your biggest problem). The last arrow is deterministic as well: sales revenue usually varies directly with purchase rates.

149

But the third and fourth arrows indicate probabilistic relationships. It's not guaranteed that any given staff member will absorb new skills or apply them at work, or that those skills will impact customer behavior. But in a large sample size, it's a good bet that at least some of them will. So theoretically, we should be able to quantify these effects by how likely they are to occur. In other words, we can't use the relationships to compute a specific, reliable outcome, but we can use their probabilities to help us make decisions about where to focus our efforts.

We can look at the training investment diagram (Figure 4.4) in several ways:

- If we were to look only at the first three boxes, we'd have a deterministic model because it's based exclusively on deterministic relationships.
- If we only looked at the middle section (Attend training session → Apply skills → Increase purchase rate), we'd have a probabilistic model because it's based on two probabilistic relationships.
- The complete model of all six nodes is hybrid because it involves both kinds of relationships.

In big, complex, real-world systems, a single event often has multiple causes and effects. This is where even a simple visualization can be incredibly powerful. Human brains are great at spotting individual causes and effects, but terrible at keeping multiple cause-effect relationships in mind at once. Diagrams can solve this problem, especially for groups of people.

Figure 4.5 is a simple diagram that shows the flow of capital on a balance sheet over time.

The two loops demonstrate that there's a balance between the payoff of an investment and the rate at which it depreciates. The direction of the arrows shows that more investment *increases* capital (+) and that depreciation on the asset *decreases* capital (–). The insight is that, if capital is to grow over time, the flow between these nodes needs to be considered.

Figure 4.5 **Causal Loop Diagram**

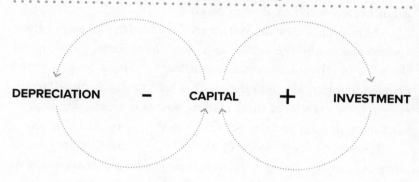

Figure 4.6 **Dynamics of the Biofuels Industry**

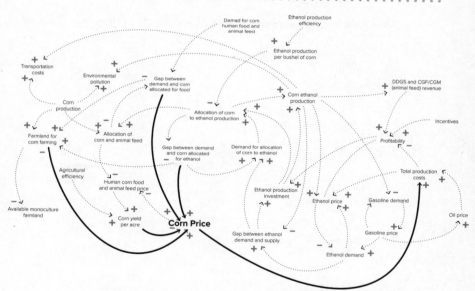

Source: Enze Jin and John W. Sutherland, "A Proposed Integrated Sustainability Model for a Bioenergy System," *Procedia CIRP* 48 (2016), 358–63, doi: 10.1016/j.procir.2016.03.159.

Figure 4.6 is a more complex causal loop diagram describing the dynamics of the biofuels industry. There's no need to dig in and fully understand it. The point is that it shows *recursion*: how one process changes several other processes that then loop back to change the first one. Often, these feedback loops counterbalance each other to keep the system stable. Systems geeks separate these further into balancing loops and reinforcing loops.

The ones that slow the system are called balancing loops. These are represented by the minus signs (–). The price of gasoline and the price of ethanol, for example, are kept in check by supply and demand, but they also influence each other's demand. Any dynamic system you can think of that's holding relatively steady, despite having a lot of moving parts, must include one or more balancing loops.

Reinforcing loops work in the other direction, taking small changes and magnifying them, so that they move a system away from stasis with increasing speed. These are represented by plus signs (+).

Figure 4.7 **Upstream Indicators of Future Corn Price**

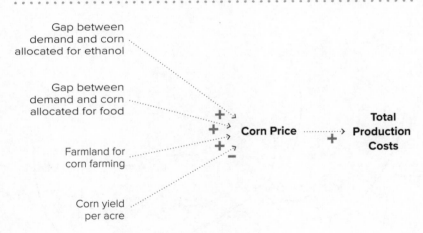

While this example might seem complex at first glance, it allows you, and more importantly, a group to see the forest, but it also helps everyone track the trees. For instance, if you zoom out on Corn Price (Figure 4.7), the larger diagram quickly shows that it affects a lot more than just production costs, getting you all thinking about second- and third-order drivers. If you zoom in, it also helps you track the details.

You can often get an early warning or create disproportionate change by focusing on these upstream and downstream indicators. For example, you might only get a near-term forecast of total production costs by looking at first-order drivers, like the price of corn. But you can look further out and get a more accurate forecast by monitoring things like corn yield per acre. Perhaps you could also push down prices by adding upstream nodes, like lobbying the government to simultaneously increase corn subsidies and decrease human corn syrup consumption.

In the diagram of global climate change (Figure 4.8), when something like higher carbon emissions strengthens the reinforcing loop, the system moves away from inertia and toward entropy. Melting permafrost (previously frozen biomass) begins to rot, emitting methane, which further increases global temperature. Left unchecked, a reinforcing loop can give rise to an exponential growth situation. This is a central concept in both identifying threats and maximizing opportunities that we'll explore later.

Causal loops help you rapidly make sense of a system from a qualitative perspective. They can help you identify what information and which relationships are still unknown. They can also point out which indicators need to be tracked in order to quantify changes in the system. All of this can help you to find the cracks in your systemic intuition—when, where, and how your probability of success is changing—so that you can address it. Causal loop diagrams are powerful tools for revealing nonintuitive but highly plausible futures. Perhaps, as importantly, they can help you identify the trigger points where a small change will cause one future instead of another.

The *New York Times* famously used the diagram of the war in Afghanistan shown in Figure 4.9 in an article. General Stanley McChrystal, one of America's great military strategists, was quoted, apparently out of context, as saying, "When we understand that slide, we'll have won the war."[12]

The chart looked crazy to journalists, but it was no joke. For one thing, the act of creating something like this forces you to think

Figure 4.8 **How Climate Change Is Modeled**

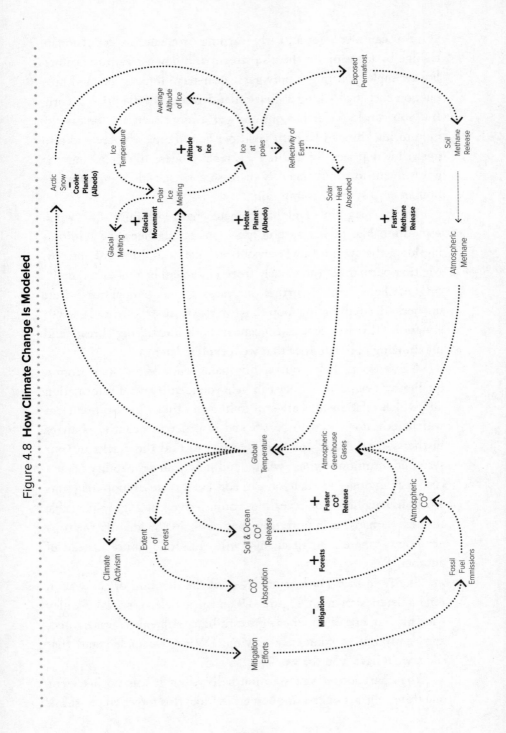

Figure 4.9 **Diagram of Afghanistan Conflict**

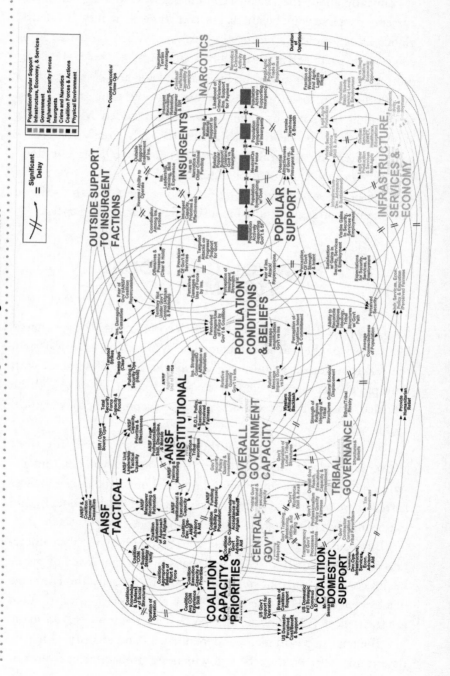

155

systemically about the social, economic, and technological under-currents shaping your business. As confusing as it may be at first glance, it can rapidly align group thinking. When presented in its component parts and then brought together as a whole, the chart did precisely what it aimed to: lay out the logic and objectives for a 300,000-person force operating across multiple time zones across the world. The common mental model it provided McChrystal's staff allowed it to operate with agility through a daily conference call, sidestepping the military's traditional and reliable but slow-moving command and control architecture.

The boost in context awareness among the team and shift in management strategy resulted in a significant increase in speed.

HOW YOU CAN MODEL SYSTEMS TOO

Mendel's peas. Elon's rockets. Palantir's correlations. The spaghetti-like tracery of the war in Afghanistan. While these examples span the realm of human genius, they are all the result of systems, with multiple elements connected by cause and effect. They can all be modeled, and while those models may be incomplete, they are still useful.

So how does this relate to the challenges you face? The short answer is simple: if there's a system whose outputs you don't under-stand but need to, it's time to build a model of it. The longer answer is that there are several different ways to build system models, and mastering that process takes effort and practice.

But you can do it. Whether you're grappling with an uncer-tain supply chain, an unstable political situation, or a web of public health concerns, the first step is to list all of the parts. The Elements of a System Model list (see Figure 4.1) is a good place to start: What are the nodes? What are the links? What are the inputs? And so on.

The next step is to map out dependencies and identify which are deterministic (if A, then B) and which are probabilistic. Even this level of modeling, which can often be done in a matter of hours or minutes, can make things surprisingly clear and reveal second- or third-order effects and evidence of silent players that you need to address. In the SpaceX example, simply understanding the costs of a launch opened up a huge opportunity.

Models can do much more. Forecasting likely futures is one of their key uses, allowing you to identify places where air gaps could eliminate threats and where changing the timing of decisions will modify the future. The winners of the next decade will be the organizations who understand where and when small changes can create exponential impact. In the next few chapters, we'll master the techniques for doing just that.

SUMMARY

Find Your Range of Futures

1. **Map the system.**
   - Identify the boundaries of the system in which you're working.
   - Identify the nodes, links, inputs, and outputs that you understand. Place "black boxes" around those you don't yet.
   - Identify the balancing and reinforcing loops that keep the system in equilibrium.
   - Determine which subsystems are tightly coupled, loosely coupled, and uncoupled.

2. **Identify the subsystems that are worth investigating.**
   - Isolate the subsystem around each of the black boxes.
   - Perform direct investigations where you can (as described in Chapter 3).
   - In the subsystems where you cannot directly investigate, infer what is going on inside the by looking at rates and frequencies throughout the system.

3. **Imagine possible causes of disruption.**
   - Consider what would cause the reinforcing or balancing loops to accelerate, decelerate, reverse direction, or break.
   - Consider the impact of the 10 undercurrents (as described in Chapter 2) on your system as you've mapped it out.

4. **Identify which uncertainties are most important to understand and manage.**
   - Consider the range of futures that are possible within the timeline you're concerned with.
   - Identify the elements of the system that are both impactful and practical to address.

Today's To-Dos for Tomorrow

- **Find unnecessary brittleness and redundancy.** Assign a sponsor to assess where unforced errors or inefficiencies are occurring because of tactical decisions that fail to consider their systemic implications.

- **Increase the organization's focus on systems.** Make a list of actions you could take to build a common awareness of how systems operate, as well as a common language for discussing it.

- **Benchmark your goals versus your budgeting.** Compare your systems modeling objectives for the organization as a whole with your funding for: IT, training, and intelligence capabilities. Are they in alignment?

- **Coordinate modeling in your organization.** Identify the people with modeling skills within your organization. Such people and data are often siloed within business functions, which limits their impact. Encourage them to work on common models, coordinate business intelligence data, and teach others.

5

G: Generate Your Futures

Build scenarios that explore the full range of
likely futures—not just the future you want.

used to live on a decommissioned Navy base. I'd walk around the old Pacific Command building where much of the American effort in World War II was planned. The warehouse where I had my office was one of the largest clear span hangars in the world when it was built.

On the far side of the island were bizarre steel structures that cut into the sky. They looked as if someone had assembled the inside of an aircraft carrier but forgotten to build the hull (Figure 5.1). And that's essentially what they were. This was the Navy's fire school. They lit the building on fire, every morning, so that generations of kids in asbestos suits could put it out while rising, frigid water encircled their waists. This exercise prepared sailors for radical situations so that, when everything went wrong, they had a plan. That's the nature of "pressure testing."

Military leaders have used similar simulation programs for centuries to improve group performance and survival when the radical unknown rears its head.

This approach has proven effective outside of the military as well. In the early 1980s, United Airlines responded to a string of airplane

Figure 5.1 **US Navy Fire Simulator**

crashes by instituting the Crew Resource Management[1] (CRM) system, which dramatically improved the safety of commercial air travel. At its core was a set of protocols that forced flight crews to communicate more openly in stressful circumstances. CRM figures prominently in books about risk management[2] and is rightly celebrated as an innovation that's saved thousands of lives. It wasn't the only safety innovation of the era. During that same period, flight simulators became a major component of aviation training as well. Today, before commercial jet pilots take their first real flight, they are almost fully trained in hyperrealistic simulators.

This revolution was led by a company called CAE that trains 135,000 pilots a year.[3] They give lectures and administer tests, but fundamentally believe that the best way to keep passengers safe is by putting pilots in "sweat boxes"—multimillion-dollar simulators that immerse them in situations that are too difficult and dangerous for the real world.[4]

Simulations let you explore how different actions impact what-if scenarios. They allow users to identify more possible futures. When applied to business, they can rapidly accelerate organizational learning, find unlikely opportunities, and prevent threats before a plan is deployed. They can help you better blend strategy and execution.

Large organizations do this type of strategic modeling, simulation, and risk management all of the time. The private equity behemoth BlackRock, for example, uses real-time statistical models to assess risk, helping to ensure that their trading strategies make money in good times and bad.[5] Good modeling can help any leader shrink risk and shed light on three questions:

- **Uncertainty:** What is the likelihood of an event occurring?
- **Impact:** How significant will its impact be if it does?
- **Timeline:** Are the uncertainties and potential impacts relevant on the timeline being considered?

All three questions need to be asked simultaneously to yield useful insights about what opportunities to take and what risks to manage. It is nearly 100 percent certain, for example, that a large meteorite will hit the earth at some point, with enormous impact. It has already happened multiple times, killing off much of the life on the planet. But its likelihood during any one human lifetime, much less during your current job role, is incredibly low. And there's the rub: a cataclysmic meteor strike is just as likely to happen during your lifetime as anyone else's. The probability is static, not dynamic.

Beyond the human cost, even a small strike would have a catastrophic impact on the global economy, so it's worth investing a limited, but meaningful, amount of time and effort in planetary defense. NASA spends $150 million per year—about three-quarters of 1 percent of its budget—preparing for such an event. Some of the world's brightest minds, including Freeman Dyson, Peter Norvig, and Lord Martin Rees, have devoted many brain cycles to the problem.[6]

On the other hand, highly uncertain events that happen frequently but have low impact can actually be higher risk. Friendster, the failed predecessor to Facebook, prioritized speed to market over efficiency and scalability. When it became a sudden global hit, growing from thousands to millions of users, the inefficiencies began stacking up.[7] Individually, each was trivial, but in aggregate, they regularly crashed the service. This effectively killed the business.

In the real world, one of the best ways a teenager can increase his or her chance of financial success is to borrow $300,000 and invest it in a STEM degree from a prestigious university. But if you already have $300,000 on hand when you're 18, you might be better off putting it in a tax-protected index fund and getting a stable, low-paying job. The past doesn't predict the future, but index funds have earned 7 percent a year on average over the past 75 years. Assuming that holds true for another 50 years (when that teenager retires at age 68), the investment would have earned around $8 million. While results may vary, this is far more than the average increase in lifetime earnings that a typical STEM degree from a prestigious university enables. I have a friend who did this. He got a job as a dog catcher. Today, he's a very wealthy man.

A prestigious degree isn't necessarily a bad investment. But given the economics of education, investment advisors now question if it's the universally good bet we've long believed. For most young people planning their education and career path, the approach my friend used isn't even considered. Had they modeled the full range of options, most would still invest in the degree, but many should go the dog catcher route.

Modeling systems and performing simulations is a great way to correct biases that lead to poor decisions. Some of the most common errors that stem from cognitive illusions are:

Failing to time probability. A "hundred-year storm" doesn't happen every hundred years. Much like roulette, unless there is a change in the environment, it has a 1 in 100 chance of happening every year— and just because one happened last year doesn't make this year any safer. Counting on sequencing to reduce static risk is a surprisingly common bias.

Failing to understand a change in probability over time. In card games like War and Blackjack, the probabilities in a specific hand change dramatically over the course of the game if the dealer shuffles after each hand instead of playing through the deck. Counting cards, for example, becomes essentially pointless.

Failing to understand a change in impact over time. As we have seen, that $300,000 has much more potential at age 18. If you lose it, you also have many more chances to recover. You would have done quite well over many decades, even if you had timed the market terribly. But if you were to invest at 55, you would have much less time to recover from a loss. Previously, I mentioned the impact of investing in the stock market just before it crashed in 1929 versus just after.

Investment institutions have long used modeling to prepare for a variety of scenarios, but as data and data analytics have burgeoned, other businesses are taking up the practice. Amazon's unique advantage in e-commerce is that it continually gathers useful data about its customers, suppliers, products, and anything else you can think of. Its army of economists plugs this data into sophisticated computer programs that are effectively flight simulators for business—sexy, fun, expensive video games that require an army of PhDs to take full advantage of. Turn the knob left and see what happens. Turn the knob right and see the impact. Amazon uses them to make constant improvements to its user experience, reduce its costs, and increase sales. They minimize unpleasant surprises by running simulations. It helps them to explore what is possible and ensure that most of the kinks have been worked out before they go live.

In many cases, you don't need Amazon's or BlackRock's resources to answer what-if questions. As with many of the approaches outlined in this book, simulation follows the 80/20 rule: 80 percent of its value can often be realized with 20 percent of the effort of doing it "properly." Yet, because simulation is seen as an expensive, specialized pursuit, few organizations bother with it.

Most make decisions based on simple linear forecasting or (surprisingly often) gut instinct in new situations. In known situations, experience and experts can help you focus on the most common issues and ignore the outliers. But in a novel situation, they can't tell you what the outliers are. Their zombie assumptions are just as likely to gloss over the critical insight. This is why running even a rough simulation of your possible futures gives you a leg up on competitors.

Simulation can be a simple mental exercise, performed with a pencil and paper, some reconnaissance and discussion, and possibly a spreadsheet or two. The important thing is structuring it in the proper way, asking the right questions, and being rigorous about the logic.

THE TREE OF POSSIBILITY

The obvious way to develop a future scenario is to list everything you know about your current situation and extrapolate. This is largely what we were doing in the previous chapters when we conducted reconnaissance, created systems models, and drew causal loop diagrams. This approach can help you understand current relationships in the system and the categories of events that would cause them to change.

When it's time to look closely at future possibilities, though, the better approach is to go backward. When you start with a future situation and work back to the present, your ability to plot out the best course of action improves. Some decision science researchers suggest that a future-first approach is successful 30 percent more often than extrapolating from the present.[8]

Starting at the end requires you to define your goals precisely. This is something nearly every organization neglects but should be doing as a matter of habit. Creating a clear target forces important questions, and each suggests a different path:

- Are we looking to increase volume?
- Increase price or margin?
- Make a lucrative exit?

There's no need to choose just one end, either. Pilot trainees don't simulate flights with the same airports, the same emergencies, or the same weather. They switch things up, putting themselves through a wide range of scenarios—bad as well as good—to test their skills and improve their communication. This helps them to spot hazards earlier and respond to them more effectively when they crop up in real life. In the business world, this means creating what we call the Tree of Possibility (Figure 5.2).

Figure 5.2 **The Tree of Possibility**

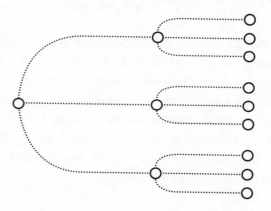

This exercise works because it expands your universe of possibilities, presenting a wide range of plausible outcomes, from optimal success to total disaster, depending on major shifts in your supply chain, customers, or competitive landscape. When you forecast from your current situation forward, you're likely to do more of what you've done before. When you trace back from a desired future or a possible catastrophe, reconstructing why you ended up there, you'll think more broadly *and* specifically about new ways of doing things.

The Tree of Possibility is also useful because it can be scaled. Once one person in an organization maps out a possible scenario, it's relatively easy for others to build on it, each bringing in their unique perspective. It's useful for a CEO to map out how to respond to a US-China trade war, but far more useful if product and supply chain managers do it too. Sharing a future scenario within the organization inevitably generates powerful discussion and feedback. If managed well, it results in a better plan and the ability to respond wisely when the future works out differently than imagined.

ENVISION THE EXTREMES

If you want to understand something, take it
to the extremes or examine its opposites.
—COL. JOHN BOYD, USAF

In the past decade or so, there's been a steady trend to view failure as a learning experience. Business books admonish us to "fail fast" and "fail forward," to have a growth mindset, and to see missteps as an indication that we're pushing the boundaries of the possible. That's all true, and it's also a common excuse for wasted effort.

Simulation reduces the cost of failure because we can learn the lessons of a mistake without suffering the consequences. But to enjoy its full value, we need to do two things:

1. **Imagine failure in its fullest extreme.** When the *Challenger* exploded, it wasn't because a particular O-ring was defective, but because the O-rings that the boosters depended on *did not work in cold weather.* The flaw was systemic. A catastrophe occurred because the people who greenlighted the launch thought the worst-case scenario was political fallout from millions of schoolchildren missing the launch on TV. As I discovered when spending an afternoon with the mother of *Challenger* astronaut Christa McAuliffe, things can always get far, far worse. When analyzed thoroughly, many, if not most, failures turn out to have root causes that occurred long before the failure itself.

2. **Imagine success in its fullest extreme.** Envisioning a positive outcome is fairly simple—most of us know what our organization is trying to achieve, even if only vaguely. But dramatic success is also possible. And it's rarely achieved by organizations that haven't considered it. Friendster's viral growth spelled its doom.

We tend to compare the present to the past—to what has happened instead of what can happen, to the largest wave we have seen, instead of the biggest one we'll see. This is why defining a broad range of possibilities beyond our lived experience is so transformative—it gives us the mental frame to take advantage of it.

Asking about best and worst extremes also helps us identify what we should pay attention to. If a threat or opportunity comes up repeatedly in a range of possible futures, that suggests it's worth focusing on. Later in the book, I'll talk about prioritizing and mitigating uncertainties, and using them as sources of innovation.

But in this chapter, let's look at possibilities: how to define them, how to estimate their likelihood, and how to make sure we're considering a wide enough range of them. The approach we'll use considers optimal outcomes, likely outcomes, and terrifying, nearly unimaginable ones. In other words, let's look at the Good, the Bad, and the Ugly.

The Good

You probably have a healthy idea of your company's goals. In many cases, this is purely financial and takes the form of a revenue or profit target or a successful exit. It may also be something more abstract, like market share, sustainability, or a level of innovation.

However, in most cases, the goals we set for ourselves are nowhere near good enough. Silicon Valley yahoos love to talk about order-of-magnitude improvements, or "10x outcomes," which is a good starting mindset. But in many categories, even 10x is not ambitious enough, especially if you're creating a new product or platform. The reality in many fields is that it takes five to seven years to get a new category product from idea to scale. Once you take the existing competition into account and factor in the cost of capital over that period, a 10x improvement is barely enough to stay competitive. Real breakthroughs are much bigger than that.

100x Outcomes

Thirty years ago, the concept of an amputee running was considered absurd. Since then, the science of prosthetics has improved dramatically, to the point where amputees using custom-built prostheses can outrun top athletes who are unassisted. Prostheses have been banned from many competitions, like the Olympics, because they give an unfair advantage.

This seems like a 10x future: a device that gives amputees superior performance in specific circumstances. I thought so, too, until I met Hugh Herr, the world's leading prostheticist, in 2014. He's known for putting motors into prostheses that significantly improve mobility.[9] As a double amputee, Herr has a personal interest in these developments.

When I first met him, he walked with a slightly off-kilter gait. While he could control his feet, he couldn't feel what they were doing. Our paths crossed a second time in 2019, when he introduced me to his college roommate, Jim Ewing, at a conference. Jim had also lost a leg, after a climbing accident a few years earlier. Hugh took on Jim as a personal crusade, making sure he had access to the most advanced prostheses, surgeons, and treatments on the planet. Jim didn't walk the way Hugh had five years earlier. In fact, I only realized he was an amputee when he pulled out his phone and showed me a video of himself rock climbing in the Cayman Islands.[10] He was hanging from a sheer cliff wall hundreds of feet above the Caribbean. It was the cinematic sort of climb that Tom Cruise does in *Mission Impossible* movies. It was also the same climb on which Ewing had handicapped himself years earlier. He was moving up the face with grace and competence, using the same prosthesis he was wearing beneath his suit as he showed me the video.

Thanks to a recent surgery, Jim can sense force feedback from his prosthetic foot. So when he thinks about moving his limb, he literally feels it moving the way he intends, just as a nonamputee would.[11] These prosthetic innovations have done more than allow Jim to walk. They have returned him to a state of near-complete mobility. This kind of advance alters the whole idea of what is possible with prosthetics: it is at least a 100x outcome, if not more.

The strategy of modeling 100x outcomes has led to some of the great success stories of the modern era.

In the 1980s, a brick-and-mortar specialty store typically turned its inventory over once or twice a year. Amazon.com turns inventory an impressive nine times a year. JD.com, Amazon's Chinese doppelganger, turns its inventory almost 12 times a year.[12] And while these are impressive results, consider that eBay's inventory turns by the minute because it doesn't have inventory. Founder Pierre Omidyar thought past the store and to the future.

In 1981, the Space Shuttle could put a kilogram of payload into low Earth orbit at a cost of $85,216. Today, SpaceX can do the same at a few percent of that (Figure 5.3). But its ultimate aim is even bolder. SpaceX's Starship project aims to bring the cost down to $22 per kilogram by 2025 with larger launch volumes and fully reusable rockets.[13] Elon Musk is notorious for ambitious schedules, and his projections are decades ahead of some analysts'. But given SpaceX's track record to this point, such a shift seems feasible, if not guaranteed.

How Many Miracles Do You Need?

Dramatic improvements begin with envisioning 100x outcomes: starting from a future perspective, with the things you had done— instead of starting in the present with the things you'll do. The next step is to trace that outcome back from the future to the present day and see what would have had to happen for it to come true.

Figure 5.3 **The Dropping Cost of Space**

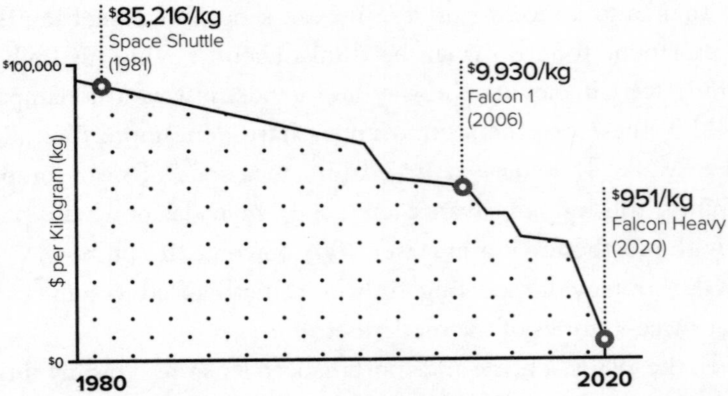

$85,216/kg
Space Shuttle
(1981)

$9,930/kg
Falcon 1
(2006)

$951/kg
Falcon Heavy
(2020)

$100,000

$ per Kilogram (kg)

$0

1980   2020

Source: "Launch Costs to Low Earth Orbit, 1980–2100," Future Timeline, September 1, 2018, https://www.futuretimeline.net/data-trends/6.htm.

In Jim's case, it took a string of unlikely events, none of which were altogether implausible. He needed to survive the initial accident, and he had to have been buddies with Hugh. Motors and lithium ion batteries had to have become small, powerful, and safe enough to fit into the prosthesis and power it. He needed to be healthy enough to survive his many surgeries and able to find a surgeon who could carry out the operations.

If we make a list of all of these miracles, we can start to see both our to-dos and the potential risks we face. The questions to ask are:

1. How likely is each of these conditions?
2. How might we make each one more likely to occur?
3. When and where do we need them to happen?
4. How will we know if they have?
5. How should we respond if they didn't?

The CEO of an IT hardware startup recently asked my team to look at their product pipeline. He knew something was wrong with the planning for their augmented reality products. Their headsets would be the best, highest-end devices on the market, but something was amiss that he couldn't put his finger on.

His team was looking one product cycle out—18 months—and they were confident they could make back their $10 million investment. The problem was that the investors weren't looking to be paid back. They had assessed the growth potential of the company and expected a billion-dollar valuation. That required it to be making $100 million in annual net profits by year five.

We used a causal loop diagram to examine how the industry would change over time. It showed that the third generation of his headset (the one that would be on the market in five years) would likely fail because the industry was certain to have changed. In five years, 5G technology will have become widespread, upending the AR industry, especially at its high end. Large cloud computing providers like Amazon will move into the market on the content side, and network equipment manufacturers like Huawei will be selling devices that are optimized for their network clients. At the same time, service providers like T-Mobile, Comcast, and Verizon will be pushing low-cost hardware solutions for their own benefit.

All of these competitors will have learned how to dominate the mobile market from Apple's use of closed hardware/software ecosystems. Each will have a vested interest in building their own walled gardens by selling as many devices as possible. Competition will be fierce, and some major players are likely to sell their devices at a loss to lock in their customers. To avoid getting crowded out, two key miracles would need to occur:

1. The startup would have to retain its pricing power over time.
2. It would have to overcome direct competition from much larger players.

The result of this exercise was a complete change in the way the startup approached building its new platform. The specific products didn't change much. But after listing and analyzing the number of miracles it needed, we shifted everything from its pricing strategy to its marketing plans. The result is a company that has been redesigned from the ground up for sustainability in a hostile market, with different goals but vastly better chances for survival.

SpaceX's 100x question was, "What miracles need to occur to plant a colony on Mars?" It has to be one of the most batshit-crazy missions a private company ever dreamed up. Analysts in the early 2000s wrote them off as lunatics. Despite the opposition, Musk & Co. identified the key components that would enable it. They got granular about the wins and changes that had to occur: in market demand, technology, public perception, government policy, and industrial structure. This granularity led them to focus on underserved markets, it informed the design of their initial rockets, and it drove their quest for a reusable launch platform. Without a 100x goal, it's unlikely they'd have been able to sustain the decade-long effort (and the dozens of crashes) it took to get there.

Many times, managers—particularly middle managers—avoid suggesting 100x ideas because they know they're out of line with the company's operating model or short-term strategy. I once heard a Fortune 100 CEO berating a junior executive by telling him to "get out of the troposphere." It was a career-limiting moment, but the junior guy was right: the company was too caught up in incrementalism; what it needed was to make a step change. Shortly thereafter, the executive was fired, the CEO was let go, and the company was snapped up by a corporate raider and sold off in pieces. The junior executive's idea didn't guarantee a better outcome, but it was certainly worth considering.

Thinking big—and then getting specific—opens up the range of options. But it also decreases the risk of failure by normal standards. This is because it decomposes the problem, exposes the core issue, and clarifies priorities. Even if SpaceX never goes to Mars, they've already built a spectacularly successful business with their profits planted firmly here on planet Earth.

The Bad and the Ugly

The simple fact is that you can't tell whether an idea is likely to work unless you consider all the possible negatives.

—CHARLES MUNGER

The "How Many Miracles" approach also works for negative outcomes. When systems break down, it's generally because we didn't anticipate the right threats, or put measures in place to manage them. Often, these measures are obvious. You put the money in the safe. You put a stoplight at the intersection. You read a checklist out loud. You deliver critical news in person instead of by mail.

Big opportunities and risks appear when less obvious problems occur. Several years ago, I was working on a team studying data center failures. It should come as no surprise that most of the failures we saw were caused by multiple overlapping human errors. In one case, management didn't consider that:

- The janitorial crew might use cleaning fluids.
- Procurement was cutting corners on safety equipment.
- A critical component would be exposed to those liquids.
- The component would short-circuit.
- And it would be impossible to replace in a timely way.

A major company then lost tens of millions of dollars because it had to stop processing transactions.

More frequently than not, failures occur due to links within systems. Nodes (the servers, the engineering teams, the finance systems) are typically better protected. Half measures and duct tape can keep them functioning, even if they function inefficiently. But the communication links between the nodes aren't as well protected, because no one is incentivized to keep them open—or to notice when their resilience decreases.

In the meantime, leaders play the ostrich, assuming that the right number of miracles will keep occurring, in the right order, at the right time. The problem with miracles is that they are hard to predict unless you make them happen. And when the wrong ones occur, you need to be prepared for them.

Who Sank My Battleship?
Seeing from the Other Side

Army Lieutenant General B. B. Bell looked out over the sunbaked sea. He was stunned. Just 10 minutes earlier, he had commanded the most powerful fighting force in the Persian Gulf. Now his navy was sunk and 20,000 service men and women had perished. As he surveyed the decimation, he had one question: What the hell just happened?

If you want to see how fragile a miracle is, attack it as hard as you can. People who deal with systemic risk in their jobs often stress-test plans by acting like an adversary. These include public health professionals, enterprise risk managers, and unsurprisingly, the military.

In 2002, just months before the Iraq War, the US Department of Defense's Joint Forces Command (JFCOM) decided to test an invasion plan for a fictional country that bore a striking resemblance to Iraq. It had been decades since they had tested the power of a US carrier strike group—a city-sized system of ships, aircraft, and assault vehicles with enough firepower to take out a small nation's air force. The Millennium 2002 battle exercise (MC02) would be the most public, complex, and expensive war simulation in the history of the US military. Congress allocated $250 million for it.

Secretary of Defense Donald Rumsfeld described it as something that "will help us create a force that is not only interoperable, responsive, agile and lethal, but one that is capable of capitalizing on the information revolution and the advanced technologies that are available today."[14] Anticipating war, he wanted to ensure that the military could withstand a rogue wave.

The exercise was a catastrophic embarrassment.[15] The US military's complex, detailed, forward-looking strategy for the simulation had taken 350 people to develop. It was undone by a counterstrategy that was essentially worked out on the back of a napkin.[16]

During what was supposed to be a two-week exercise, the bad guys—called OPFOR—were led by retired Marine Lieutenant General Paul K. Van Riper. His job was to attack the most powerful fighting system on the planet, a veritable iron mountain, with the limited resources of a ragtag nation. He had no destroyers, few heavy aircraft, and none of the stealth equipment of his opponent. What he did have was a large flotilla of speedboats and a crayon box full of decades-old cruise missiles left over from the Cold War.

Recognizing his own limitations but also understanding his opponents', Van Riper had his forces make the first move, much to the JFCOM's surprise. OPFOR overwhelmed the fleet by launching dozens of missiles simultaneously, followed quickly by a swarm of bomb-carrying speedboats. Faced with so many small, fast-moving targets, the fleet's command and control systems couldn't track them quickly enough to intercept them. Dozens made it through the fleet's defenses, inflicting enormous damage before JFCOM had begun to put its carefully planned strategy into motion. The timing of the attack also shifted the conflict closer to the edge of the wargame area, which was bounded by shipping lanes and commercial air traffic. The practical reality of peacetime politics limited the strike group's movements.

In just a few minutes, OPFOR managed to sink 16 major warships, including an aircraft carrier, 10 cruisers, and 5 of 6 amphibious crafts. It was one of the most devastating naval defeats ever suffered by the United States—had it been real.

While few of us are in the business of sinking ships, we're all in the business of surviving unexpected threats. It's not that JFCOM was helpless against the kind of attack OPFOR mounted—it's that they hadn't considered its possibility. If JFCOM had someone like Van Riper on their side, things would likely have gone differently, even in the same situation with the same resources.

So how can your organization prepare for the unexpected? Plenty has been written about the mistakes that the JFCOM made during MC02, but they mostly boil down to these three:

- They didn't take the larger context into account.
- They hadn't sufficiently probed their own vulnerabilities.
- They hadn't fully considered how an informed opponent might attack—in JFCOM's case, mounting a decentralized attack on a decentralized network.

Each of these causes has a remedy:

- Look at all of the data.
- Look for unexpected vulnerabilities that could compound.
- Don't assume that a decentralized network will automatically make you more resilient.

These remedies are so useful, in so many situations, that each is worth a closer look.

Looking at All of the Data

When preparing for the unexpected, it's helpful to take Van Riper's point of view and look at the larger system, considering how an informed opponent might take advantage of it. This helps identify which categories of threat and opportunity are worth paying attention to.

Pandemics, for instance, weren't on the radar for most American businesses prior to Covid–19. A pandemic was something that happened in science fiction movies, or distant parts of Africa or Asia. As with most large-scale crises, the direct cause (the virus itself) wasn't really the issue. The world is full of things that can cause large-scale harm—including viruses—but most are naturally constrained by the systems in which they operate.

It's easy to think of Covid as a black swan, but it's not. If you look at the miracles that need to occur for a novel virus to become a pandemic, it's clear that the constraints preventing them are being progressively removed:

- Widespread habitat destruction makes it easier for viruses to jump from wild animals to humans.

- Increased international air travel accelerates the rate of global spread.
- Greater mobility in general means that instantly locking off an affected region is a nonstarter.
- Greater urbanization means faster transmission within cities.
- Aging demographics mean larger vulnerable populations.

Even before Covid-19 came along, we'd seen a rising tide of small pandemics (SARS, MERS) and big ones (HIV, influenza, polio) over the past hundred years.

Civilization has made great strides in speeding the detection of infections, developing vaccines and therapeutics—but a deadly pandemic was guaranteed to occur eventually, and a realistic response plan wasn't in place.

What corporate leaders had failed to appreciate in their risk assessments is that events that used to happen every 50 or 100 years are now happening every decade or two. A doubling in Chinese air travel combined with a deeper push into the nation's biome increased the likelihood and speed at which a new bug could flit—undetected—from a wild animal to all the major cities of the world.

But if you'll recall from Chapter 1, pandemics are dynamic, symmetrical, and synchronous rogue waves. World wars or solar flares that disrupt electronics globally fall into the same category. The chance of a major solar flare is less than 1 percent in any given year.[17] But in the twentieth century, the chance of a new rogue wave hitting a US business in a given year was in excess of 20 percent. If the business survived, it typically took a number of years to bail out. While a specific wave may be unlikely, rogue waves aren't.

One company that was resilient enough to take advantage of pandemic-caused instability was Amazon. In interviews with Amazon's leaders, they made it clear that they didn't have a preexisting "pandemic playbook" that told them which knobs to turn. Yet they hit the ground running when it struck. To deal with increased demand, they hired an additional 175,000 workers—a labor force the size of the Ford Motor Company—in about 90 days.[18] In doing so, they became one of the few genuine winners of 2020.

Amazon's agility wasn't the result of planning for *this* event. Amazon experienced the pains of change, like other retailers, but it had taken a long view of potential threats and designed its organization to be resilient to a broad range of rogue waves. Its leaders quickly figured out which knobs to turn because they had a detailed system model of their organization (remember all those economists they hired?). They already knew how to rewire links and scale the capacity of nodes. And through simulation, they knew exactly how far they could push their system before it broke.

This is a big business example, but smaller companies can use the same thinking to respond to the same range of threats. I recently worked with a forager that sells truffles to high-end restaurants. Pre-Covid, they would receive orders from chefs and deliver them the next day. Because luxury dining correlates closely with consumer confidence, they were able to review their orders and determine down to the zip code where people were getting nervous. A drop in orders from lower Manhattan suggested an impending downturn in the stock market.

Combining this insight with publicly available information about the epidemic, we recommended that the forager begin to short hospitality stocks. Our calculations suggested, and then bore out, that they would make more money from the speculation than they did from their usual business, which would give them much-needed capital to weather the downturn.

Amazon and the forager both did what the US military didn't—they looked beyond the immediate situation to the broader context. Amazon's quarter-to-quarter performance doesn't depend on having a meticulous model of its entire business and hundreds of contingency plans. But its leaders understand that succeeding over years or decades means dealing with things that aren't traditionally "business" concerns: external events like pandemics, civil unrest, climate change, demographic shifts, and other undercurrents discussed in Chapter 2.

The forager's leaders recognized that they were participating in a massive network of production and consumption, which brought risks but also information. They saw that their "game" was part of a larger system, which presented opportunities—much like Van Riper did when he noticed that the shipping lanes would constrain the wargames.

Spotting Unexpected Vulnerabilities

Nearly every system has critical nodes—people, places, or software through which command, control, and communication pass. These nodes act as filters, helping to keep out bad information and decisions, but they also act as choke points. We call them *centers of gravity*. When they are disrupted, bad things happen.

There are two basic strategies for recovering from attacks on a center of gravity: accelerate movement through them or replace them.

Amazon's Covid strategy demonstrated world-beating levels of resilience. But leaders in the organization considered it an obvious response—just tweaking variables in a well-understood system. Amazon wasn't explicitly designed for a sustained, one-third increase in shipments in a single quarter. There were brief hiccups, but it was able to absorb that opportunity by rapidly expanding warehousing, running equipment harder, and using digitized hiring and onboarding systems to ramp up.

One of history's great examples of a failed center of gravity is the Maginot line. After World War I, France's Minister of War, André Maginot, directed construction of a massive line of fortifications along the German border, with concrete bunkers, roadblocks, and artillery installations to deter a German invasion. Designed to withstand aerial bombings and tank attacks, the line even had its own underground railways to move troops and matériel around.[19] He was determined that the Germans weren't going to traipse into France as they had at the start of World War I and that any conflict would occur on the Belgian frontier.

Although the Maginot Line was effectively impenetrable, Maginot's strategy lacked resilience (Figure 5.4). The French spread their nodes broadly, but only along part of their border, trusting in the rough terrain of the Ardennes forest in Belgium to protect their northern flank.[20] Unfortunately, the French hadn't kept tabs on Germany's advances in air power, radio communication, and rapid deployment of pontoon bridges. Reality wasn't as they had imagined.

Figure 5.4 **The Maginot Line**

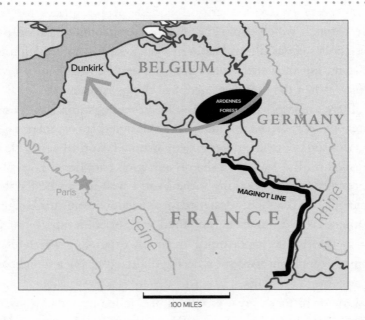

100 MILES

In 1940, shortly after invading Poland, the German army moved westward into Belgium and flitted around the Maginot Line into northern France. What was supposed to be a 10-day slog through the rugged Ardennes took the German army and infantry just four days. This was one of the great drubbings in modern military history. When it evacuated from France a few days later, the British Army abandoned 80 percent of its matériel on the beach at Dunkirk: 700 tanks, 20,000 motorcycles, and 45,000 motor vehicles.[21] Not long after, the French came to terms with reality and surrendered.

The Line had advanced communications, and the troops could be moved swiftly along it by underground rail and be concentrated where they were needed. But because the Line was focused on the German border, the country's overall defenses lacked redundancy. France hadn't seriously considered the possibility that the Germans would so easily cross different terrain, rendering the Line irrelevant. As a result, the Allies nearly lost the war shortly after it had begun.

The moral of the story is that you need to do more than just consider the worst-case scenario when making plans. At some point, the French almost certainly discussed the possibility of the Germans plowing through the Ardennes, but they didn't treat it as likely. Even if something seems incredibly improbable, it's not enough to simply acknowledge it and dismiss it. You have to follow through as if it were going to happen, and see what you learn. Only then can it be dismissed. In other words, you need to act as if Plan B is the likely path. Plan A often works, but the more competitive or unknown the environment, the more likely something unexpected will come along and derail it.

Negative Miracles

Achieving something extraordinary requires positive miracles, which can be mapped out and incorporated into strategic plans. But miracles can cause good or bad. Often it's a matter of perspective. That's why negative miracles require just as much attention.

We've already talked about the importance of imagining a 100x outcome. The same effort should go into imagining catastrophic outcomes: Germany sweeps through the Ardennes, a pandemic disrupts the globe, an automated startup undercuts your market, and so on. Planning for these outcomes means determining what steps you can take now to minimize their likelihood, recover from their impact, or flip them to your advantage.

The French, for example, had no clear way of tracking German progress through the Ardennes, no contingency plan for slowing them down, and no withering surprise parry. If they had considered this catastrophic outcome, they might have drastically changed the course of the war with a small shift in effort—for example, by concentrating troops and fortifications at a number of different choke points.

A "negative miracle" can take many forms in the business world: a new technology that undermines your business model, a global event that disrupts markets or supply chains, or a competitor that does what you do, but faster, cheaper, or smarter.

One powerful question is, "What's the worst that could happen?" Terrifyingly, this is typically asked in jest. You would be wise to answer it seriously.

After this, the next step is to assess likelihood and impact. This can be done for categories of events. Pandemics and economic crises could crash the global economy, so impact is high, and likelihood low (but not zero). Other negative miracles are almost certain over a longer timeline. Artificial intelligence and digital currencies are guaranteed to disrupt the way we handle contracts and finances, so the important question to ask is: how long do you have to respond before it impacts your business?

Once these scenarios are defined, you can start playing out your organization's possible responses, and then identify the best course of action. It may be diversifying lines of business so that a negative impact on one means a boost for another. Or, like Amazon, it might mean putting systems in place that let you adjust quickly in the face of change. How your organization responds will depend on your current situation, existing strengths and weaknesses, and plausible threats.

Realizing a Decentralized Network Is Not a Fortress

Avoiding death is best possible and most robust advice.

—NASSIM TALEB

Networks are inherently more resilient than rigid hierarchies. Giving individual units more autonomy is a great way to encourage innovation and speed up reaction times. But networks have weaknesses, too.

The US Joint Forces strike group was a very decentralized organization. Individual ships had considerable autonomy, and the Aegis information systems they relied on were spread across multiple cruisers; no single foundered ship could cripple the armada. So Van Riper's success in taking it down is all the more impressive.

Ironically, his plan was absolutely textbook. The US military has a manual on how to attack networks,[22] and the strategies it recommends are almost perfectly in line with what Van Riper planned and executed. The manual focuses on five tactics that complement each other, what I call the 5Ds: Deceive, Disrupt, Degrade, Deny, Destroy (Figure 5.5). OPFOR was unconventional in its specific tactics, but it did a better job of delivering on these 5Ds than the JFCOM's more complex plan.

Lt. Gen. B. B. Bell, who led the Blue Team (the "good guys" in this exercise), has since become one of the US military's most outspoken fans of this type of simulation. He called it "a watershed 'eureka' moment" because it exposed so many of JFCOM's untested what-ifs. Over the next several years, he ordered more than 20 similar simulations.[24]

The 5Ds are useful in any situation in which you need to assess threats to a network. Statisticians use similar techniques to understand the implications of policy during public health emergencies. In banking and insurance, they can be used to stress test organizations, and internet companies use them to defend against competitors as well as cyberattacks. They can also be used offensively, to develop viral business models by evaluating the vulnerability of competition or existing market leaders to different types of challenges. They can also be used to find pain points your customers aren't yet aware exist.

The best organizations consider the 5Ds both defensively and offensively. How could they be used to change the wave's characteristics (Figure 1.4)? How could they disrupt the Four FOES of Growth (Figures 1.2 and 5.6)? What opportunities could they open up?

Figure 5.5 **The 5Ds**

Deceive	OPFOR used low-tech communications such as light signals and motorcycle messengers to coordinate actions without tipping its hand. JFCOM's surveillance systems were so advanced, it didn't occur to them that they might be missing communications at this scale.
Disrupt	Van Riper's decision to launch a preemptive strike before JFCOM was prepared allowed them to attack the links within the strike group, reducing the effectiveness of each ship.
Degrade	We've already discussed how OPFOR used the surrounding shipping lanes to box JFCOM in. Through careful maneuvering, they were able to limit where the strike group's ships could navigate, and where its planes could safely fly.
Deny	OPFOR overwhelmed the central nodes— in this case, the Aegis cruisers—with a barrage of missiles from ground-based launchers, commercial ships, and low-flying planes. As a result, critical information, systems, and services were taken off line, crippling the more powerful fleet.
Destroy	Swarms of speedboats loaded with explosives made kamikaze strikes on many ships simultaneously, overwhelming the nodes. One attack can usually be fended off, or its damage absorbed. A synchronized attack can be debilitating.[23]

Figure 5.6 **Using the 5Ds to Identify the Impact of Radical Change**

	Financial	Operational	External	Strategic
Deceive				
Disrupt				
Degrade				
Deny				
Destroy				

HOW TO WIN THROUGH PRACTICAL WARGAMING

Few companies or countries have a quarter billion dollars to burn on a wargame. But small or medium-sized businesses can realize many of the benefits through a half- or full-day exercise that takes place in a single room, without an Aegis cruiser. The key is to have the right people in the room, to get them communicating openly, and to keep them focused on a well-defined and constrained set of future possibilities. If you've never tried this kind of exercise, here's why you should simulate your future:

- Use it to practice effective teamwork and communication.
- Use it to find blind spots.
- Consider the entire set of the knowable data instead of fixating on the known data.
- Consider the positive and negative extremes as well as your acceptable outcomes.

Assemble Your Team

The best team includes as many different perspectives as possible. Your finance department has different motivations than your legal department. A challenge that's obvious to your operations people is often invisible to the CEO. Consider bringing in participants from outside the organization, whether vendors, customers, or subject matter experts. Lt. General Van Riper was retired, and was brought in specifically to make moves that weren't part of JFCOM's current doctrine. You should also include people who operate at multiple levels in the organization. Extraordinary insights can emerge when the smart intern and the jaded CTO get talking. Don't be too quick to defer to seniority and superior knowledge. As Jeff Bezos has pointed out, innovation requires both domain expertise and the ability to refrain from being "corrupted by that domain knowledge."[25]

Collaboration can be a challenge on diverse teams. They work well when they have clear roles, but not a rigid hierarchy. This can mean tasking individuals to be the Builder, Disruptor, Connector, Pessimist, etc., so they have more license to push the edges. Occasionally shifting the roles, as Ted Selker and I do during Chess Tournaments, can help to diversify thinking and limit politics.

You'll also get better ideas when people aren't worried about losing their jobs or upsetting the boss. Creating a safe space for free expression is a critical but difficult task. As a leader, it's far too easy to be coercive, when your goal is to be the opposite. Consider holding sessions in unfamiliar, neutral spaces. Create a situation where your people attack the problem and not each other. Provide specific stimuli to react to and questions to answer—anything to get people out of the familiar hierarchy and into an open flow of ideas. The ideal wargaming situation has a "sandbox" feeling: everyone needs to understand that whatever is said in the room won't have a negative impact outside of it.

Set Your Ground Rules

In addition to clear roles, any team that's trying to model future scenarios needs to set explicit goals and boundaries. The goals should be concrete and few in number: a simulation that's trying to do too much ends up doing nothing. So it's useful to focus on one or two key issues.

Perhaps you're modeling a particular 100x outcome, like dominating a category into which you recently moved. Or you need to understand your response to a specific threat, like a sudden labor shortage or a massive new set of tariffs. Whatever the goal, articulate it clearly and *write it down*, ideally in specific terms of what "success" looks like. For instance: *Deliver a 40 percent increase in margins in the UK market in the next three years, without increasing capital investment or acquiring new customers.*

Then make sure everyone in the room knows what the goal is. Ideally, post it on the wall.

Rules and boundaries for a simulation should identify what's assumed and what's off limits. If there's a particular product, process, location, or principle that you're unwilling to abandon, then say so. Similarly, if you know that the company is going to go public next year, that needs to be included in every scenario.

None of this is new, of course. The idea of "scenario planning" was first articulated in the 1950s by Herman Kahn at the RAND Corporation as an exercise in which short stories (scenarios) were written from the point of view of someone in the future. Each depicted a different future in which a key variable goes one way or another.

A company whose success depends on trade between the United States and China might consider scenarios in which trade tensions are the variable: one may assume a trade war, another a compromise and a new agreement. By developing plans for both extremes of a spectrum, you're theoretically prepared for most of the situations in between. In the US–China example, the company could develop contingency plans that minimize the downsides of a trade war (or take advantage of it), while also creating systems that could flourish under a new trade agreement. Since negative events affect competitors, too, better preparation offers a relative advantage, even in a catastrophe.

You can't create a scenario for every situation, so determine which variables are assumed to be stable and which are less relevant. You might assume a growing global middle class and, if you sell completely in Southeast Asia, that South American trade patterns are less important. This allows you to focus on the variables that have a high enough probability and a significant enough impact to be relevant.

For each scenario, the right team can make reasonable predictions about the future environment and how the organization can thrive in it. By creating detailed narratives, you ensure that you're thinking about a concrete reality instead of an abstract possibility, exposing future implications that might otherwise be missed.

Facilitate the Session

The specifics of running a simulation or scenario planning session can vary widely, depending on the goals, the kind of organization, and the participants. There are, however, a few best practices worth following:

1. **Orient the room:** Distribute a clear agenda in advance that lays out the meeting objective, the work that has already been done, and the expected outcomes of the meeting and of the rest of the process.

2. **Go around the room:** For sessions with more than a few participants, it's a good idea to give everyone a chance to speak before starting. A simple introduction is the minimum, but they should also explain their unique skills and expertise. The goal is to dissolve some of the hierarchy while establishing each person as a source of potential

insights. This is why the boss shouldn't sit at the head of the table.

3. **Have a facilitator:** It's tempting to run a session like this as an informal, "headless" affair, but having a designated facilitator, preferably an external one, is always a good idea. Ideally, this is someone who's not part of any existing power structures in the room, and who has experience leading groups in workshop or cocreation settings (in other words, not the boss). The facilitator establishes objectives and boundaries for the exercise and presents relevant information and stimuli.

4. **Stay on topic:** Future thinking can be exciting and inspiring, so it's easy to wander off topic. It's up to the facilitator to monitor progress and ensure that everyone stays on task.

5. **Add some structure:** Without clear advance planning, scenario-building sessions tend to degrade into just another meeting, where people sit around a table chatting about what they think is going to happen. While robust discussion is important to the process, you won't get far if that's all you do. There are many ways to flesh out a future scenario, and a lot depends on matching the activity to the goals and the group. Writing first-person narratives, as Kahn did at RAND, can be a powerful approach, but it depends on having people who are comfortable writing long-form fiction. Other techniques include:

   a. Write a newspaper story or press release from the future, describing a new product, service, business development, or news event.
   b. Conduct a well-structured brainstorm of scenario ideas, then rate and rank them to identify the most promising.
   c. Create a familiar artifact from your current business process but in a fictional future situation. This could

        include org charts, project plans, budgets, business plans, or product concepts.

   d. Modify causal loop diagrams, as described earlier in the book, to reflect future scenarios.

6. **Schedule more time than you need:** Because scenario-building is such an unfamiliar task for many people, it can take a while for the group to get into the right mindset. Many of the best ideas occur toward the end of a session, after the team has loosened up. It's worth allowing time for some overflow to avoid having to shut things down just as they're getting interesting.

7. **Coach instead of lead:** If you're the boss, share how you think, not what you think.

   a. Write down your thoughts, but don't share them yet.

   b. Ask people what they see that you might not.

   c. Then share your opinions.

   d. Perhaps most importantly, describe how others have shifted your thinking.

8. **Look for insights and share them with the organization:** The value of future scenarios is the way they affect what you do today. You're not done when you've painted a picture of the future. You're done when you've looked at the "miracles" that will get you to the future that you want *and* determined what principles you need to adopt to make them happen. This can be a slow, difficult task, but it's incredibly valuable, and its results should be socialized throughout the organization.

In the next chapter, you'll learn how to use these insights to make your system more resilient, enhance your processes and management methods, and, ultimately, change the incentives that reinforce your culture.

CHART YOUR POSSIBLE FUTURES

Everyone should walk out of these exercises with a better understanding of the assumptions and a larger range of possibilities.

Memory changes over time, so whether you're doing this as an individual or working as a group, it's always useful to write down what you learned from each scenario that was developed.

- What is the *situation*, and what are the underlying drivers that will create your good (100x), bad, and ugly outcomes?
- What sequence of miracles does each outcome require?
- What triggers could cause them to happen?
- What is the *certainty* of those miracles occurring?
- What is the *impact* if the miracles do or don't occur?
- How would the outcome change if the *timeline* or sequence of events changed?
- What *actions* could you take to influence the likelihood of triggers occurring?
- What indicators would give an early warning that the likelihood is changing?
- How will you change your current programs and investment priorities in light of the risks and opportunities you've identified?

In addition, it's always helpful to ask what high-impact events might suddenly become low-impact tomorrow—and how likely that change is. For instance, Covid-19 was a massive disruption to human existence without a vaccine. With a vaccine, it is potentially far more manageable.

Make sure to compare the possible futures you have identified by both likelihood and impact. The best tool for doing this is a simple chart on which you plot your future scenarios and rank them by these metrics. This is helpful when making initial assessments, but it becomes even more useful if you check back regularly to see whether your priorities are still in line with the possible futures you face (Figure 5.7).

Figure 5.7 **Chart Your Possible Futures**

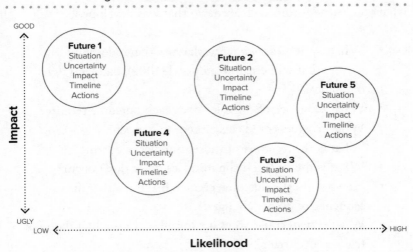

SUMMARY

Your Sensitivity to Change

1. **Build your Tree of Possibility.**
   - The Good: Imagine a larger, transformational goal, your 100x future.
   - The Bad: Reframe your current goal as a minimum acceptable outcome.
   - The Ugly: Lay out the worst possible scenario.
   - Determine the necessary miracles for each scenario by laying out its financial, operational, external, and strategic drivers.

2. **Grow your tree and consider your sensitivity to it.**
   - Consider how you might apply the 5Ds (Deceive, Disrupt, Degrade, Deny, Destroy) to gain a competitive advantage. Examine your vulnerabilities should they occur.
   - Consider how the 10 undercurrents (from Chapter 2) could invalidate or amplify your assumptions.

3. **Maintain a chart with your range of possible futures.**
   - Rank the likelihood of each future and its likely impact on your organization.
   - Identify the events that could cause each future and which indicators you can watch to see them coming.
   - Rank actions you can take now, based on:

     a. Their potential to shift the future to your advantage
     b. The timeline on which they need to be completed
     c. Their impact on your financial, operational, and strategic position

Today's To-Dos for Tomorrow

- **Perform a threat-opportunity analysis.** Have a conversation within your organization about where you could be better at managing the future, and make investments in response.

- **Run more frequent simulations.** Run—or ideally, have a facilitator run—scenario planning and simulation programs on a regular basis. Test the key threats and opportunities these identify, and distribute the insights to the larger organization for discussion. Collate learnings from other groups that do similar work.

- **Maintain a ranked list of opportunities and threats.** Quantify each of your primary threats and opportunities by its degree of uncertainty, its impact, and the time you have to prepare for it. Assess your spending in relation to the payoffs. Do a quarterly reassessment against investments.

6

U: Uncouple Your Opportunities from Your Threats

Work backward from your potential futures to identify and exploit key decision and trigger points.

Born in Florence in 1454, Amerigo Vespucci was a scholar, a geographer, and a businessman. One of the merchants he worked for invested in Cristobal Columbus's 1492 expedition and won a contract to provision his second. After outfitting several other voyages of discovery, Vespucci got the itch to go west himself, first on commission from others, then as captain of his own ship.

Little was known about the far side of the Atlantic at that time. Columbus had gotten no further south than the north coast of modern-day Colombia. Was it a large island, like Madagascar? The west coast of Asia, as Columbus died believing? Or something else entirely?

Vespucci's fleet was tasked with seeing how far south the land went, and what riches or trade could be claimed for Spain. A series of papal decrees had divided the unknown land with a meridian, a demarcation line that ran from pole to pole. The land east of the line belonged to Portugal, while the land to the west belonged to Spain, so whether the coast curved east, west, or allowed a passage to Asia had enormous implications for the wealth and power of the two burgeoning empires.

Columbus had identified fresh water flows in Colombia that suggested that it was a continent, not an island—something Vespucci confirmed when he reached the mouth of the Amazon. By the time he turned east to head back to Europe, Vespucci was certain that he'd explored farther south than any landmass in Asia. Not only was this a continent, it was a New World.

In many ways, Vespucci was the ideal captain for this expedition (Figure 6.1). Its ultimate destination was unknown, and so were the conditions under which the crew would have to operate. Having a professional outfitter in the lead ensured that the fleet was prepared for a wide range of outcomes.

Vespucci already knew how much and what kind of supplies they would need to get to South America. But he also knew they'd have to reprovision before they headed farther south.

Near modern-day Buenos Aires, he took on another six months' worth of food and water—the entire amount used on his trip to that point—before heading east to discover what is believed to be South Georgia Island, the southernmost large landmass in the Atlantic. From there he turned north toward Portugal, stopping in Sierra Leone and the Azores along the way.[1]

Like most Europeans sailing west in that era, Vespucci hoped to get to India. But unlike many of his contemporaries, he didn't approach it as an all-or-nothing big bet. He built plenty of flexibility into his plans. Even if he didn't get to India, he understood that there was plenty of value to discover along the way. But most importantly, he approached the journey not as one trip, but as a series of smaller connected ones. Each of the stages of his journey—from Lisbon to the Canary Islands to Brazil, down the coast, and then east to South Georgia Island—was a much shorter journey than that of Columbus. Every landfall presented an opportunity to stock up on food, water,

Figure 6.1 **Vespucci's Third Voyage**

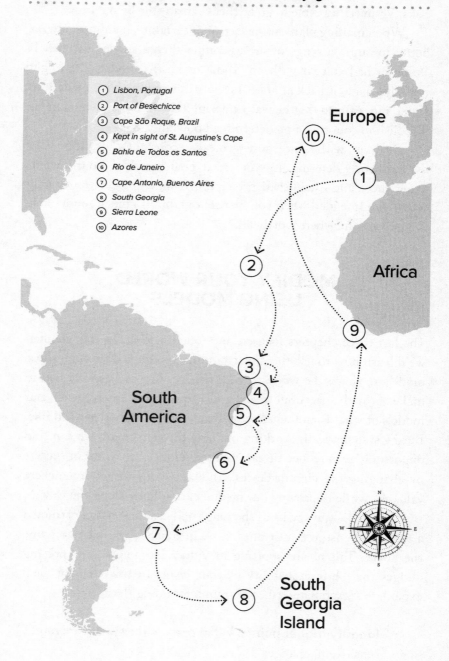

1. Lisbon, Portugal
2. Port of Besechicce
3. Cape São Roque, Brazil
4. Kept in sight of St. Augustine's Cape
5. Bahia de Todos os Santos
6. Rio de Janeiro
7. Cape Antonio, Buenos Aires
8. South Georgia
9. Sierra Leone
10. Azores

Europe

Africa

South America

South Georgia Island

and wood—and to turn back to Europe if necessary. By limiting his risks, Vespucci was able to go farther than anyone before him.

When making plans in the face of uncertainty, it's almost always better to target a range of success rather than a single outcome. If Vespucci had started with an "India or bust!" mindset, he might not have made it back at all—and he still wouldn't have made it to India. He realized that he was exploring the unknown, which made it foolish to count on a predetermined outcome.

Dealing with uncertainty means constantly testing your assumptions—determining your next goal based on your current experiences and established principles. It may not get you exactly where you intended when you first set out, but it's much more likely to get you somewhere worthwhile.

MODIFY YOUR WORLD USING MODELS

The last three chapters focused on model-making. In this chapter, we'll learn how to use the understanding you gained through those models to shape the world to your benefit. Just as Vespucci had to make do with inaccurate maps and rudimentary instruments, our models of what is and what could be are never as good as we'd like. But by systematically working our way through them, we can find opportunities to reduce threats and maximize our chance of success by changing the circumstances. This allows us to get somewhere valuable, while improving our mental cartography along the way.

A casino always wins in the long run because it has constructed a system to ensure that it does. To win reliably, you have to game the house. This means spotting its vulnerable points and applying nudges that shift probability in your favor. In this chapter, we'll explore four tactics and rules of thumb for doing that:

- **Identify trigger points:** What parts of the system are most sensitive to change?

- **Nudge the system:** How can your organization adjust the trigger points to shift the larger system to your benefit?
- **Prioritize threats and opportunities:** How can your organization decrease the uncertainty that surrounds each and determine the best order and time to address them?
- **Shift certainty and impact:** How do you build and communicate a strategy for changing the likelihood of events and their degree of impact?

These tactics aren't meant to be applied in any particular order. As Vespucci demonstrated, a successful long voyage is composed of many short voyages, which are constantly reviewed and adjusted based on new knowledge. That's why it's best to look at these tactics as iterative processes, to be performed many times in whatever order makes sense for the situation.

IDENTIFY TRIGGER POINTS

In a Rube Goldberg–style chain reaction, one action causes the next. A falling domino triggers a hammer, which drops onto a lever that starts a bicycle wheel turning. As a kid, it's easy to think of this as a perpetual motion machine, in which a small amount of energy is passed from one step to the next. But that's not what's happening at all.

Each action releases stored energy, often the potential energy of a heavy object that's poised to fall. By linking actions together, a small amount of energy from one can release the potential stored in the next, and so on.

Such transitions are common in the real world. We'll call them trigger points: interactions in which a small amount of effort can release a large amount of pent-up energy. By "point," we mean some combination of a moment in time, a convergence of multiple elements, and possibly a physical location. As in the Rube Goldberg machine, the trigger point isn't primarily a transfer of energy, but a release of potential energy.

The assassination of Archduke Ferdinand is a dramatic example of a trigger point, in which a single death unleashed the armies of many nations, fundamentally reshaping half the globe. But Ferdinand's death didn't *cause* the war and what came after. The energies that his death released had built up over the course of decades of enmity, alliances, trade pacts, and secret treaties throughout Europe. Without them, his death would've been a footnote.

Similarly, the short circuit that shut down the data center that I wrote about in Chapter 5 was triggered by a janitor who used cleaning fluid in the wrong place. It cost the company millions. But you can't blame the janitor. A whole series of mistakes provided the kindling; the poor guy just lit the match.

Identifying trigger points in the systems around you is crucial for two reasons. First, it helps you spot ways to focus the force the trigger releases in the direction you want. In the case of Ferdinand's assassination, better communication channels between and within the great empires of Europe might have defused the bomb before it exploded (or at least pointed it in a less destructive direction). A clear contingency plan and the right spare parts would've made that janitorial screw-up a tiny blip.

The second reason is that you can use trigger points to your advantage. The most successful businesses aren't the ones that build entire industries from the ground up or fight single-handedly against established leaders. They're the ones that see the pent-up forces and prepare themselves to ride the wave they release. That is what McDonald's did when it rode the wave of automobile-dependent suburbanization in the 1950s. It's what Apple did when it helped schools and universities ramp up their technology in the 1980s.

We're mixing metaphors a little here, but catching a wave is a useful image: position yourself at the right spot, and you can paddle a few strokes and then ride it. Position yourself at the wrong point, and you'll miss it or get wiped out.

Welcome to VEGAS

*We had all the momentum; we were riding the crest of a high
and beautiful wave. . . . So, now, less than five years later, you
can go up on a steep hill in Las Vegas and look West, and with
the right kind of eyes you can almost see the High Water Mark—
that place where the wave finally broke and rolled back.*

—HUNTER S. THOMPSON,
FEAR AND LOATHING IN LAS VEGAS

We've highlighted a lot of unpredictability in this book, but the fact
is most things don't go haywire. Most epidemics don't upend the
world economy, most financial disasters don't become 2008, and
most business crises don't result in bankruptcy. The world is full of
systems that could go nonlinear but don't because of external controls that keep them in check.

So how do we know which limiters will work? What clues do
we have that *this* event is a trigger point that will cause an uncon-
trollable crisis (or exponential opportunity) when the previous 10
events weren't? The key is to look beyond the trigger point to the
controls that contain it. As you might expect, having gotten this far
in the book, there's a handy acronym that can help systematically
identify these controls: VEGAS, which stands for Visibility, Effect,
Gestation, Accessibility, and Security (Figure 6.2).

The easiest way to understand VEGAS is through examples.
The first is from my own career, back in my data center days. At
that time, we were dealing with the serious issue of thermal management in server arrays. In the days of car-sized computers, an air
conditioner (called a CRAC unit) would blow cool air under a raised
floor, pressurizing the subarea where the power and network cables
ran. Holes were cut out of the floor in front of the computers, and
the pressurized air would rise to cool them. But as servers got hotter
and more dense, the air conditioners couldn't keep up.

The obvious solution was to simply turn up the air conditioner,
but the amount of heat to be dissipated was getting prohibitively

Figure 6.2 **Why Things Don't Stay in VEGAS**

V

Visibility
How easy is it to identify problems in the system?

E

Effect
How might a mundane event cause unexpected second- or third-order effects that lead to failure?

G

Gestation
How much time is there between a catastrophic action and its result?

A

Accessibility
Can you actually get to the points of failure in order to fix them?

S

Security
How likely are each of the key components to break? And what abilities do they have to self-correct or recover?

expensive due to mechanical issues and the electricity required. Another option was to space out the servers. Again, the economics didn't work: reducing density would require additional data centers, making them less profitable. It was actually cheaper to take a third approach and simply let the servers burn out every few months. For a while, big companies like Google were treating servers as disposable, swapping them in and out frequently (and doing extensive backups to avoid data loss).

Faced with three bad options, our team drew up a causal loop diagram to map out how the facilities worked. Then we built a specialized sensor and went around different data centers, mapping their airflows. What we discovered was that, as more servers per square foot had been added, more cutouts had been made in the floor to accommodate cabling to them. Air was escaping through those cutouts. The result was that as much as 80 percent of the chilled air was recirculating through ducts in the ceiling before it got anywhere near the computers. The openings, we realized, were a trigger point, where a relatively small effort could have a large consequence. We identified it by looking at the five VEGAS issues:

Visibility: How easy is it to identify problems in the system? In a data center, air flow is crucial but invisible. It was only after we'd invented a tool for measuring it in different locations that the real source of the problem became clear. Solving the airflow problem was relatively straightforward, as we'll see in a minute. Identifying it was hard.

Effect: How might a mundane event cause unexpected second- or third-order effects that lead to failure? The data center team had noticed that there was a huge difference between projected and actual performance of the CRAC units. But the difference couldn't be explained by anything we could directly measure. To isolate the air circulation problem, we had to use a causal loop diagram to look at the larger system and find failure points.

Gestation: How much time is there between a catastrophic action and its result? Since the late 1990s, data processing has moved from mainframes to servers to co-location, with incremental improvements along the way. This tepid progress doesn't encourage investment in R&D. As a result, facilities managers made short-term investments, based on the equipment that was easily available, without considering the long-term costs and consequences. By contrast, Amazon, knowing that it would build many data centers, saw the negative impact of inefficient cooling and dealt with it proactively. It designed its data centers, and eventually its cloud services company, AWS, from scratch. It did more than pioneer a new approach to the cooling problem. It was able to reinvent how data centers are run by rethinking the inefficient legacy systems that burdened its competitors.

Accessibility: Can you actually get to a point of failure in order to fix it? The cooling system in a data center is massive, powerful, and essential to operations. This makes replacing certain parts nearly impossible without shutting the whole system down. While we could have developed more exotic solutions, our team realized that the best approach would be one that a maintenance worker could easily retrofit while the system was running.

Security: How likely are each of the key components to break? And what abilities do they have to self-correct or recover? This comes last in the acronym but is actually the most fundamental: If a data center's servers can't be cooled, they can't function, resulting in millions of dollars of lost income. These cooling systems are still one of the most vulnerable elements of the internet. They've prompted giants like Facebook, Microsoft, and Google to spend billions of dollars on highly redundant data centers, located in far-flung places (including the bottom of the ocean[2]) chosen for their climates and access to cheap electricity.

A VEGAS of the Heart

If data centers are a little too tech-heavy for you, let's try applying VEGAS to understand rogue wave risk in something closer to home: the human circulatory system. Heart disease is still the number one killer of Americans. Spotting and preventing heart problems is one of our greatest medical challenges. We can use the VEGAS approach to better understand the vulnerabilities and possible trigger points in this crucial system.

Visibility: Like data center infrastructure, the circulatory system is crucial but invisible. Plenty of instruments exist to measure circulatory health, but you have to know how to use them. The biggest obstacle to reducing fatal heart attacks isn't poor measurement—it's people not realizing they need to get tested.

Effect: Heart attack risk can't be measured directly, but many things that increase it can. This is why doctors look at the weight, age, and genetic background of a patient, as well as blood pressure and cholesterol levels. None of these factors causes a heart attack on its own, but the interaction of several can be strong indicators.

Gestation: One of the things that makes heart disease so hard to prevent is the long lag between unhealthy behaviors—like poor diet, smoking, and lack of exercise—and negative outcomes. Having a model that links today's behavior with heart conditions 15 years from now is a crucial part of prevention.

Accessibility: Open-heart surgery is expensive, disruptive, and potentially life-threatening. The less invasive surgical techniques that have been perfected over the past decades have made a huge difference. But nothing can change the fact that most of the human circulatory system is irreplaceable, which is why heart disease is still so deadly.

Security: The human heart is an incredibly reliable muscle, but it's also very vulnerable. It has no backup, and while it can recover from minor damage, something as simple as a sticky valve can cause sudden death. Despite decades of medical advancements, 356,000 Americans still die every year due to sudden cardiac arrest.[3]

NUDGE YOUR SYSTEM

Once you've identified a trigger point, what should you do about it?

There's an old thought experiment called Maxwell's Daemon that helps illustrate how small efforts can have a big impact if performed at the right point. Imagine two boxes, connected by a door, filled with gas at the same temperature. The "daemon" is an intelligent actor that selectively opens and closes the door, shepherding faster moving molecules into one box and keeping slower ones out. This raises the temperature in one box while lowering it in another.

In the field of thermodynamics, Maxwell's Daemon helps us understand why hot and cold things in contact eventually reach equilibrium if left alone. If you put ice in hot water, the ice will melt and the water will cool. With no daemon guarding the door, the molecule speeds will balance out. This gives rise to the idea of entropy (or disorder) and the second law of thermodynamics, which states that a closed system can't spontaneously become more orderly without some external effort.

But there's a broader insight here, which is that a small amount of effort, applied selectively, can transform a system. In the real world, devices like heat pumps, air conditioners, and refrigerators act as daemons, using electrical power to separate hot from cold. In each case, the work the system does can be far greater than what's done by the daemon. A heat pump is more efficient than a simple electric heater because it doesn't generate heat itself. It separates existing warm air into hotter and cooler air. It then routes the cold air outside. This is perhaps the greatest value of looking holistically at systems: it's typically far more efficient to organize or release existing energy than to be the source of energy oneself.

Creating daemons that can nudge systems at their trigger points is a powerful way to shape change in your favor. Similar daemons are frequently used to nudge financial, demographic, and political systems. When the German government subsidized the development and manufacture of solar panels, for example, it accelerated a decline in their cost. It suddenly made something improbable, a green energy revolution, much more likely.[4] The nudges don't have to be dramatic to cause or offset the impacts of a rogue wave. They just have to be cumulative.

In the case of the cooling problem in the data centers, our team invented a surprisingly simple product called the Koldlok. It's a plastic insert that allows cables to pass through cutouts in a raised floor but keeps cold air from escaping. It's a small nudge in exactly the right place, and it transformed an industry. At the time of Koldlok's invention, data centers were the fastest-growing consumers of electricity in the United States. This thirst for power touched all four FOES of Growth (financial, operational, external, and strategic risk). A plastic fixture costing a couple of dollars allowed them to start saving electricity on the scale of cities, and it's still on the market decades later.

There are as many different ways to nudge a system as there are trigger points to address. What's most effective depends on the specific case. It might be a product like the Koldlok, but it might also be a government policy, a checklist, or a contingency plan.

While researching the VEGAS system for spotting trigger points, my team has paid careful attention to the kinds of solutions clients deploy and sorted them into the five most effective nudges (Figure 6.3).

Figure 6.3 **The Five Nudges**

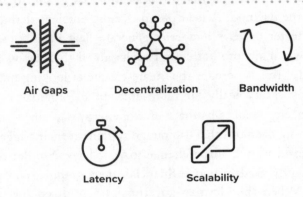

Air Gaps

One way to make a big bet and reduce the impact of a potential catastrophe is to disconnect it from the things it could affect. Web and software developers often create "sandboxes" where they can test new features in isolation before connecting them to an existing system. For organizations, a similar approach is to separate high-risk projects or departments from the rest of the company, giving them their own finite resources and staff. This allows them to be more effective because they don't have to be so concerned with the consequences of failure. On the flip side, removing an air gap can shift the risk in your favor, for instance, by paying a new salesperson on commission instead of a salary. You might have to pay them more money, but you won't have to pay for any inefficiency.

Decentralization

Having just a few key nodes that everything must go through—whether that's information, resources, or approval—creates a point of control, but it can also make those nodes especially vulnerable. Devolving resources and decision-making to the edges of a network helps ensure that it keeps functioning even if a central entity is overwhelmed. This strategy has driven the development of the world's most resilient networks, from the modern internet to terrorist organizations like Al-Qaeda. It's also why multinational consumer brands like McDonald's put so much effort into localizing their offerings, from *ebi* (shrimp) burgers in Japan to lobster rolls in Maine. On the flip side, centralization often increases rigor and efficiency. HP split into two companies so its cash cow business units could increase their focus on performance. Unlike Xerox, it kept a diversified portfolio and didn't cut too far. This saved HP when Covid hit.

Bandwidth

At the same time, it's possible to create an advantage by changing the amount of information being shared. The data center failure mentioned earlier could have been prevented if management and operations had talked to each other more often. World War I might've been averted if the military and diplomatic corps within each country were more aware of what their counterparts were up to. It can also be useful to decrease bandwidth. For instance, mattress stores have different names for similar products so customers can't price compare.

Latency

In addition to increasing communication between parts of the network, it's often useful to change the time between gathering and sharing information. High-risk environments like emergency rooms and air traffic control centers have robust real-time information systems that allow everyone to see exactly what's going on at a glance. One of the most popular strategies for fighting climate change—carbon taxes—works by decreasing the lag between when a company emits carbon and when it feels an impact. By making the effect immediate (financially, at least), the link between cause and effect is clearer, which encourages different investment decisions. On the flip side, real estate developers often choose materials that are cheaper up front but cost more to maintain after they have offloaded the property.

Scalability

It's natural for some links and nodes in a network to get bigger and faster than others. But left unchecked, this creates vulnerabilities. When you decentralize, you have to scale up capacity in neglected parts of the network to make sure they can take up slack when needed. And crucially, you need to study the process of scaling up so it can be repeated quickly. During the Covid pandemic, for example, Amazon Web Services enabled Zoom to scale quickly by providing infrastructure as it needed it.[5] On the flip side, it's worth considering the challenges of scaling down. Throughout the first year of Covid, Carnival Cruise Lines' run rate was three times its revenue as over 80 ships sat idle.[6]

Keeping What Happens in Vegas in VEGAS

It doesn't matter whether you want to disrupt a system or increase its reliability, the tools are essentially the same. You study strengths and weaknesses using VEGAS, and then consider the combination of nudges that would create the change you desire with the least effort on your part (Figure 6.4).

PRIORITIZE YOUR OPPORTUNITIES AND THREATS

Spotting trigger points and understanding where your system needs resilience is only the first half of the task. Then you need to actually

Figure 6.4 **Choosing the Right Combination of Nudges to Change the System**

	Air Gaps	Decentral-ization	Bandwidth	Latency	Scalability
Visibility					
Effect					
Gestation					
Accessibility					
Security					

build that resilience—and usually you can't do it all at once. This raises the issue of prioritizing risk: which opportunities and threats do you need to address first, second, and third? This isn't just a matter of efficiency. With a wave approaching, it can be the difference between sinking and success.

There are a number of strategies that can help you bend the future to your benefit:

- **Slice your risk onion:** Look at all the challenges you will face instead of just the challenges you face right now.
- **Start with Plan B:** Develop your backup plan first.
- **Understand your risk levels:** Consider the impact of systemic risks that come from other systems.
- **Expand your awareness of uncertainty:** Use techniques that increase your contextual awareness.
- **Exploit your information advantage:** Apply nudges based on your superior understanding of the system to shape it to your advantage.

Slice Your Risk Onion

Netscape founder Marc Andreessen, now a prolific startup investor, describes entrepreneurial risk management as "peeling an onion." On day one of a startup, you have a bulb full of every possible kind of risk. Then you peel it away, one layer at a time. There are seven layers to consider. You start with the founding team, making it as reliable and prepared as possible. You validate the product concept. Then you examine the needed technology to minimize reliance on uncertain breakthroughs. This derisking continues through four more layers—product launch, market acceptance, cost of sales, and cost of growth—until the whole process is as low stakes as possible.

All of this needs to happen for a startup to become viable. But in the hypergrowth markets where Andreessen's venture capital firm invests, it rarely does. According to a study of 350 failed tech startups, 70 percent of those that made it past the earliest stages failed within 20 months. Of those:

- 42 percent went bust because they weren't making something people wanted.
- 29 percent ran out of cash (though they raised an average of $1.3 million each).
- 23 percent had the wrong team.[7]

Juicero is a classic example of a company that failed to manage risk effectively. Cold-pressed juice was a growing market in 2017, and the idea was to have it available on demand in your home or office. Doug Evans was a seductive CEO with experience in the juice business. Yves Behar and Apple's Jony Ive, two of the most famous product designers in the world, were involved. Kleiner Perkins and Sequoia Capital were investing. Even Campbell's Soup was backing it.[8]

A whopping 97 percent of hardware startups fail,[9] yet investors were drawn to the product like drunken sailors to a siren. "It's software. It's consumer electronics. It's produce and packaging," said

David Krane from Google Ventures.[10] The high complexity should have been a warning, but the financiers were high on Doug's juice, buying into the team and the product concept instead of the miracles necessary to make it succeed.

In fact, Juicero needed a *lot* of miracles to occur:

- Every city where it operated would have to build a multimillion-dollar "fruit factory."
- Each customer had to buy a massively complicated $700 juice machine that could apply 8,000 pounds of pressure to the packets of fruit.[11]
- Customers had to download and order through a mobile app.
- Most of all, they had to want an $8 glass of fresh juice on demand on an ongoing basis.

As the onion was peeled, it became clear that Juicero was destined to fail. The machine made it to market, but hardly anyone bought it. People loved cold-pressed juice, but they weren't prepared to invest in it at that level. And once it was revealed that the $700 machine was simply squeezing a pouch—which you could do nearly as efficiently with your hands—demand virtually evaporated.

"I was just naive," Evans said. "I was like Forrest Gump. I had no idea what it took to make a piece of hardware that could ship to consumers safely."[12] The problem with the "onion peel" approach is that it implies you can address threats and opportunities in the order that they surface. Juicero had a great founding team, a product that reviewers fawned over, and technology that had been sweated out in every detail. What killed it were the final layers: it cost too much to make, and the market didn't accept it.

In my experience, the more successful strategy is to slice through the onion rather than peeling it. In many cases, the most fatal risks are based on decisions made early on that don't impact the outcome until much later (that's Gestation, the G in VEGAS). At the same time, many of the elements that get derisked early on change so much before the launch that they must be reexamined. If you're a typical tech startup founder, by the time you launch you can expect to:

- Lose 20 to 50 percent of your founding team
- Deliver using a different technology than you prototyped with
- Change your product concept as you talk to customers
- Switch to a different sales channel than you originally thought you'd use

Notably, Andreessen Horowitz did not invest in Juicero.[13]

So what are your layers of risk, and are they worth the opportunity? No matter what you're attempting, these layers are likely knowable, and even if you don't know them, someone else does and is probably willing to tell you. More urgently, what can you do now to offset those risks later? Much of the answer comes down to performing the right experiments and having the right backup plans.

Start with Plan B

Much of my career has been focused on inventing the new—but new things rarely work the first time. Ralph Guggenheim was an early mentor. He's one of the founders of Pixar and the executive producer of *Toy Story*, the first 3D-animated feature film. Ralph taught me one of the great lessons of my early career, which is to start with Plan B.

When making *Toy Story*, Pixar had two scary moments. A quarter of the way through production, they realized they had the wrong characters. Then three-quarters of the way through, they realized they had the wrong story.

In most cases, either of these challenges would have killed the film. But the Pixar team had anticipated having problems along the way. They were, after all, making a kind of movie that no one had ever tried to make, using new technology. So instead of starting with a beginning-to-end plan, they built a modular system that could be recombined later on if needed.

In practice, this meant creating each character independently and cataloging a full range of movements, gestures, and expressions for each. The same was done with environments and lighting setups. It was a lot of extra work at the front end, but when crises struck, the modularity made it much easier to adjust the characters and story lines and then "reshoot" with relatively little time lost. Had they not been able to adjust along the way, it's almost certain *Toy Story* would've been a box office bomb, despite its groundbreaking technology. More likely, it wouldn't have been released at all.

This approach—which parallels Vespucci's step-by-step exploration strategy—applies to a huge variety of projects. When the opportunity is too big to avoid taking on risk, modularity is a good plan. This is true whether you're building a business, a product, a research program, or an investment strategy. When one thing breaks, you can isolate and fix it. It's a concept that sits at the heart of planning for resilience.

Understand Your Risk Levels

As overplayed as the *Titanic* story is, it's still one of the best case studies on the consequences of not fully understanding risk. The *Titanic* was, after all, specifically designed to be invincible and sold itself largely on how safe it was (in addition to how big, how luxurious, how modern, and so on). A lesser-known element of the story is that the White Star Line, which operated the *Titanic*, was getting overtaken by competitors. White Star saw a massive, "unsinkable" ship as a high-profile investment and marketing coup, an opportunity that could reverse its fortunes.

The *Titanic*'s reputation was based on its innovative hull, with 16 watertight compartments that could be sealed in the event of a breach—a maritime version of an air gap strategy. But when disaster struck, water flooded six compartments at once, causing the bow to tilt forward.[14] Harland and Wolff, the shipbuilders, had designed the compartments with bulkheads that reached much higher than the waterline, but not up to the ceilings. As the ship pitched forward, water poured over the bulkheads, slowly dragging the bow underwater until the ship snapped in two.

Perhaps they should have foreseen this kind of catastrophe, but there are hundreds of ways a ship can sink. Their real mistake was believing that they understood all the ways that things could go wrong, which led them to skimp on innovative redundancies, like high-volume pumps to remove the water. The *Titanic* was designed to a high standard, but that didn't remove the danger of a rogue wave—or its iceberg equivalent.

Risk is often misunderstood this way, even (perhaps especially) by experienced, well-informed professionals. They assume that the future will match their lived experience:

- Before September 11, 2001, art insurers didn't seriously consider that the World Trade Center could be destroyed, even though a terrorist bomb had been detonated there less than a decade earlier. It was a "surprise" when Al-Qaeda's attack caused perhaps the largest art loss in the history of the insurance industry.[15]
- In the late summer of 2020, during the Covid-19 pandemic, a Montessori school in Mountain View, California, opened its doors to students. They'd read the latest research on child safety and believed they could keep the kids masked and spaced apart. They kept the windows open and served lunch in the yard outside. Three days after opening, they had to close the windows to keep out the smoke from a forest fire that had been sparked by lightning. With one bolt, all their months of planning and preparation were defeated, and the school was closed.[16]
- In the 1990s, Long-Term Capital Management leveraged $5 billion in assets to borrow $120 billion against positions

worth over $1 trillion dollars. Long-Term was led by Salomon Brothers' former head of bond trading, John Meriwether, and the Nobel Prize–winning economist Myron Scholes.[17] Lenders assumed that Meriwether and Scholes were the smartest people in the room. Had they investigated, they'd have realized that a single change in the market would take down the company—in this case, the 1998 default of the Russian government.

In each of these examples, the experts solved for risk at one level of a system without understanding it at the next level up. A mechanical engineer might understand steel, but not personnel changes. A facilities engineer comprehends air conditioning, but not forest fires. A hedge fund manager knows how to sell to investors, but might have a shaky understanding of geopolitics. A great operations executive might know how to serve current customers and optimize labor, but not win new markets with innovative technologies. All of these experts understand risk, but only in one arena. What's obvious at one level can be opaque at another, and that's why you need tools to look at the same challenge at different scales.

Expand Your Awareness of Uncertainty

At this point, it should be clear that dealing with rogue waves is primarily a function of how well you understand uncertainty: where it comes from, how likely it is, and what its impact will be. Hopefully, it's also clear that there are nearly infinite ways of misunderstanding uncertainty. You can get it wrong by addressing risk in the wrong order, like Juicero did. You can also get it wrong by assuming the possibilities you're most familiar with are the most likely or will have the biggest impact. Given how many smart people have fallen prey to these traps, how do you avoid them?

The best answer is to expand your awareness. This may sound overly philosophical, but it's the truth. Part of the reason this book uses so many analogies and examples from seemingly random fields is to help illustrate this.

So far, you've learned about wine tasting, oil drilling platforms, ocean exploration, data centers, power-generating kites, world wars, demographics in China, Sherlock Holmes, rocket ships, genetics, hurricanes, bicycle pumps, failed startups, terrorist attacks, prosthetic limbs, and a dozen other things (and we're not done yet!). Each of these has served a purpose in explaining a concept, and none of them would be able to carry the book on its own. But combined, they tell a bigger story.

There's nothing magical about this particular combination of examples and analogies; someone else could've made the same points just as well using an entirely different set. It's the variety and range of topics that matters. The unavoidable fact is that *nobody* has all the answers or understands all the alternatives, no matter how much the experts would like you to believe otherwise. You need multiple perspectives to get an accurate, relevant picture of the present so that you can better prepare for the future.

I'm not spectacularly intelligent or well educated, but I'm extremely curious, and this has probably been my greatest asset as an advisor. It means that I have to gather a wider range of information and perspectives than most of the people I work with. So if there's one lesson to take from this book, it's to be more curious and trust that it will make you better at making decisions.

Barring that, there's a short list of concrete steps you can take to expand your perspective and thereby improve your understanding of the possibilities, threats, and opportunities you're likely to confront.

1. **Talk to someone outside your field or level of seniority.**
   Perhaps this is obvious, but in practice it's rare: when was the last time you had lunch with someone who makes half as much as you, or asked in-depth questions of an expert in a field you know little about? Chatting with a call center worker in your organization will yield plenty of interesting anecdotes; one or two of them could transform your perspective.

2. **Read some history, especially about times and places you don't know well.** Most mistakes have been made before, as have most good decisions. Looking at an unfamiliar era or place helps remove some of the bias that we all bring to stories about our own field or time, which makes it easier to be surprised by insight.

3. **Consider corollaries in other fields.** This is just an action-oriented version of the previous step. When you're faced with uncertainty or a difficult decision, look for a field in which such decisions are commonplace. You might not deal with rapid staff turnover very often, but the managers of a McDonald's do. How do they handle it? Assessing risk might not be central to your business, but it is for an insurance agent or a beat cop.

There's also a fourth step you can take, which is to **learn how to think probabilistically.** This is different from the others because it's not about revealing unknown possibilities. It's about pushing the ignored ones into the spotlight, and letting go of attractive but far-fetched alternatives.

It's not enough to just be aware of what could happen. It's also important to get in the habit of assessing how likely each alternative is, or asking someone more knowledgeable about the topic to do it with you. Many of the great investors and entrepreneurs you've encountered in the book—Jeff Bezos, Charlie Munger, Elon Musk, Ray Dalio, and others—have built much of their success on knowing what's likely and what's not, in areas where others are going on unquestioned assumptions.

To better explain the value of this approach, I'm going to introduce one more investor, whom you probably haven't heard of.

Exploit Your Information Advantage

One of my colleagues, let's call him Bill, aggregates hundreds of opportunities a year for a large investment consortium. About one in a thousand of the consortium's investors win big, yet Bill does so consistently. What's he doing differently?

This consortium of angel investors acts as a hook to attract desperate startups, and Bill performs a service, researching the startups and making recommendations. His office charges a fee for this, but that's not where the bulk of his success comes from. Because he's the one doing the research, and has done it for years, he's got a far broader range of investing experience than any of the other angels. He draws on thousands of examples, while the others might be referencing half a dozen. He's also extremely curious, and he talks regularly with experts from a wide range of fields, having faith that this knowledge will someday serve him well.

Bill is able to make very credible assessments of each startup's chance of success by gathering all this information and making comparisons. This enables him to keep the very best investments for himself. In a game with a 1 percent payoff, that can shift the chances from something like 1 in a 1,000 for the consortium to 1 in 10 for Bill.

Of course, no bet is certain, especially in the world of venture capital. If you've read Nassim Taleb's book *The Black Swan*, you might remember his advice for dealing with risk-taking: make reliable low-risk investments with most of your money, putting a small percentage in ultra-high payoff bets with huge (even incalculable) risk, and buy insurance or hedge against the downside. It's good advice.

In the terms we've been using, this recommendation comes down to:

- Design a stable system with low but reliable payoffs
- Use impact amplifiers and air gaps to isolate yourself from major threats
- Make a small number of high impact, low probability bets that will pay off if the right rogue wave hits
- Use nudges to maximize your leverage when the rogue wave wells up

This is sound advice when dealing with a truly random system in which every player has access to the same information and is equally likely to guess right. But in many cases, you can improve on these odds if you have an information advantage, which is what Bill does.

An information advantage can bend the future in your favor if it helps you control the timing, sequencing, or hedging of events. Bill does this in three ways:

1. First, he does the prospecting and due diligence work that others don't want to do to *develop granular knowledge*. This gives him a leg up over the majority of investors.
2. With that knowledge comes *early access*; he can choose the best projects for himself.
3. Finally, Bill always makes sure that he has enough free capital in reserve to *double down when he sees an advantage or when probabilities shift*.

If you think of investing and other business decisions as a casino, Bill's approach is equivalent to gaming the house. Many aspects of a situation may be truly chaotic, but some are reliably knowable. In any business decision, there are aspects that:

- Are truly chaotic
- Are probabilistic
- Can be predicted
- Can be managed at a different scale

Understanding the difference between them is what separates the house from the casual player.

SHIFT CERTAINTY AND IMPACT

Growing up, one of my favorite songs was Kenny Rogers's "The Gambler." I'm not alone; it's one of the top-selling country songs of all time. Perhaps it's because it tells a simple story, or has a great musical hook, or because "You've got to know when to hold 'em, know when to fold 'em" is still one of the best choruses in country music. But what's stuck with me the most is this pair of simple truths: "Every hand's a winner, and every hand's a loser," and "That the secret to survivin' is knowin' what to throw away and knowin' what to keep."

In many cases, the real game isn't in the cards. It's in understanding how to use the cards you have to shift the operating environment to your favor.

In business, it's too easy to get caught up in our beliefs instead of distrusting our understanding of reality. We look at a weak hand without considering the limitations our competitors face. We get caught up in how we value the cards, rather than the cards themselves. Everyone wants a royal straight flush, but sometimes a pair of threes can win the hand. In online poker, the best hand, on average, only wins about 12 percent of the time, and bluffs are only challenged about a third of the time.[18] You can turn a poor hand into a winner if you can create change in the right places. But most inexperienced players either bet on everything or wait for the straight flush.

One of the most important skills to master when trying to shift the odds is to know what changes *not* to pursue. It rarely pays off to focus on big systemic issues that are beyond your control. Conversely, small things that don't add up to significant change can be a waste of effort. It's also crucial to make sure you're solving actual problems, not just symptoms.

The way to avoid making these mistakes is to be honest and accurate about what changes you can actually make, and how much impact those changes are going to have, before deciding what combination of them to pursue. Beating the house reliably starts with identifying trigger points (using VEGAS or something similar) and then nudging the system by air gapping, changing the bandwidth, latency, and such.

Select the Right Combination
of Interventions

If you want to put the techniques in this chapter into practice, first make a list of interventions that minimize threats or create opportunities. Once you have this list, one good way to prioritize is to cluster them into low, medium, and high impact interventions.

Low impact: A change that shifts the incentives in the system. Often, these are items like standards and subsidies, such as offering incentives to employees and partners who complete certain tasks. Because these don't actually change the system, everyone immediately goes about trying to game them. If you know what game you want them to play, this can be a very powerful technique.

Medium impact: A change that shifts probabilities within the system. Typically, this is done using nudges to change the rates, frequencies, and inputs to the system. One example of this is SpaceX. It accelerated development throughout the organization by building faster feedback loops into its design and production processes.

High impact: A change to the underlying structure of the system. This is typically done with nudges *and* impact amplifiers (timing, sequencing, and hedging) that change the connections between links and nodes in a system. For instance, in the case of heart disease, surgeons bypass the blocked vein by installing a new one. In business, structural shifts often change the distribution of power and the goals of the system. Social media tools like Twitter and Parler have shifted mindsets and power. Everyone can tune into the voices they want to hear, bypassing the gatekeepers of the old establishment. Amerigo Vespucci, a relative unknown in European circles of influence, shifted the priorities for European exploration (the high-risk, high-reward business of the day) by getting his idea of the "New World" on maps. In the process, he got the Americas named after him.

Time Your Threats and Opportunities

Most major events are preceded by one or more indicators going off the charts, and if you know what to look for, this offers an information advantage. Ray Dalio, for example, tells the story of the "Depression Indicator" he tracks, which went off prior to the economic collapse in 2008.[19] The threat and opportunity dashboard later in this section (Figure 6.5) is a similar tool for identifying the indicators that are most relevant to you.

It's important to remember, though, that tracking an indicator doesn't mean responding whenever it shifts: a spike on the graph doesn't automatically indicate a crisis. It often makes sense to ignore, if the trouble is too far in the future to be statistically relevant. The sun will go supernova someday, but, God bless Elon, we don't need to prepare our escape to another solar system today.

Sometimes the indicator is ambiguous. Climate modelers, for example, use similar techniques to stock market analysts, but instead of trying to predict a day or a year ahead, they project out decades or centuries, which stretches their credibility. At the same time, the consistent trends of the past two decades suggest change is afoot. The questions are how big will the change actually be, what types of responses should be mounted, and when?

One way to overcome arguments about poor modeling and political blindness is to explicitly identify which triggers require action and when: *When is the latest and when is the earliest we need to be prepared?*

The politics of leadership typically incentivize us to view the future through the lens of the past. People are rarely rewarded for saying that the next wave could be bigger than the last. Instead, they are forced to walk the plank for interrupting the party. By the time the ship founders they, and their warnings, will have been carefully deleted from history.

This is why it's useful to create a dashboard that tracks the likelihood of threats and opportunities over time so that everyone can watch it to see:

- Which are increasing
- Which are decreasing
- Which triggers might cause things to accelerate, decelerate, or break

This approach takes the politics out of the conversation. It also allows groups to work with the same strategic snapshot of the environment when discussing the priorities that need to be reset.

Build Your Threat and Opportunity Dashboard

When I work with clients to track threats and opportunities, we build out two dashboards, one focused on opportunities and the other on threats (Figure 6.5).

Figure 6.5 **Threat and Opportunity Dashboard**

Radical Change	Undercurrents to Track	Likelihood of Change			
		3 months	6 months	12 months	24 months
Financial					
Operational					
External					
Strategic					
Triggers to Watch					
Trigger 1					
Trigger 2					
Trigger 3					
Trigger 4					

In the left column is a list of FOES (Financial, Operational, External, and Strategic) events that could change your ecosystem. Reviewing the Four FOES from Chapter 1 provides a good initial list (see Figure 1.2). The second column lays out the undercurrent that would drive that change. The 10 undercurrents in Chapter 2 (see Figure 2.3) provide a good start point. The remaining columns are assessments of the impact of those issues over time. At the bottom is a calendar of known potential triggers. Change is often driven by the tempo of events like trade shows, earnings reports, elections, trade negotiations, and major holidays like Christmas and Chinese New Year. Your calendar may tip you to the "when" and the "where" something will happen, even if the "what" can't be known. For instance, it was entirely knowable that countries around the world would start asserting their power the first quarter of 2021—to test the new Biden administration. It was also likely that China would push hard for an EU trade deal in the weeks just before.

Governments and hedge funds have entire buildings full of analysts tracking this sort of thing, and they hire contractors for second opinions. But in most cases, the future of nations isn't at stake. The goal is simply to prevent unforced errors without putting in huge effort. You can gain most of the insights you need from a quick brainstorming session and a spreadsheet. The key is to draw input from people with different points of view who might know more than you do about evolving opportunities, threats, triggers, or techniques to turn them to your advantage.

Peter Drucker was right: what gets measured gets done. This is particularly true in performance-driven organizations, and it's why you should measure both opportunities and threats on an ongoing basis. Beyond just keeping you oriented toward the future, this will help you set priorities. When there's an inferno coming toward you from the other direction, fighting small fires is a waste of time.

Consider Reversibility

Leaders often get caught up in analysis paralysis, forgetting to ask the first and most important question before taking on the responsibility of thinking it through: How reversible is this decision? In his 2016 letter to Amazon's shareholders, Jeff Bezos explained how he prioritizes risks:

> Some decisions are consequential and irreversible or nearly irreversible—one-way doors—and these decisions must be made methodically, carefully, slowly, with great deliberation and consultation. If you walk through and don't like what you see on the other side, you can't get back to where you were before. We can call these Type 1 decisions.
>
> But most decisions aren't like that—they are changeable, reversible—they're two-way doors. If you've made a suboptimal Type 2 decision, you don't have to live with the consequences for that long. You can reopen the door and go back through. Type 2 decisions can and should be made quickly by high judgment individuals or small groups.

The failure at Harland and Wolff was to prioritize Type 2 decisions *(if we don't have a great marketing story for the* Titanic, *we'll have a bad quarter)* over Type 1 decisions *(if the* Titanic *fills up with water and sinks on its maiden voyage, people will die and it will be our fault)*.

So the first step in prioritizing risk is to figure out what decisions you can walk back and which ones you can't. Vespucci designed the legs of his voyages so that they were Type 2 decisions, which let him proceed relatively quickly down the coast of South America. Most of Pixar's decisions when making the first *Toy Story* were explicitly designed to be walked back. This is one of the best uses of the Tree of Possibility. It can show you where to unbundle your threats and your opportunities so that you have more Type 2 decisions and fewer Type 1 decisions.

For decisions that can't be walked back, the main task is to understand what kind of consequences you can accept, independent of uncertainty, and insure against the rest.

Decide What Actions to Take

There are four approaches that you can take to shift the impact of uncertainties (Figure 6.6).

Figure 6.6 **Action Tracks**

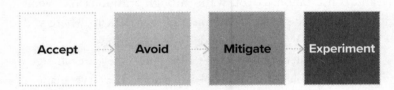

Different personality types tend toward different approaches. One way to minimize bias is to (yet again) create a dashboard, and consciously list out how you'll approach the problem, putting a disproportionate focus on the options that go against your instincts.

Avoid or Accept

There are threats and opportunities we can handle, and there are ones that we can't. While the threats we need to avoid are obvious and frequently cause gnashing of teeth, the opportunities we should avoid are less so.

Let me share an example from my advisory work. I was helping a service company grow. We were generating $2 million of services when we were approached with a $16 million opportunity. After thinking about it, we turned it down.

Why? Because even if we succeeded in putting in place the capabilities we needed, there wasn't a continuous stream of jobs of the same scale that would pay for the added infrastructure, recruiting, and training.

Mitigate or Experiment

Sometimes you can have your cake and eat it, too, through mitigation. Mitigation simply means applying tools you already know to minimize the downside of a decision. Or in some cases, maximize the upside. In the past three chapters, you've learned techniques to position yourself for a better future. We've discussed how to nudge systems by decreasing latency and air gapping, and how to improve your timing, sequencing, and hedging. All of these are ultimately tools for managing uncertainty.

This kind of thinking has practical implications. Here are more examples from my consulting practice:

- A client wanted us to create a user experience that collected a range of customer data, including fingerprints, photographs, and personal information. While the client's goals were benign, the potential PR optics were explosive. We air gapped the threat by being clear with the client about the issue and the processes we would use to mitigate it (we stored the data securely on an air gapped network and deleted it as quickly as possible), and addressed any potential liability in our contract. The result was that we won a major project without taking on the downside risk.

- An IT company I work with uses memory chips, the cost of which fluctuates widely. When the costs are low, its product is profitable. When they're high, it could kill the company. To mitigate the threat, the company pays a third party to buy components when their prices are low and hold them until it needs them. This VEGAS approach is good for everybody: the client knows what it will pay for chips and can lock in profitable margins, while the third party collects reliable fees from a thousand customers like my client.

All of the processes, techniques, and approaches I've described in this chapter can help you identify and prioritize the changes you need to make to deconstruct them into small, executable nudges. Breaking the issue into digestible bits will maximize your potential for success while minimizing your chances of failure. While these approaches may be new to you, they aren't new to the world. They are used by successful leaders and organizations every day.

When you can't change the process, or if changing it won't fix your problem, you can often innovate your way out of the box. That is the topic of the next chapter.

SUMMARY

Bend the Future to Your Benefit

1. **Identify the changes you need to manage.**
   - Consider the order in which you need to manage new threats and opportunities, instead of the order in which they will occur.
   - Identify the triggers that would cause change to sneak up on you.
   - Assess how probability will evolve over time, your potential responses, and when you should act to constrain it.
   - Build a dashboard of opportunities and threats. Put them on a timeline and track them.

2. **Assess your options.**
   - Identify where you can make tweaks to the system and the changes you could observe.
   - Place your opportunities and threats into tracks.
   - Prioritize where you will accept, avoid, mitigate, and experiment.

3. **Shift the odds in your favor.**
   - Identify the combination of nudges and impact amplifiers that will change the system.
   - Decide how you will time, sequence, and hedge your responses.

Today's To-Dos for Tomorrow

- **Plan from the future back.** Teach your team to think through project risks, working back from after project completion, identifying triggers that would cause failure, and then making process tweaks to shift probability in your favor.

- **Do threat and opportunity assessments on a regular cadence.** Assign a sponsor to conduct systematic threat and opportunity assessments, and develop management strategies around them. Take care to do this at a level and frequency that's appropriate for your organization.

- **Support active opportunity and threat management.** Create a defined budget to actively shift the probability of success and adjust project plans to support that work.

- **Talk to low-level managers.** Find out whether they are getting the context they need to assess threats and opportunities and what they would require to feel more comfortable responding proactively and discussing ambiguous concerns with senior leaders.

7

E: Experiment

Build a portfolio of experiments that maximize the benefits of success and minimize the impact of failure.

n Sausalito, the town where I live on the San Francisco Bay, I often walk past a building with a rusty sign out front that reads "Bay Model." For years, I wondered what on earth it referred to. The San Francisco Bay, presumably, but how in the world can you model a body of water? Then one day during my lunch break, I finally walked in, and what I saw blew my mind.

It was a 128,000-square-foot hydraulic model of the entire San Francisco Bay Area. It was built by the Army Corps of Engineers in the 1950s to understand how water flows in and out of the Bay and the Sacramento–San Joaquin River Delta (Figure 7.1). It isn't just a visual representation; the model actually moves water back and forth between simulated land masses, sloshing it through scaled-down shipping channels, rivers, creeks, inlets, and the canals in the delta. The tides and flows move around the major wharfs, piers, slips, dikes, bridges, and breakwaters that interrupt its flow. The model includes every significant node and link in the entire system of the largest estuary on the West Coast of North America.[1]

Figure 7.1 **The Bay Model**

Credit: Cary Bass-Deschenes[2]

Having a visible model of a system this complex does more than enable engineers to account for change. It allows people who might not know the details of the system to understand how it works and identify the right combination of low, medium, and high impact interventions to achieve their goals.

What I, like most techies, hadn't understood about the San Francisco Bay area is that it's much more than Silicon Valley. It's a financial center, a regional shipping and shipbuilding hub, and an agricultural powerhouse. California's Central Valley produces 25 percent of America's food and consumes about half of the state's water. The rivers that supply it are of life-sustaining importance. As the region's underground aquifers get pumped out, parts of the valley floor have dropped as much as 28 feet. Farmers are becoming increasingly dependent on the delta's water, which would otherwise drain into the ocean through the San Francisco Bay.[3] The collision of urban and rural has created political and economic tensions since California became a state. City-dwellers have complained about the traffic since the 1940s; country folk have complained about water rights since long before that.

Back in the 1950s, John Reber had a grandiose idea to kill two birds (traffic and flood control) with millions of stones. He wanted to fill in the bay with a 36-lane superhighway, transforming it into two freshwater lakes (Figure 7.2).[4] Reber's proposal was taken seriously—perhaps because the Dutch were in the process of doing something just as audacious at the time, the Zuiderzee and Delta Works, which effectively dammed the Rhine delta from the sea. The project protected 700 kilometers of the Netherlands' coastline from flooding.

Figure 7.2 **Proposed Development of the San Francisco Bay**

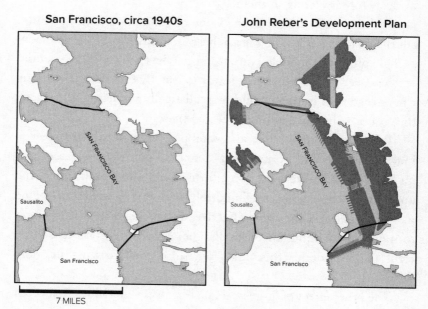

Credit: Cary Bass-Deschenes, https://creativecommons.org/licenses/by-sa/2.0/

Reber got the country's leading civil engineer to design and draft his scheme, and the region's leading newspaper to promote it. San Francisco's city supervisor called it "destiny." Reber even convinced

Congress to spring for the Bay Model, at a cost of about $25 million in today's dollars, which he hoped would silence naysayers.

In fact, it had the opposite effect. The Army Corps of Engineers called the plan "infeasible by any frame of reference" in its official report. The model illuminated second- and third-order effects that were simply too large to ignore, such as flooding, shipping disruptions, and water pollution.

Some big ideas work, but this one didn't—at least, not in the way Reber intended. The Bay Model was used for a half-century to test projects out: everything from dredging ship channels to digging irrigation canals. It paid for itself many times over and benefited the whole region—planners were suddenly able to simulate big public works before investing in them.

We've already looked at the value of simulation and modeling, but there's a deeper lesson to learn here. The Bay Model didn't model a single project; it modeled hundreds, maybe thousands of potential projects over the 50-plus years it was in use. By providing a sandbox where costs and impacts could be realistically predicted, it reduced the cost of failure of any project tested there.

Its enormous size and all-encompassing nature also allowed multiple projects to be modeled at once. Planners could see how multiple canal and reclamation efforts would affect each other. The unexpected consequences of multiple events is a recurring theme in this book, and the most effective way of dealing with them is to model them simultaneously. Parallel experimentation is a powerful tool for doing this, and something we'll discuss in more detail.

The other effect of large-scale platforms for modeling that often goes unappreciated is how it encourages experimentation. Coming up with ideas for things to try out is easy, but feeling justified in pursuing them is much harder. Most humans are naturally risk-averse. But when failure is cheap, you tend to try a lot of things out. And when you try a lot of things, some of them eventually succeed.

MORE INNOVATION DOESN'T ALWAYS MAKE YOU MORE PROFITABLE

When it's impractical to avoid, accept, or mitigate risk, you need to innovate your way around it. This means taking on tasks that increase, test, or integrate knowledge into better processes. These tasks are experiments.

Long-term performance is highly correlated with increased experimentation, according to a recent cross-sectoral study of R&D investment at 103 firms over 23 years.[5] In particular, the study found positive correlations between R&D and:

- The standard deviation of future earnings
- Subsequent operating performance
- Profitability
- Stock value
- Revenue growth

Perhaps the most important finding is that R&D investments had twice the impact on market capitalization as similar investments in tangible assets.

As Jeff Bezos puts it, "If you double the number of experiments you do per year, you're going to double your inventiveness." The obvious conclusion is to increase your R&D budget, right?

Unfortunately, there are plenty of other studies that show more tenuous links between R&D budgets and growth. Between 2014 and 2018, for example, the Chinese electronics giant Huawei averaged more than a 10 percent return on its R&D each year, while its rival Xiaomi only got around half that (Figure 7.3).

Why the big difference?

It helps to think of experiments as investments. Some succeed, some fail, and different groups have different strategies for choosing where to invest. The foolish investor picks just a few bets, often for

Figure 7.3 **Return on Research Capital**

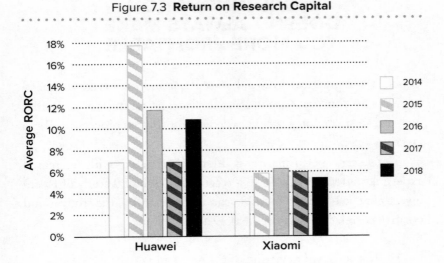

Source: Diego Santizo, "The Other War Between the US and China: Investment in Research and Development," UFM Market Trends, February 12, 2019, https://trends.ufm.edu/en/article/other-war-us-between-china/.

emotional reasons, instead of as part of a strategic response to the Four FOES of Growth.

In the case of Huawei, it is attempting to control the global 5G wireless ecosystem, from chipsets to operating systems to handsets to cell towers. If it win, it'll win the whole pot. Xiaomi, on the other hand, is focused on building consumer loyalty and a consistent brand experience. It works with a broad range of third-party innovators to customize preexisting technologies and continuously launch new products in response to rapidly changing consumer demand.

Huawei makes big bets because the potential revenue is long term and deep. Xiaomi avoids the risk of R&D because consumers are fickle and the technology churn is fast. Both portfolio approaches are valid; what matters is that they are strategic.

A portfolio approach means more than just investing in many different things. The portfolio must be well-designed. One big bet is a bad idea, but a thousand small bets that aren't coordinated or well-distributed can be even worse.

You can see this play out in the stock market. My father invested in a dozen equities that he believed in. They were diversified across industries, but all of them were high-risk stocks that would fall in the event of a financial crash. In 2008, their value dropped 70 percent. While he thought he had a diversified investment strategy, he hadn't considered systemic risks.

A good portfolio considers timing so that the upside and downside of investments are asynchronous and have limiters. This way, it's not possible for everything to go wrong at the same time. Investors often use what they call a "barbell" strategy, like Nassim Nicholas Taleb's, to decrease the risk of high-growth investments:

- They put most of their money into reliable investment instruments, like bonds.
- They put a small percentage in risky bets with the potential to put a ding in the universe.
- And then they hedge or insure against any unforecast downside of those bets.

The same challenges apply to a portfolio of innovation. In any case where there are many unknowns and high volatility, you can count on something going wrong. The field of innovation is defined by the potential for failure. You can prevent a program from failing, though, by sequencing and hedging to make sure things don't go wrong all at once, and that you have the time and resources to recover if they do.

CHOOSING THE RIGHT EXPERIMENTS

Experiment portfolios often fail because they're poorly balanced. This lack of balance usually comes from a desire to reward success. Imagine a junior manager who comes to you with an idea for a new initiative. It's got a 20 percent chance of success but promises to teach the team a huge amount about a rapidly growing new category, even if it fails. Do you say yes?

The smart manager gives her the go-ahead, congratulates her in front of her peers for her boldness, and then doubles down on praise and protects her if it fails. The initiative is an experiment: yes, it'd be nice if it proves your hunch, but getting the most insight out of the process matters more. This kind of approach sounds counterintuitive on the surface, and if all the experiments you do are like this one, that's a problem. But if you look at your experiments as a portfolio, this kind of high-risk investment can make a lot of sense. Leaders need to reward well-designed experiments and well-designed portfolios, instead of their outcomes. Otherwise, you get "science fair" experiments whose outcomes are predestined and staff who avoid risk instead of manage it. You get hard problems that go unfaced. Most importantly, you expend effort on experiments that don't pay off.

When my team audits experiment portfolios, we inevitably discover that, on the whole, they tend to:

- Line up with the organization's cultural beliefs around risk management
- Be out of line with its larger strategy for risk-taking

You can avoid this is by looking at experiments as a group and asking the following questions:

- Are your efforts focused on the threats and opportunities you have identified? (You can assess this using the Threat and Opportunity Dashboard in the previous chapter.)
- Are the experiments in line with the avoidance, mitigation, and innovation strategy you have laid out in response?

Ideally, you can work with your team to ask if the experiments are weighted appropriately to achieve a desired organizational outcome.

Types of Experiments

The first step is sorting your portfolio into categories (Figure 7.4). Broadly speaking, there are three, which I'll illustrate with different aspects of the Spanish–Portuguese competition for Asia in the late 1400s. Their Royal courts were some of the largest, most aggressive venture capital investors of the day.

Growth experiments are the ones that move you to the good scenario by enabling a 100x outcome. This is what the Spanish monarchs did when they decided to fund Columbus's westward voyages in the face of Portuguese dominance in Africa and Asia. It was highly unlikely to succeed, but still worth the gamble.

Sustaining experiments decrease the chances of an ugly outcome by protecting existing interests. This is what the Portuguese did when they employed Columbus and his brother for years. The court impeded Cristobal's ability to find another investor, while funding in its own exploration of Africa.

Insurance experiments are the ones that increase your resilience if bad or ugly futures occur. When Columbus announced his discovery of the Americas, the Portuguese met with Spanish diplomats to clarify their property rights in the New World and the Atlantic. The result was the Treaty of Tordesillas, which moved existing boundary lines nearly 1,000 miles (270 leagues) to the west. Some scholars argue that the Portuguese wanted to protect their ships' ability to navigate the trade winds around Africa, but the king likely already knew of Brazil and wanted to block Spanish access to any Southern passage to Asia.[6]

Once the goals of your experiments are appropriately diversified, you need to ensure that your team is focused on achieving the right objectives. In the Columbus examples above, each investor was pushing to achieve a different type of control:

- The Spanish were attempting to *rewire* the system.

- The Portuguese wanted to slow exploration of an easterly route to Asia, driven by a desire to increase their *leverage*.
- The Portuguese also pursued the Treaty of Tordesillas, an attempt to add variables to the existing system—to create *knobs*, in other words.

Figure 7.4 **How Diversified Is Your Portfolio Around These Criteria?**

	Rewiring	Leverage	Knobs
Growth Experiments			
Security Experiments			
Insurance			

The cost of an experiment and the value of the information it yields aren't necessarily correlated. For example, Queen Isabella's up-front cost of Columbus's initial journey was less than $5 million, adjusted for inflation.[7] That's pennies for a nation state, especially compared to something similarly significant in the modern era (like a trip to the moon).

For organizations today, the tools needed to perform valuable experiments are constantly getting better and cheaper. This suggests that you should prioritize experiments by their potential to advance your goals, not the amount of effort or money they take to complete.

Parallel Versus Serial Experimentation

When we consider running a lot of experiments, we often think in series, running one after another, like Vespucci on the legs of his voyages. But today's world moves a lot faster than the world of 1501, and parallel experimentation is often necessary to deal with it.

The development and distribution of Covid-19 vaccines is a vivid example of parallel experimentation and why its payoff is often worth the greater cost and lower efficiency.

Vaccines typically take a decade or more to develop; before Covid, the speed record went to the mumps vaccine, which took four years. There are good reasons for this slow pace. A vaccine starts with a broad range of candidate compounds. Only a handful make it to market. They're run in stages to weed out less effective candidates, before too much is spent testing them. Much of that time, in fact, isn't spent determining efficacy and safety. It's spent assessing economic viability.

Operation Warp Speed, the US government's public-private effort to accelerate vaccine development, turned this on its head. The government decided to cover the labs' development costs even if the vaccine wasn't successful, while monitoring the process to ensure safety and test for efficacy. It also worked with pharmaceutical companies to start building production lines for several vaccine candidates before they'd completed trials. This way, the winners could hit the ground running. It meant spending billions on infrastructure that may never be used. But given a pandemic that was costing the economy trillions, it was the wisest possible investment.

By shifting incentives, Warp Speed was able to expand the range of approaches by enlisting partners who would normally focus on different issues, such as startups, university labs, and big pharma companies. The result is that the speed of vaccine development dropped from a decade to a year. While this drove the costs up, they were dwarfed by the overall economic benefit.

Elon Musk took a similar portfolio strategy when he founded SpaceX, Tesla, and the solar power company SolarCity, all within a four-year period. Each was set up as an independent company at first so it would be easy to cut losses. But as their markets matured, they began to consolidate. Tesla acquired SolarCity, enabling the development of electrical distribution and transportation infrastructure across the United States, while Tesla's Cybertruck is being produced using technologies originally developed by SpaceX.

I was retained by a Fortune 500 packaged food company that was concerned that the traditional "center of the store" was being hollowed out by changing demographics, as both silver spenders and young parents headed for fresh foods at the store's edge. This trend meant their existing customers were aging out and they weren't being replaced by new ones. They needed to find billions of dollars of new revenue every year to offset the decline.

Companies often look for large, fundamental responses when faced with large, fundamental threats. They want a single big answer that makes all the questions go away. This can mean launching a new brand or acquiring a new company. These are appealing strategies because they feel grand and bold. They let you tell your boss or your shareholders that you're really doing something. But they're also full of uncertainty and the potential for unintended second- and third-order consequences.

So we pursued a portfolio approach instead. We built a team of chefs, food scientists, and market researchers to develop new products across all of the client's brands simultaneously. Over the course of several months, we proposed over a thousand new product concepts, and refined them down to a hundred that we could prototype and test. Ultimately, we launched a range of new products under a variety of brands. This took about a third of the time required to build a new brand from scratch.

Working in parallel like this brought several advantages. It gave us an additional layer of testing: we could compare the performance of different products in the best testing environment of all—the market. It spread out the risk so the overall project could be successful, even if multiple products failed. And it reduced costs by letting us copy and combine concepts from one product and brand to another. It avoided the overhead and marketing costs associated with launching a new brand or acquiring a company.

The end result was a change in the organization's strategic approach to innovation. This positioned them to thrive in the midst of a rapidly consolidating market.

The approach was much like what occurs in radiation therapy. Radiation therapy treats cancer by using a large number of low-intensity energy beams, all aimed from different directions. By overlapping at just the right point, they attack the cancerous region without causing major damage to the surrounding tissue. You've probably heard the term "death by a thousand cuts," but a thousand tiny efforts can combine to solve a problem—in medicine and in business.

DESIGNING PORTFOLIOS

Dozens of low-impact experiments can add up to a high-impact outcome, if the effort is sustained and the probabilities are cumulative. When portfolios don't deliver their expected value, the culprit is usually a failure to consider the type of randomness they are trying to overcome.

The success of an experiment portfolio depends on how well the organization delivers and exploits its results. In many cases, this requires a combination of timing, sequencing, and hedging (Figure 7.5).

Figure 7.5 **Impact Amplifiers**

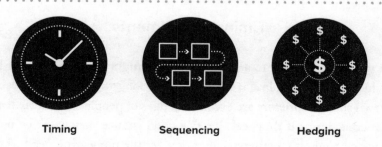

Timing   Sequencing   Hedging

Timing: Mendel's breakthrough work on plant genetics was nearly forgotten because it was ahead of its time. When he started his experiments, Darwin hadn't yet presented his theory of natural selection, and the mathematical and chemical methods that would transform biology weren't available yet. In the first 35 years after it was published, it was only cited by three people.[8]

Something similar can happen in business. In the 1990s, Iridium, a Motorola-backed communications company, spent $5 billion to launch 66 satellites into space. The technology was janky, the service was expensive, and the market wasn't ready to adopt it.[9] In 2021, the world's tech billionaires are in a scramble to build their own private satellite communication networks.

Sequencing: It appears that the technology to make inexpensive satellites, launch them into space, and build reasonably priced terrestrial transmitters is now available. Elon Musk's SpaceX took a different approach from Iridium. They built a launch capability that dropped the cost of rockets and waited for the cost of satellites to drop. We'll see what the future holds, but SpaceX believes that its StarLink Satellite communications business could generate six times as much revenue as its rocket business by 2025.[10]

Hedging: SpaceX went a step further, hedging their bets by allowing StarLink's competitors, including Iridium's NEXT satellites, to launch on Space X's rockets.[11]

Timing Experiments

If you bring a watch to a pawn shop, you might get 65 percent of its value as a loan and lose it if you take too long to pay back the debt. Pawn shop proprietors are excellent judges of people and may extend generous terms if they feel there's a good chance they won't be paid back on time. It's a fair exchange: you get the money you need when you need it, and the pawn shop's proprietor makes his profit—either from the markup on your loan when it's paid back or when he sells your goods for their full value.

Even a high certainty, high impact experiment is foolish if it can't deliver value on a short enough timeline. Companies frequently make the mistake of investing in projects that could pay off big but have no chance of paying off in time. They pawn their future on a knowable failure.

Edwin Land is primarily known as the father of the instant camera, which became ubiquitous in the 1960s and 1970s. What's less known is that his company, Polaroid, also made a disastrous attempt to enter the 8mm movie film market. Safi Bahcall writes eloquently about it in his book *Loonshots*, and I remember it well because many of my friends' parents worked at Polaroid.

It wasn't that Polaroid lacked the ability to make good film. It was that it got the timing incredibly wrong. Handheld movie cameras were all the rage in the 1970s, but by the time Polavision 8mm film came out in 1977, the world was already shifting to magnetic tape. First reel-to-reel, then the audiocassette, and then VHS and Betamax. Land knew this better than anyone, but a combination of hubris and sunk costs drove him to launch the film anyway. The result was the beginning of the end for Polaroid, with losses that moved it from leading player to near bankruptcy—when they should have been focused on the early camcorder market.

Doing Experiments in the Right Sequence

The order in which you do experiments should be based on the type of randomness you're dealing with. As I said in the Introduction, your poker face won't work at the roulette wheel.

A brilliant example of sequencing comes from the breaking of the Enigma code in World War II. The Germans had a seemingly impenetrable cryptographic system that translated messages into any of 15,354,393,600 possible codes. It was so good that, if you wrote a word like *wetterbericht* (German for "weather report"), it would look like gibberish. Not even the two Ts would be duplicated; they could be a Q and a B. There was no way to look at the code and use brute force parallel experimentation to break it.

But English and Polish cryptographers were able to decrypt communiques every morning because the Germans, being German, felt they needed to send out a daily *wetterbericht*. And, being German, they needed to have it in a consistent format. So while the code itself was seemingly random, the coded message was suddenly breakable because two rules restricted randomness elsewhere in the system:

- Some words were frequently used in a typical order.
- Certain letter combinations, like TT, could not occur in certain parts of the message.

The result was that a seemingly impenetrable, constantly changing code could be broken. How did they do it?

Their first step was to run an experiment in sequence. Given the knowledge that a couple of words like w*etterbericht* had to exist in a certain section of the message, code breakers identified the places where encoded patterns, like double Ts, must exist, given the rules of the system.

With this knowledge, a machine called The Bombe performed a parallel search for all of the possible combinations that could match the rest of the coded gobbledygook, given the known words. Once one bit of code was confirmed—the first T really was a Q and the second T a B—the system would shrink its search area (discussed in Chapter 3), removing the options that were no longer possible. Suddenly, contrary to its name, Enigma was an easily solvable mystery.

The most consistently useful approach to spotting patterns is to thoughtfully combine sequencing and parallel analysis. If you're attempting to understand the type of system you're looking at, start by trying as many sequences as possible. See if patterns start to appear. Does TT never end up as QQ? If you know that, you can shrink the search area to gain an advantage.[12] Are there additional opportunities to restrict the randomness elsewhere in the system? If, as with Enigma, things that are consistent at one level restrict randomness at another, you can solve the problem more effectively by choosing where to operate in parallel and where to operate in sequence. Does one thing being true, like the need to transmit *wetterbericht*, make something else possible?

When to Hedge with an Experiment

Steve Jobs famously said that Apple doesn't do market research, and thousands of CEOs took note. It's a seductive statement because experimentation is expensive and time consuming, often comes with corporate political baggage, and most of us would rather not deal with it. But while Apple didn't do market research in the traditional sense, it did plenty of experimentation and testing of a different sort. In 2000, a year before the first Apple Store opened in Tyson's Corner, Virginia,[13] I was developing a retail concept for another electronics company with Pompei A.D., a boutique retail designer in New York.

We were based in Manhattan's SoHo neighborhood, the trend-making capital of the Western world in those days. I'd meander down its cobblestoned streets at lunchtime, popping into empty art galleries and specialty stores in search of ideas. For several days I walked past a tiny mom-and-pop electronics store with a gorgeous window display. It stood out, not just because it looked out of place but because in 2000, in the shadow of the dot-com crash, the timing was all wrong.

By the end of the week, the window display and the incongruity had reeled me in. The store (which didn't have a sign in front) was a dream. Boxes of Macromedia Flash software and cool peripherals were in the center of the store, each lit like a sculpture in a museum. Sexy computers, including the most lusted-after tech product of the time—the Mac Cube—just begged to be touched. It was a sharp contrast to Circuit City and other electronics stores, with their dented linoleum floors, drab metal shelving, and prison-inspired fluorescent lighting.

When I walked in, I was greeted by a polished man with silver-flecked executive hair, wearing expensive titanium glasses and gabardine slacks. He definitely wasn't your typical computer store employee. He welcomed me and asked if I'd like to sit at the bar and enjoy a sandwich or a cup of coffee, and then he sent his bespectacled, turtleneck-wearing colleague to pick those up at the bakery next door. We had a great conversation about technology and how I wanted to purchase it. If I had tried to buy anything, I don't think they would have known what to do—I didn't see a cash register anywhere.

When I returned to the office, I asked my boss if he knew anything about the store, and he clammed up in the way that only Steve Jobs could make people clam up. This was clearly a test of what would become the Apple Store—now the world's most profitable retail chain, per square foot, on earth.[14] As far as I can tell, they were experimenting with new service concepts and figuring out how to categorize products before opening their Virginia venue. They had even tested to see if customers wanted to have food at a Genius Bar. And they had done this for the cost of some shelves and a month-to-month lease on a storefront.

The prototype Apple Store was worth the time and money because it met all of the criteria for a good experiment:

- Goals were clearly defined.
- New knowledge would significantly increase the likelihood of program success, even if the experiment failed.
- Cost and scale of the experiment were proportionate to the value of the gained knowledge.
- Risk of failure was known and acceptable.
- Results could be profitably integrated back into the organization.

BALANCING YOUR PORTFOLIO

Rumor had it that Jobs felt his Apple Store experiment was worthwhile, even though it set back the launch by six months.[15]

When running NeXT, he wanted its factory tours to be memorable, and made the mistake of investing in a splashy museum-quality factory with custom-painted robots and reengineered pick-and-place machines. In his book *Steve Jobs and the NeXT Big Thing*, Randall E. Stross describes it as the "single most expensive, and easily the most unwise, commitment that Jobs made."

With the retail stores, Jobs pushed back against the pawnshop promise of easy terms on a too-short timeline. He made a careful calculation: the SoHo experiment extended his timeline for opening the Virginia store, but it promised a more certain outcome for all the products he would place in it. It's easy to look at an individual experiment and judge it a success or failure. The real issue is whether it's a success or failure in the context of the larger portfolio.

Following are some challenges worth considering when balancing your portfolio (Figure 7.6).

Figure 7.6 **Balancing Your Portfolio**

New Knowledge	VS.	Costs
Likelihood of Success	VS.	Impact
Experimental Risk	VS.	Project Risk

Will It Produce Enough New Knowledge?

It's tempting to pursue experiments just because it's possible to perform them. But experiments aren't an opportunity to show off your capabilities, and they're not a place to indulge personal curiosity. They're a way to gain actionable information. The Portuguese had one of the world's largest fleets in the late fifteenth century, and were sending ships on numerous long journeys, around the Cape of Good Hope and all the way to India. They weren't interested in funding Columbus's journey west because the knowledge he'd discover wasn't as useful to them. If successful, it could cause an ugly future.

The Spanish, on the other hand, had plenty to gain from discovering a new route to Asia. And the cost of sending a fleet to do so was comparatively small, even if the likelihood of failure was high. They also sponsored Magellan, a Portuguese navigator, 25 years later, and used the knowledge his crew brought back to expand their reach into east Asia.

Both kingdoms probably made the right decisions for their circumstances, but leaders often make three miscalculations:

- Avoiding risks that can't be measured when they should invest in learning more about them
- Investing in contradictory knowledge that won't impact decisions
- Investing in knowledge that won't shrink the search area

I recently worked with a company that spent seven years and $17 million exploring the market for a new piece of sports equipment. It rebuilt the development team three times as project leaders peeled off to develop similar startups. When they finally did launch, the market wasn't there. Instead of modeling and researching, they could have performed a fairly straightforward experiment. They already knew how to produce the product; they could have simply thrown up a website and seen if people wanted to buy it.

Does the Risk Match the Reward?

In June 1939, German physicist Siegfried Flügge published the first paper describing how nuclear fission could be used to build an atom bomb.[16] In August, Albert Einstein warned President Roosevelt that this was a real possibility.[17] By October, the US government was funding the research that grew into the Manhattan Project.[18] By the time the first bomb was tested, the initiative involved over 130,000 people and had cost more than $2 billion (the equivalent of $23 billion today).[19]

Knowing how to make a nuclear bomb was considered so important that the cost of new knowledge was irrelevant. At one point, the copper needed to build industrial magnets proved scarce because it was being used in shell casings. So the team requisitioned 28 million pounds of silver from the United States Treasury and used it as a substitute. It's easy to ignore pie-in-the-sky ideas, but the cost of failing to pursue this one would have been incalculable if a parallel German effort had succeeded.

The same kinds of land grabs occur in business, but often without understanding the cost. YP, the company that makes the Yellow Pages telephone book in the United States, saw that online advertising products like Google AdWords were shrinking its business and decided it needed to make a big bet: it would create a competitor to Google Search that focused on local searches where its existing salesforce could drive advertising. The company clearly needed to bet the farm to survive, but the probability of beating Google and local advertising competitors like Yelp was clearly an uphill battle. Not long after, YP's parent company was purchased for $1.5 billion by Cerberus Capital. Today, its remnants have been repackaged into an incomprehensible business called Thryv.

The moral of the story: the effort of innovation is only worth it if you survive long enough to collect the reward.

What Is the Risk to the Project if the Experiment Fails?

The United States Centers for Disease Control has a long history of producing its own tests for citizens instead of relying on off-the-shelf or foreign solutions. When Covid-19 came along, the test it produced failed, leaving the American medical establishment in the dark about Covid's spread in the US population for months. While the CDC was following long-established procedures, its leaders hadn't taken the risks of their approach into full account.[20]

This happens in business all the time. Sometimes managers try to protect their divisions, even when it decreases the larger group's ability to compete. Other times inventors triple down on experiments that have no chance of paying off in the given time frame.

It's always a better option to give up a chance at winning if the pursuit is more likely to bankrupt you first. This is where leaders have to make hard choices. When do you avoid throwing out the baby with the bathwater, and when do you need to throw out the baby?

Making ethically challenging decisions is probably the hardest part of being an executive. In terms of creating an experiment portfolio, it requires asking some difficult questions. Most fundamentally: does this experiment improve the standing of the larger portfolio?

DESIGN YOUR PORTFOLIO FOR RESILIENCE AS WELL AS PERFORMANCE

Terry Gilliam is one of the most critically acclaimed cinematic directors in the world. His wildly inventive films include *Time Bandits*, *Brazil*, and *12 Monkeys*. In 1999, Gilliam started production on a film adaptation of the classic Spanish novel *Don Quixote*. The $32-million project encountered disaster after disaster, from the injury of its leading man, Jean Rochefort, to an actual avalanche. Production was canceled in 2000, costing $15 million in insurance claims. Several attempts to revive the production also met with failure over the next 16 years. Eventually, the entire film was reshot and released in 2018 as *The Man Who Killed Don Quixote*. It was a critical and box office disappointment.[21]

Film is an art form, of course, so it's understandable that a director like Gilliam would want complete control over the process. He approaches films as a kind of quest to realize his unique vision. It's an approach that's worked on many other movies. But film is also a high-stakes business. *Don Quixote* was entirely dependent on one person, which gave it tremendous artistic focus but made it fragile. When things went wrong, there wasn't much to do but start over.

As recounted earlier, *Toy Story* was also hit by a series of rogue waves and survived them because it built so many redundancies into its pipeline. The contrast plays out daily in innovation processes across industries. If you break them down, they suggest a few key ways of designing for resilience:

- **Time your experiments so that the upside and downside are asynchronous and have limiters.** A number of years ago, I worked with a high-end retailer who was excited about a new concept and wanted to launch it in a store in Times Square. We recommended trying the experience as a pop-up first, and then building a store in a smaller city before making a much larger, hard-to-undo investment. As with Apple's low-cost SoHo experiment, the result was improved sales and greater customer retention when the concept was fully launched.

- **Have clear metrics for when to initiate experiments and when to stop them.** *Toy Story* halted production when its producers soured on its script. In many ways, the production was lucky. In business, "zombie" projects often continue while good ones get cut because the highest-paid person's opinion is valued more than the objective reality.

  I was once tasked to improve a product for a Fortune 500 software company that was looking to get into hardware. The program had been lumbering along with the support of its founder for a number of years, with no checks to assess whether it was achieving its goals. It didn't take us long to realize that the product didn't have a market. While we were able to develop a strategy for its second generation, we insisted that better governance be put in place to keep the program on the rails.

- **Design a modular pipeline so that you can retool your portfolio as you learn more.** Pixar's modular approach to production made it possible to retool the film without having to rebuild it from the ground up.

The Fortune 500 packaged food company discussed earlier used the same strategy, developing a massive volume of projects that could be swapped in to fill out its product portfolio. I call this the Taco Bell theory of product development: You can create a seemingly endless number of dishes with beans, cheese, tortillas, tomatoes, and ground beef.

MAINTAINING YOUR BACKLOG

When it was still open, I liked to bring clients over to the Hidden City Café in Point Richmond for innovation sessions. Beyond providing a comfortable setting and a great cup of coffee, Hidden City had a great story. Four of Pixar's most successful films—*A Bug's Life*, *Finding Nemo*, *Monsters, Inc.*, and *Wall-E*—were sketched out during a single meeting in the café, literally on the backs of napkins.[22] (In one scene in *Monsters, Inc.*, there's a car with a California license plate that says "HIDNCTY"; in another, the café itself can be seen in the background.)

That meeting was held specifically to create a backlog of projects, and it succeeded. This was no fluke. It was the outcome of a principle that has guided Pixar since its early days. Animated filmmaking is different from live action because you can depict literally anything. This is great for imagination and artistic freedom, but it also puts a lot of pressure on the ideas that drive the films—they have to be strong so you don't end up with an unfocused mess. Having plenty of solid ideas to try out, refine, and develop is crucial, even if it means bringing in outside help like the Hollywood supertalents Joss Whedon and Joel Cohen, who were hired to script-doctor *Toy Story* three-quarters of the way into production.[23]

It might be the director's vision and taste that count, but it's math that puts the images on the screen. Each pixel is a calculation, and the layers upon layers of technology required to create them are more than any one person can track, so Pixar invests in experimentation at every level. A colleague of mine spent over a year directing a single shot in the movie *Cars*, changing it as the rest of the script evolved. But at the same time, he was tasked with creating experimental animations, some assigned by director John Lasseter and others that he conceived himself.

These experiments are another example of the backlog principle. Everyone at Pixar is creative in some way, and they are expected to apply their creativity to future projects as well as current ones. It might be an idea for a character, a new lighting technique, a way of animating a particular animal or vehicle, or a concept for a short film. Develop enough of these assets and when it's time to start developing the next film, you have plenty to react to and put to use.

INNOVATE AT THE RIGHT LEVEL

In the early 1990s there was a company called General Magic whose goal was to invent the smartphone. It was staffed by people who went on to change the world: Andy Rubin, who later invented Android; Tony Fadell, the man behind the iPhone and iPod; Kevin Lynch, who became the head of technology at Apple; John Giannandrea, who became head of search and AI at Google.

It was perhaps the most inventive startup team ever assembled. They raised $90 million in an IPO based on their vision and got industry powerhouses like Apple, AT&T, and Sony behind them. The first device based on their technology, the Sony Magic Link, launched to great fanfare—but only sold about 3,000 units.[24]

Why did the Magic Link fail so spectacularly? It wasn't the talent, the vision, or the funding. General Magic had plenty of all three. But these were the outer layers of the "risk onion." If they'd sliced it instead of peeling it, they'd have realized that the timing of the project contained a fatal flaw. It was 1994, and most people still hadn't even heard of the internet or used email. The product General Magic shipped was absolutely earthshaking, but the market wasn't ready for it.

More fundamentally, General Magic was innovating at the wrong level. It had created a wide range of innovative features, an innovative product, and an innovative process for developing it, but what it really needed was to innovate at the ecosystem and regulatory levels (Figure 7.7).

The team at General Magic thought *they were* the rogue wave. What they actually needed to do was ride one. As a result, they hadn't innovated around the real threats facing their business:

- **Financial:** They didn't have a plan to maintain liquidity and goodwill if their product failed.
- **Operational:** The organization's R&D budget was out of line with its ability to recoup it.
- **External:** They hadn't considered that being so far ahead of their industry and standards would make them irrelevant.
- **Strategic:** Their demand forecasts weren't based on a customer use case.

The lesson here is to make sure that the necessary portfolio of experiments occurs at the right time and in the right order to shift the probability of success. No amount of technological wizardry could have saved General Magic.

I often see similar things when I walk through research labs. Brilliant scientists and engineers have spectacular demos that require nonexistent ecosystems to thrive. That said, it might be worth talking through that ecosystem's requirements with your experts because they might be onto something. You hired them because they are smarter than you, after all.

Figure 7.7 **Levels of Innovation**

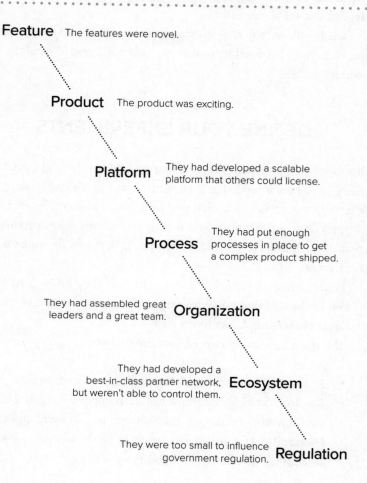

Feature   The features were novel.

Product   The product was exciting.

Platform   They had developed a scalable platform that others could license.

Process   They had put enough processes in place to get a complex product shipped.

They had assembled great leaders and a great team.   **Organization**

They had developed a best-in-class partner network, but weren't able to control them.   **Ecosystem**

They were too small to influence government regulation.   **Regulation**

General Magic's saving grace was sitting in the basement, and they never put it to use. In the wake of the Magic Link disaster, the customer support guy pitched pivoting from making PDAs to becoming an internet flea market called AuctionWeb. Michael Stern, the company's chief counsel said, "That's the dumbest idea I've ever heard. We're not interested. Have fun." The smart business-folk missed the boat, but Pierre Omidyar didn't. He left General

Magic and founded eBay, where you can now buy a mint condition Magic Link for about $130.

The lesson here is that it's important to focus on the bigger picture. But you also need to remember that someone else might have a better picture.

DEFINE YOUR EXPERIMENTS

Choose the right type of experiment to achieve the right goal. The objective of new knowledge is either to improve an impact amplifier or to create a nudge that changes your performance (faster, better, cheaper). If you don't understand how you want your experiment to impact the system, it's unlikely that you'll perform the right sort of experiment.

People often choose the experiment that they know how to do, instead of the one that will achieve their objective. When you have a hammer, everything looks like a nail.

The most common goals of experiments are:

- **Scanning:** Identifying changes to the environment
- **Control:** Testing the impact of an independent variable
- **Verification:** Trialing a new solution in a known application
- **Flexibility:** Testing an existing solution in a new application
- **Durability:** Measuring reliability over time

Columbus and Vespucci both sailed to the New World, but they were running different experiments. Columbus was verifying a calculation of the circumference of the world. Vespucci was scanning to see if there was a break in South America which would allow navigation to Asia.

In complex systems, like the ones you encounter in life sciences and economics, one of the major issues is simplifying the problem enough to isolate causes and effects. For example, in food product development, one of the major issues is durability. How long is the shelf life of a good? In climate engineering, one of the major issues is flexibility. Can a known technology, like plant hybridization, be leveraged to the task of increasing a plant's capacities to suck carbon dioxide out of the atmosphere?

The methods to address these issues fall broadly into four categories:

- **Systematic observation:** Examining quantifiable behavior
- **Modeling:** Representing a phenomenon in a way that captures its causal and corollary relationships
- **Simulation:** Reproductions of events and processes under test conditions
- **Field study:** Collection of raw data outside a laboratory

It's important to match the method to the right goal (see Figure 7.8, next page).

Often, companies get obsessed with the hammers they already have. Finance organizations like modeling and simulation. Engineering organizations demand perfectly controlled experiments. Marketing teams need field research. But as Feynman showed NASA, sometimes a glass of ice water, a clamp, and a 10-cent O-ring are more than enough.

An alcoholic beverage producer once asked me to do a national study of how their brand was perceived by 21-to-25-year-old women. Instead of flying around to carry out the requested million-dollar ethnography, we went online, looked at social media around the world, and then reached out to consumers on Facebook. It was cheaper and faster, but even more importantly, it allowed us to home in on the right questions and on the precise demographic we needed to answer them.

You don't always need more data or better data—what you need is useful data. Choose the experiment that best helps you improve your system on the time frame that you need.

Figure 7.8 **Experimental Goals and Methods**

	Systematic Observation	Modeling	Simulation	Field Study
Scanning				
Control				
Verification				
Flexibility				
Durability				

EVALUATE YOUR RESULTS EFFECTIVELY

It is easy to inadvertently optimize for the calculable rather than the important.

—DANIEL DAVIS

Perhaps the most important thing to remember when experimenting is that failure can teach you as much as success. Prototyping a new process can yield a sea change if successful, but if it fails it could yield even more: an understanding of why something doesn't work, and possibly a new insight that can inform the next prototype.

If you conduct an experiment that succeeds, don't assume it happened because you're smart. Conversely, don't assume that a failed experiment indicates someone is dumb. It's often the case that an untried idea has no way of succeeding—but you'll never know that for sure until you try it out.

A failed experiment doesn't automatically mean a failed idea, and distinguishing between them is a crucial skill for building an effective experiment portfolio. It may be that the idea was sound, but the way of testing it was flawed.

We're all primed to make mistakes. If you want to push back against that tendency, you need to understand the nature of those mistakes and the reasons behind them.

The Dirty Dozen Test

Here are a dozen rules of thumb that will radically decrease your chances of misunderstanding the meaning of data. I keep a copy of this list by my desk.

1. **Probable doesn't mean inevitable.** Just because something is improbable doesn't mean it can't happen. This is called the "Coin Flip Problem" because if you flip a coin 1,000 times, you don't get 500 heads and 500 tails. If you do, it's almost certainly *not* random. So be wary of data that fits too closely with an expected probability.

2. **What's true of the group may not be true of the subgroup.** This might seem like an obvious statement, but it frequently trips people up because we're taught that larger sample sizes are always more reliable. Remember that aggregate results are the average of many individual results, and that variation within the group may not be random.

It's always worth doing a gut check when looking at the numbers: Is it possible you'd see something different if you looked at a different slice of the sample?

3. **You can't make inferences about a group until you understand the group.** If a retailer based in New York City purchases a chain of stores in the Midwest, team members might be tempted to apply existing store designs to the new locations. But what works in Manhattan might not work in Minnesota. Instead of rubber-stamping an existing solution, spend time with your customers to determine what can be readily adapted and what needs to be modified.

4. **Experts aren't fortune-tellers.** Experts are excellent at explaining what has happened in the past, but they're rarely better than the rest of us at predicting the future, especially in areas outside their expertise. The halo created by their superior knowledge in one area can often blind us to this fact. When dealing with their field of expertise, it's often helpful to run information past them that you consider surprising and ask if it matches up with their experience. If it doesn't align, ask what would have to happen to change their minds.

5. **Variation usually has a cause.** Organizing data into groups can yield important insights. But if you don't understand what causes the groups to be different, it's easy to solve for symptoms and not causes. For example, if customers who are in a loyalty program spend more, is it because of the loyalty program or because they were better customers to begin with? Finding the real cause of a variation often requires breaking it down further to see where the difference is actually occurring.

6. **Data can't replace logic.** Data can illuminate the truth, but it's also effective at amplifying lies. Every time you review data, there are two important questions you should ask:

    a. Why is this specific variable a good predictor?
    b. Is the relationship reliable enough to be useful?

I once worked with an IT services company that was extremely data-driven; its leaders wouldn't do business with any customer that didn't fit specific criteria. But after performing field reconnaissance and extensive interviews, we found that a lot of the "unacceptable" customers were potentially profitable. The issue wasn't that the company screened its customers, but that leaders hadn't taken commonsense measures to ensure they were using the right criteria to do so.

7. **A data point is not a data set.** A picture is worth a thousand words; it can also convey a thousand numbers. Charts, animations, and interactive media can help us make sense of anomalies that get lost when an argument focuses on an individual point. Noting that promotions increase sales is one thing, but plotting the relationship between spending and sales on a curve can show you how much you need to spend on promotions to get an optimal return on your investment.

8. **Correlation often looks like causation.** Correlation (on its own) is not causation, as any introductory statistics class teaches on day one. For instance, in 2008, there was an almost perfect correlation between people who worked themselves to death in the United States and billions of dollars in sales of General Mills' cereal.[25] If you see an outcome rising along with an indicator, it's worth probing the connection before you accept it. For example, are your telemarketing sales increasing because you've chosen the right prospects or because you're calling when they're more likely to be at home?

9. **Oversimplified framing can leave you solving the wrong problem.** There's enormous pressure to present challenges and solutions in a short, pithy way; executives are notoriously impatient. But if we oversimplify, we might miss the real problem entirely.

A toy manufacturer's executives, for example, once came to my team thinking they had a marketing problem because their sales were flagging. But after deeper probing, we realized they ran promotions year-round, but did the majority of their business between Thanksgiving and New Year's. So we worked with them to develop toys that either required smaller accessories that could be sold year-round, or came with a subscription for more items that would be shipped and billed throughout the year.

10. **Overfocusing can make you over- or undershoot.** When a company focuses on itself instead of its customers, it frequently undershoots or overshoots their needs. This often takes the form of obsessing over improvements that its customers don't really care about. BlackBerry's determination to improve the keyboards and security on its smartphones is a classic example. It lost its entire market share to the iPhone and Android by failing to see how much more a touch screen and app store mattered.

11. **What works at one scale might not work at another.** When we were prototyping Koldlok, we thought we had a winning solution. Then we brought it to the manufacturing engineer, who took one look at our over-clever fastening mechanism and sent us right back to the drawing board because it wasn't mass-producible. Testing first at a small scale is always a good idea, but make sure you're not missing a key factor that will change dramatically when scaling up.

12. **To solve the problem, you need to get outside of it.** "Think outside the box" is such a cliché that it's easy to forget what good advice it is. Innovative thinking rarely happens when we're wrapped up in the details of a problem. Force yourself to think about it in new ways, for instance, asking someone who isn't an expert to help you solve your problem, taking your competitor's viewpoint or

working back from the end state instead of starting from where you are.

This often means putting yourself in a situation that pushes you to take on a different perspective. Some people have their most creative thoughts when they take walks or sit in a sauna; others take a nap or go for a drink. My best thoughts occur in the shower, so I often take one in the middle of the day—specifically to encourage innovative thinking. These kinds of habits might seem odd, but if you want to prioritize innovation, just do what works.

It's not enough to change your own thinking, however. You need to change the way your whole organization approaches its planning and problem-solving. In the next part, we'll explore how you can change your culture without changing your DNA.

SUMMARY

Experiment to Future-Proof Your Business

1. **Plan your experiments like an investment portfolio.**
   - Balance the effort you spend pursuing growth, sustaining, and insurance innovations.
   - For each experiment you set up, consider the timing and sequencing that will make it most effective, and how to hedge against its failure.

2. **Structure your portfolio to maximize payoffs.**
   - Choose experiments that you can exploit if they are successful.
   - Do the riskiest experiments that will provide the most important information first.
   - Maintain a backlog of shovel-ready experiments that you can perform quickly if the world changes or your experiment portfolio progresses differently than expected.

3. **Develop and follow clear rules for financing experiments.**
   - Focus on managing overall project risk, rather than the risk in any individual experiment.
   - When setting budgets, consider each experiment's impact on the overall portfolio's long-term optionality, near-term impact, resilience, and performance.
   - Aim to have a spread of experiments with high and low impact, and high and low success rates.
   - Compare the knowledge gained with each experiment to its cost.

4. **Develop processes for designing and analyzing experiments.**
   - Consider whether the experimental design can answer the question being asked.
   - When analyzing experiments, use a standard checklist that calls out common cognitive traps.

5. **Institutionalize the use of experiment portfolios.**
   - Implement them at all levels of the organization.
   - Provide a protected budget.

Today's To-Dos for Tomorrow

- **Design your governance to deliver the innovation you want.** Assign a sponsor to identify where your organization's architecture and incentives discourage taking the right risks.

- **Use clear and consistent funding criteria.** Have each level of your organization build experiment portfolios, set metrics to track them, and clear decision-making criteria for canceling or continuing funding.

- **Treat experiments as a portfolio and look for synergies.** Create processes to capture and integrate learnings from experiments, build on them, and reprioritize them more effectively.

- **Rebalance your innovation portfolio.** Have your team assess—ideally with help from an outside facilitator—the timeline and certainty with which each innovation initiative will drive growth and increase resilience.

- **Reward risk-taking.** Protect a budget for experimental initiatives with high payoffs that are likely to fail. Penalize a lack of experimentation.

PART III

CULTURE CHANGE

*Do your processes and incentives
drive a culture of resilient growth?*

U ntil now, we've focused on the challenges facing your organization and the tools you can use to enhance its awareness and behavior. Applying them is rarely straightforward, and almost always requires a shift in culture. But institutional cultures are notoriously difficult to change. As Peter Drucker said, they "eat strategy for breakfast."

In books, articles, and talks, culture is given a thousand vague meanings, but I use the word to mean something that's very tangible and concrete. As I define it, an organization's culture is what management incentivizes and discourages, and the ethical framework that governs its expectations. More than anything, it's a consensus understanding of who gets ahead, who doesn't, and why. Everyone in an organization pays attention to this, and it shapes their behavior much more than any messaging strategy.

If you, as a leader, want to change your culture, you may have to examine your own values first. Because if you try to change an organization's behavior without changing its underlying drivers, you'll create a mismatch between your interests and the interests of the group. This dissonance causes a kind of paralysis in which people are less likely to take risks or help each other.

Not every culture that performs well in calm seas can survive a rogue wave. If everyone focuses on repeatable procedures and optimizes them, an organization can survive and even thrive in a predictable environment. Everyone simply becomes more and more specialized in their domains. That can increase your performance in the short term, but it leads to rigidity and ultimately sclerosis. To sustain your performance over time—and to be adaptable enough to weather the unexpected—you must be resilient.

There are no set processes for handling the unexpected. But it's possible to build a more intuitive culture that can innovate its response in real time.

Organizational cultures evolve, and they do so in knowable ways that you can track and control. The next chapter will show you how.

8

Leading in Stormy Seas

Shift how your leaders think about risk-taking and risk management to ensure that your change efforts are adopted and sustained.

Astro Teller heads up X, the advanced research lab at Alphabet, Google's parent company. From his name, you might think he's a character in a science fiction story. In a way he is. Some of the technologies X is working on—in augmented reality, optical communications, artificial intelligence, and renewable energy—sound more like fiction than the scalable business propositions that they'll become.

Alphabet is a trillion-dollar enterprise, and Astro's job is to double its valuation. No one has ever tried to do that before. There are no known best practices for putting such a big dent in the universe—you have to write your own rulebook. While Astro doesn't play by traditional rules, he uses the same strategy I've seen in every organization that's pulled off the impossible. Instead of building a portfolio of businesses, he's building a portfolio of experiments.

The methods he uses to do this successfully are the same ones you've encountered throughout the pages of this book. If you want to take a similar approach, you need to do several things:

1. **Incentivize failure:** It's not a good experiment if you already know the answer. The best leaders and firms incentivize smart risk. They reward good experiments, not successful experiments. By good experiments, we mean those that help the company learn more about the future, even if they fail.
2. **Do the riskiest things first:** If you want to increase your likelihood of success, incentivize people to run the experiments that tell you how likely you are to fail.
3. **Encourage tight feedback loops:** If an experiment is going to take six months or a year, measure the value of new knowledge against the cost of the lost time.
4. **Manage a portfolio of risk, instead of individual risks:** Alphabet, Google's parent company, has enshrined this philosophy in its name. They make massive Alpha bets on technologies like AI and what they call Other Bets on more far out but possibly even higher impact areas.
5. **Assign risk at the right level and make the risk parameters clear:** It doesn't matter if you're on Wall Street or in Silicon Valley, you can't move fast and break things if you don't know which china you can't break.

   Executives often pay lip service to innovation, but then they make one of two mistakes. Either they don't devote enough budget to experimentation, or they take their hand off of the cash spigot and let their teams waste piles of money on undirected research.

   Astro has two solutions that shift incentives and drive a culture of smart experimentation:
6. **Ex-ante incentives:** Most incentives are designed to reward good outcomes. In situations where you can't know the future, this is an insane strategy. Incentivizing outcomes drives most managers to decrease risk instead of taking smart risks. Risk management is very different in the unknown. You need to encourage *more* risk-taking if your aim is to learn and become more agile. That's why Astro Teller incentivizes good experiments, no matter what their results.

7. **Incentivize killing your own projects:** Projects are fiefdoms, and the best way to grow one is to avoid risk. This often leads project managers to avoid learning inconvenient truths. X flips this on its head, providing bonuses and Astro's very public admiration for the teams that cut their losses early.

When your goal is to add a trillion dollars' worth of new businesses, you need to bet big. But in a world of unknowns, you can't beat the house without decreasing your them. The best way to hedge is to adopt a portfolio strategy, spreading out both your risks and your chances of success. It's madness to only reward the experiments that achieve the best results. The way of wisdom is to reward well run experiments that are designed to provide useful information at just the right level of risk.

SOWING THE SEEDS OF AN EXPERIMENTAL MINDSET

It takes time to build a portfolio of experiments, but as your organization's playbook of options grows, so will its willingness to try new things. The first steps toward fostering your group's experimental mindset don't require investment. They require a personal shift in perspective that others in your organization will model once they see it in you. This shift has two main components.

The first is to *make room for experimentation*. This means resisting the pressure to provide (or demand) quick answers, realizing that initial reactions are frequently wrong. If you want more objective, reliable answers you often will need to budget time to model and experiment.

The second shift is to *push others to explore a wider range of options* before making decisions. This can be uncomfortable because it often requires acknowledging that a situation is not yet fully understood. Nobody likes to look dumb.

Once you've adopted these mindsets, you can start incentivizing experimentation within your organization, and removing incentives that prevent people from participating. These steps and the broader activity of building a problem-solving process are what we'll explore in this chapter.

HOW TO FUTURE-PROOF YOUR CULTURE

Perhaps the best way to understand what a leader must do to foster a culture of experimentation is through a case study. The stormy seas in this one are not metaphorical.

The place is Elephant Island, a narrow, ice-covered spray of land about 150 miles north of Antarctica. The year is 1916. On the 24th of April, Sir Ernest Shackleton undertook a last-ditch effort to save his men. They had been trapped there for the entire winter after their ship, the *Endurance*, was crushed by ice. Along with the *Endurance*'s captain and a few others, the explorer set sail for South Georgia Island, the nearest civilization. The voyage of the 22-foot *James Caird*—the ship's last functional lifeboat—was an 800-mile Hail Mary of a trip.

On the Southern Ocean's 50th parallel, there is no land. When the wind whips up the sea, its power circles the earth—a wave unimpeded, just waiting for another storm to give it an even harder kick. Here is Shackleton's account:

> At midnight I was at the tiller and suddenly noticed a line of clear sky between the south and southwest. I called to the other men that the sky was clearing, and then a moment later I realized that what I had seen was not a rift in the clouds but the white crest of an enormous wave.
>
> During twenty-six years' experience of the ocean in all its moods I had not encountered a wave so gigantic . . .

. . . White surged the foam of the breaking sea around us. We felt our boat lifted and flung forward like a cork in breaking surf.

We were in a seething chaos of tortured water; but somehow the boat lived through it, half full of water, sagging to the dead weight and shuddering under the blow. We baled with the energy of men fighting for life, flinging the water over the sides with every receptacle that came to our hands, and after ten minutes of uncertainty we felt the boat renew her life beneath us.[1]

It is also a story of teamwork. Captain Worsley describes how the crew came together to make it through the terrifying ordeal:

Navigation is an art, but words fail to give my efforts a correct name. Dead reckoning or DR—the seaman's calculation of courses and distance—had become a merry jest of guesswork . . .

. . . The procedure was: I peered out from our burrow—precious sextant cuddled under my chest to prevent seas falling on it. Sir Ernest stood by under the canvas with chronometer, pencil and book. I shouted "Stand by," and knelt on the thwart—two men holding me up on either side. I brought the sun down to where the horizon ought to be and as the boat leaped frantically upward on the crest of a wave, snapped a good guess at the altitude and yelled, "Stop," Sir Ernest took the time, and I worked out the result. . . . My navigation books had to be opened page by page till the right one was reached, then opened carefully to prevent utter destruction."[2]

After 16 days on the frigid seas, they hit land on South Georgia Island, the same isolated rock that Vespucci had discovered some 400 years before (see Figure 8.1). If the *James Caird*'s course had been off by one-tenth of a percent, they would have been lost at sea. They then took a ship back to pick up the 22 men on Elephant Island, and sailed home to England with no loss of life.

Throughout the trip, the men survived through constant experimentation. They upgraded the salvaged lifeboat, moved ballast around it to make it more stable, and worked together to keep Worsley steady so he could work his sextant. Every member of the crew innovated as necessary to ensure maximum resilience.

Figure 8.1 **The Voyage of the *James Caird***

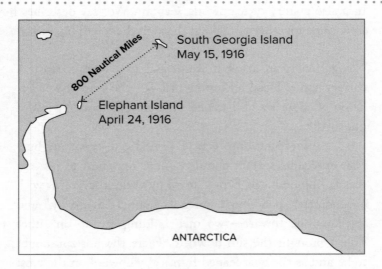

Developing a More Resilient Crew

The voyage of the *James Caird* illustrates several useful points about how teams can deal with chaos successfully.

The first has to do with leadership. Shackleton knew how to force his opinion, but in this situation it was more important that he knew how to create space for his men to experiment. Most of the innovations that kept them alive weren't Shackleton's doing. They couldn't have been. He wasn't a navigator or shipwright, and he knew that. So rather than taking total control or sitting back and doing nothing, he enabled.

Through his behavior, he ensured that meritocracy defined the crew's power structure. The person with the most knowledge about any given situation was able to pass judgment. In some cases, like when the navigator took readings, this meant that Shackleton subordinated himself, becoming an assistant and scribe so that Worsley could better do his job.

The whole crew was able to make adjustments based on new information, rather than on politics. Much of what they were doing had never been done before, so they were in a constant state of experimentation. As each experiment succeeded or failed, they'd modify their strategy to suit. If they had behaved like many modern organizations, setting a course based on who proposed it and how much authority he had, everyone would have perished.

All of this was made possible by their intense cohesion, achieved through months spent literally stranded together on an ice-covered island. If you read the memoirs of the ship's crew, it's clear that their culture had evolved from a traditional rigid hierarchy to a circle of constantly experimenting colleagues.

In modern business, that kind of cohesion is more difficult to achieve. External contractors need to be onboarded and turned into team members. New employees need to be innovating productively from day one. People get bogged down in meetings and politics when they don't have an incentive for shared survival. Anyone who is tired of it can leave at any time—and they often do.

You can't send your people to bond over roast penguin at a mandatory Antarctic team-building session, but you can help them to work together more effectively. Specifically, you need to:

- Create a common mental model
- Encourage people at all levels to report the impact of changes, in ways that everyone can comprehend
- Empower individuals to coordinate experiments without excessive intrusions from above

All this requires you to increase both bottom-up and top-down communication. New information must move up the chain of command quickly and be shared laterally, too. You need to be more than a well-coordinated group. You need to act as a single organism.

Knowing When to Captain and When to Coach

In our rapidly changing world, success is increasingly probabilistic as opposed to deterministic. This means that you can't assume that the future will play out like the past—or even like your most careful projections. The lockstep, efficiency-oriented approaches that have defined the last hundred years of management theory are no longer suited for the volatility, uncertainty, complexity, and ambiguity (VUCA, as the military calls it) that is increasingly the norm. Imagine if Shackleton had insisted on running his ship strictly by the book. Not only would he have alienated his terrified crew, he also would have missed out on all the innovations and clever workarounds they developed.

To survive in stormy seas, you need a team that can quickly make and execute decisions based on the latest information. This only happens when everyone in the organization understands and accepts the system, specifically, how power is distributed and decisions are coordinated. The decision-maker must be the person closest to the problem, and must be empowered to process information and execute action—while being held accountable for the result.

We see this in Shackleton's shift from commanding the crew to becoming Worsley's stopwatch-holding assistant. This was only possible because Shackleton had made sure that Worsley:

- Understood the overall goal of the team
- Was motivated to see the goal achieved
- Understood the context they were working in
- Had a fast feedback loop with the captain

Compare this to a traditional *captaining* authority structure (Figure 8.2). Instead of hoarding and controlling information, and assigning tasks without providing context, Shackleton was acting much more like a coach. In a *coaching* mindset, the leader informs, aligns, and motivates team members and supports them in improving their own judgment.

Figure 8.2 **When to Captain and When to Coach**

CAPTAIN		COACH
Has a Vision	vs.	Creates a Shared Mental Model
Command and Control	vs.	Coach and Learn
Maximizes Predictability	vs.	Manages Uncertainty
Simple Systems	vs.	Complex Systems
Focused on Incremental Efficiency Gains	vs.	Focused on Exponential Efficiency Gains
Clear Goals	vs.	Multiple Competing Aims

Be an Octopus, Not a Lemming

Glittering schools of fish part when you swim through them. They avoid you so skillfully that not one touches your body. No individual fish knows what all of the others are doing. Yet they're able to coordinate instantaneously to follow the ocean flows or evade a hazard.

This behavior is achieved with a simple flocking algorithm, where each fish tries to maintain a constant distance from its nearest neighbors and swims in roughly the same direction. When one fish moves to avoid a diver, the entire school moves in unison. Simple rules work well when there is a point threat or single goal, like avoid the diver or the shark. I call this a *focused threat*.

Unfortunately, this doesn't offer much help when you face a *systemic threat*. What seems smart in one case can be suicidal in the other.

Norwegian lemmings also use a kind of flocking logic when migrating. Contrary to popular depictions, they don't commit suicide en masse,[3] but they do respond to threats in a way that can have the same effect. For example, they migrate when systemic threats like food shortages appear. And when they migrate, they use a simple, predetermined strategy that's not unlike what schooling fish use. Each lemming follows the one in front of it blindly, with no understanding of what comes next. It's an effective way of moving a large herd quickly, but it has a downside. It can result in thousands of healthy animals following one another off the rocks and into the water, not knowing whether they're swimming across a fjord or fording the North Sea without a life vest.

Systemic threats are becoming more frequent, meaning that rogue waves will hit more often. When they do, many businesses react algorithmically—much like fish or lemmings. Rote strategy works fine in a world where things don't change much from year to year; it creates the slow thrum of compound growth. But when large shifts change the system itself, those tried-and-true strategies are likely to fail. When the wave hits, your approach needs to evolve dynamically and your team needs to respond in a way that's both coordinated and intelligent.

Perhaps a better role model is the octopus, an animal whose intelligence and problem-solving ability is up there with dogs' and dolphins'. Unlike vertebrates, the octopus has a sort of distributed brain, with one for each of its tentacles. These are linked by a neural ring that bypasses the central brain altogether.[4] Each "tentacle brain" can send information to the others without involving the "big" brain, allowing them to work independently, but coordinated in the pursuit of a common goal.

To do something like hunt crabs while traversing the sea floor, all of these neural brains must have a common understanding of the objective, while responding to the the constantly changing environment. This is why the efficient, balletic movement of octopodes seems both random and precise at the same time.

Teams that respond effectively to novel crises take much the same approach. They continually share information about the environment and context and course correct as necessary. And while each member of the team is independent, their communication and shared understanding allow them to coordinate effectively.

If you're a team leader in an uncertain, constantly changing environment, you're the choke point. You have the option of routing all information and all decisions through yourself, and in fact, many leaders choose to do just that. It's a leading cause of *"Titanic"* moments. If you want to innovate around the change, your team needs to think probabilistically. All of its members must know the context and the high-level goal.

Beyond that, there's another reason to emulate the octopus. It is uniquely resilient and adaptable. The genomes of octopods as a species change very, very slowly. Paradoxically, this allows them to evolve very quickly as individuals. Over the course of its lifetime, a mammal might modify 1 percent of its RNA, the chemical that tells the body how to grow and manage biological processes. Cephalopods, the family that octopods are members of, can modify 60 percent of their RNA.[5] While many marine species, like cod, will be decimated by slight changes in their environment, octopods modify their RNA so that they can survive in shallow tropical coves or a mile deep in the Antarctic. This enables them to weather ongoing systemic changes in their environment.[6]

The difference between RNA and DNA is significant here. When we talk about an organization's DNA, we're actually making a pretty good analogy: DNA is unchangeable, it's simply what exists and what makes the company (or species) what it is. But the octopus gets its tremendous adaptability from its RNA, which is more like the incentive structure in your organization. I often hear executives complaining that they can't make their company more innovative because they can't change its DNA. But that's like saying an octopus can't adapt to the arctic because it can't turn into a polar bear.

Innovative companies incentivize and focus innovation through policy, and that is something that an executive can change. Shift the incentives, and you shift what employees do. That's how you become more adaptable.

The modern executive is one of the most adaptive breeds of the human species. If you want to encourage resilient growth, start by building hard and soft incentives that promote adaptive behavior. What types of collaboration, risk-taking, and management get credit? Which get people tossed overboard or their ambitions left on Elephant Island?

ELIMINATING UNNECESSARY RISK

It may sound counterintuitive, but if you want to promote resilience, you need to create a reliable set of codified processes. In military and some corporate environments, these take the form of standard operating procedures (SOPs). A poorly designed SOP can gum up the works, but when used properly, SOPs can free up teams to innovate faster by decreasing the time individuals spend orienting themselves and each other.

I recently gave a briefing to Royal Dutch Shell. They handle over four million barrels of oil a day,[7] making them one of the largest energy companies on earth. Shell is also a legendary proponent of scenario planning. It has used scenarios to build contingency plans for everything you could think of, and many more you couldn't. It has also resulted in standard operating procedures that are followed religiously throughout the organization.

Before our team could present, we were told exactly how to address Shell's leaders when they came into the room. The first thing we were instructed to do, even before we introduced ourselves, was to point out the fire exits, lavatories, and explain what to do in case of an emergency.

As the executives began filing in, one of them picked up a laser pointer sitting on the table, thinking it was a pen, and accidentally turned it on, for less than a second. What happened next left me stupefied. He carefully set the pointer back down on the table and announced in a very even voice to the entire room that he had discharged a low power coherent light source, and that the device was now off but still active.

This all seemed a bit overboard to me at the time, but later I thought about Shell's business. Extracting, transporting, and refining oil and gas is dangerous from beginning to end. It's (literally) an explosive business. There are countless kinds of accidents that can occur at refineries, on ships, and in oil-rich developing countries where unrest is just around the corner. Amid all that, Shell makes unimaginably large investments that won't pay out for a quarter century. With so much opportunity for catastrophe, even a small communications breakdown can lead to a disaster on the high seas, or a decade-long game of telephone that ends in a poor investment.

That's why they have standard operating procedures, and that's why everyone—*everyone*—follows them. Whether you're C-suite, a rig worker, or a janitor, the rules are the same. And it works. It can seem unnecessarily conservative, but these SOPs allow employees who don't know each other to operate together safely and efficiently in some of the most challenging situations on earth. Shell routinely takes on risks that would leave most executives broken and shivering in the corner.

Since that experience, I've made a point to notice similar approaches to mind-melding in other organizations. Generally speaking, the higher performing the organization and the more ambiguous its business, the more explicit it is about its processes. Amazon drills its STAR reporting method (Situation, Task, Actions, Results), its leadership principles, and its six-page memo format into every person who works in its offices. The US Military focuses on OPORDs (Operations Orders) that clearly define a commander's intent while giving subordinates the freedom to innovate.[8]

Obviously, the military is different from an oil company or an e-commerce giant, but their SOPs have several things in common. There are always procedures that ensure that everyone is aligned on intentions: what the mission is, what problem they are solving, how they know if they've been successful, and if the problem has changed. And there are procedures that define execution: how much risk they can take on, who they are coordinating with, who's in charge, what to do if something goes wrong.

Well-defined, appropriate SOPs also let the team know why an SOP is needed in the first place. Is the goal to:

- Make things easier for the captain or the team?
- Eliminate unforced errors?
- Help your organization be more agile?

Understanding the goals can give your team the freedom to ignore the SOP when that makes sense. This last part is crucial: large organizations waste enormous amounts of effort when leaders overfocus on execution (giving orders and seeing them obeyed) but fail to articulate their intent.

Execution is critical to innovation, of course, and having a Six Sigma Triple Ninja Blackbelt or an Agile Ultra Portfolio SCRUM Master on your team is an asset when it comes to routine operations. But if you're headed for a brick wall, optimization will only help you hit it faster. Better execution results in a better work product, but that doesn't mean it will be useful.

One of the best examples of doing this right—of creating SOPs that consistently produce valuable innovations—is the Chef's Garden, a farm in Ohio. As farms go, it's very much on the cutting edge, having gained national fame as a producer of high-quality, sought-after vegetables for top restaurants around the world.

If you visit the farm, you'll see a lot of people doing their jobs independently. You also see them experimenting. The greenhouse managers have developed a system that lets one person maintain an acre of greenhouse. An electrician explored the impact of light color on the flavor of herbs. One of the account managers profitably turned the visitor center into one of the best restaurants in the state. When the Covid-19 pandemic shuttered all of their customers at once, they launched a global home delivery and packaged food product line. The packaged food business was the beekeeper's idea. The result is that, while many of their competitors sank, the Chef's Garden now ships a record amount of vegetables, but to consumers. And as their restaurant customers return, they will experience uncontested growth.

The reason they have so much successful, well-aligned innovation is that the Jones family, who runs the farm, is extremely clear about intent. Everyone who works there knows the production and financial targets, the systemic threats they're facing, and the long-term vision. The owners are very demanding—not that their orders be perfectly executed, but that there is a continuous flow of experiments. Steve Jobs famously demanded 10 working prototypes of every new concept; these guys want 100. Most companies review their product lines, doing a small nip and tuck at the end of the year; the farm cuts the bottom third.

Well-formed SOPs matter in large organizations, but if anything, they're even more important in small ones that can't afford to burn their pennies.

Keeping all this in mind, there are three generic SOPs that are worth understanding. Every organization is different and no one size fits all, but if you want to shift your culture to be more resilient—more like the octopus—they're a great place to start.

SOP #1: Actively Listen to All Your Team Members' Ideas

The leaders who make the biggest contributions to history and humanity generally are not the ones we perceive to be "strong leaders" . . . Instead, they tend to be the ones who collaborate, delegate, and negotiate—and recognize that no one person can or should have all the answers.

—BILL GATES

In uncertain situations, we avoid threats, but we also miss opportunities.

I believe we all have a chance to be a billionaire. The only problem is we usually don't recognize it, or we misread it as a bad idea. My grandfather turned down an opportunity to be an early investor in In-N-Out Burger, one of the most successful fast food chains in

California. My friend and mentor Ted Selker turned down a job as an early employee and the CTO of Google.

In each case, if they'd had just a little more information, they might have made a decision with a radically different outcome. Sam Altman, founder of the business accelerator Y Combinator, explains:

> The hardest part about coming up with great ideas is that the best ideas often look terrible at the beginning. . . . The hard part is that this is a very fine line. There's right on one side of it, and crazy on the other.
>
> The thirteenth search engine—and without all the features of a web portal—most people thought that was pointless. The tenth social network—limited only to college students with no money—also terrible. Myspace had won. Or a way to stay on strangers' couches, that just sounds terrible all around. These all sounded really bad, but they turned out to be good. If they had sounded really good, there would have been too many people working on them.[9]

Paying attention to the right issues and the right ideas is a crucial skill for your team to develop. The information you need is probably already within your organization. The tricky part is it's probably not all in one place. None of us can know the future, but we all know a piece of it, just like the tentacles of an octopus that reach out and sense more of the environment. We just need to listen and communicate more effectively as a team.

To make this "horizon scanning" pay off, your organization needs more than context awareness. It needs a process for reporting back what has been learned and turning the insights into action. For leaders, this means doing an enormous amount of listening.

In my experience, the best ideas often come from precisely the people who are the least likely to be heard. One of the most useful insights in my time at HP, for example, came out of a conversation with a call center operator in Bangalore. The pitches may be unrefined, but those ideas are the most important ones to listen to. The best insights may be counterintuitive and may come from folks who don't know how to frame their value for executives.

If you want to increase the innovation quotient of your team, you need to teach them how to:

- Explain their ideas in the larger context of the organization's goals
- Articulate what information or systemic advantage the organization has (and for how long)
- Demonstrate how their idea balances threat and opportunity

Your team can create more innovation without more effort, just by doing this. One of the most common disconnects within teams occurs when two people who are experts in different domains spot the same threat or opportunity, but don't realize they're connected. By giving them a common context and purpose, you can help them see those connections.

SOP #2: Involve Your Entire Team When Building System Models

Many of the tools I've introduced can help you think more probabilistically and improve your judgment. These include trees of possibility, system modeling tools such as causal loop diagrams, and simulation tools such as scenario planning and the five Ds.

One mistake that senior leaders often make is to embrace these tools, but only at the executive level. In fact, these kinds of mapping and planning exercises are extremely effective at getting the entire team aligned on their high-level purpose. This allows them to perform their own experiments, make their own leaps of imagination, and ultimately become more nimble and cohesive.

For individuals, these kinds of planning tools—especially system mapping tools—can help supplement the physical limits of the human brain. We all rely on rules of thumb and shortcuts when we make decisions, and this often leads to bias. When we outsource our memory to a map, we're better able to see the logic of the system and the relationships between causes and effects.

Visual diagrams help team members to understand both the forest and the trees, that is, the specific elements they might not directly encounter and the overall system connecting them. This equips everyone to make better decisions about the future by showing how their actions are going to impact others.

A shared map, tree, model, or document draws from the experience of the entire team. That's why it's almost always richer and results in more options. This helps satisfy SOP #1, and it gives you a tool for discussing system-level decisions and indicators, so nobody gets blindsided. A team that models together, plans together. And when they plan together, they can then experiment independently with a lot more confidence, and coordinate their efforts laterally rather than forcing leadership to referee. The result is an octopus structure in which the individual tentacles are linked, freeing the head to focus on the objective instead of managing traffic.

In practice, this kind of modeling can take many forms. For example, a causal loop diagram drawn on a whiteboard is a simple way of seeing the impact of a staff reduction on profit (Figure 8.3).

The layoffs might save on salary, but they'll also impact morale, which will decrease productivity. The insight here is that you might need to account for two more factors when making your decision about layoffs. Are they worth the:

1. Drag on revenue because fewer goods will be produced?
2. Higher per item production costs because workers will be less efficient?

Systems diagrams are communication tools, not persuasion tools. They can seem complicated, even impenetrable without a walk-through. While a complex diagram can take longer to walk through than a PowerPoint deck, it provides a much richer map of the territory.

Figure 8.3 **Impact of Layoffs on Profit**

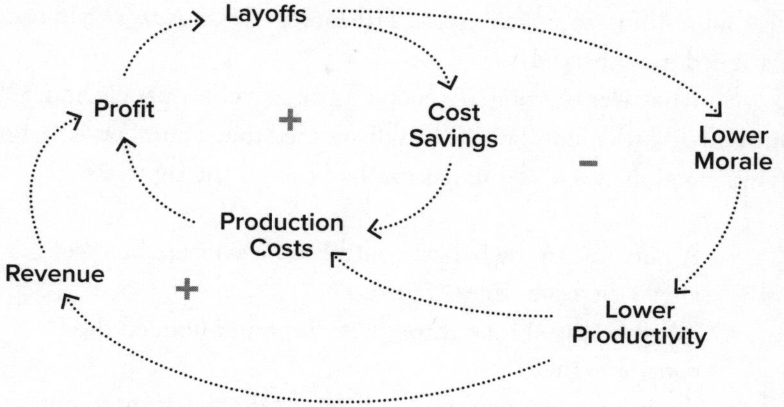

Doing this accelerates the mind meld. A two-hour exercise in model-building can help new hires or executives understand the bigger picture—where all the links, nodes, inputs, and outputs are—and will make new employees efficient far faster than letting them blindly bump up against blockers as they learn your company. Then you can use techniques like VEGAS (Visibility, Effect, Gestation, Accessibility, Security) to identify threats and opportunities, and the REAL framework (Reconnaissance method, Evidence, Alternatives, Likelihood) to uncover key information that is still unknown.

Using Scenarios to Solve Your Elephant Problem

When the people who manage a system's nodes don't have the whole picture, unforced errors occur.

On Valentine's Day 1982, a floating oil rig called the *Ocean Ranger* was drilling on the Grand Banks off the coast of Newfoundland, not far from where the ship in *The Perfect Storm* went down. As tall as a skyscraper and as wide as a football field, it was a mountain on the sea. This $125 million technological marvel was designed to live year-round in the world's roughest waters. It routinely laughed off 50-foot waves, standing on two pontoons stabilized by a sophisticated ballast system. Yet that day, it suddenly sank during a moderate storm. Rogue waves were reported by another nearby rig, but nothing approaching the 110-footers *Ocean Ranger* had been designed to withstand.

So what went wrong? A couple of blue ribbon panels and $20 million of settlements later, it was discovered that a number of design flaws, combined with human error, had caused the rig to sink:

- A porthole in the ballast control room—located 28 feet above the water line—failed.
- When a wave broke through it, the water flooded the control room.
- An improperly waterproofed electrical panel shorted out.
- That caused the controllers for the mighty pumps that pushed air into the ballast tanks to fail.
- As a result, they filled up with water and the rig went down.[10]

An expert might have been able to save the *Ocean Ranger*, but no one who was trained to control the ballast tanks was available. And while the crew had enough time to save themselves, they hadn't received the right training or equipment to get themselves off the rig.[11]

A poorly trained kid in the control room is the easy scapegoat, but that's not the real story here. The issue is the Elephant Problem, which we briefly discussed in Chapter 2. There were multiple points in the life of the rig—from design to commissioning to training—when the disaster could have been prevented, but no one ever considered the whole system. Nobody knew what the overall goal was, so everyone did their job, but no one did *the* job.

Just as with the *Titanic*, if someone had thought through what would happen if the hull *was* breached, rather than attempting to design an unbreachable hull, the outcomes would have been different. They assumed that the future would be what they had designed for. It never is.

Dealing with the Elephant Problem (and other avoidable causes of failure discussed in Chapter 2) requires direct efforts to align the team around their shared context. Group exercises, like Who Sank My Battleship?, can be useful here. More generally, exercises like VEGAS, causal loop diagrams, the tree of possibility, and threat and opportunity dashboards help your team link the details to the big picture and vice versa, as well as understand how the environment is changing the model.

In Chapter 5, we discussed the example of an augmented reality hardware startup struggling to come up with the right long-term product strategy. The Elephant Problem was their biggest challenge: everyone was focused on launching products instead of growing the business.

All the information they needed to set the right strategy was there in the room, but hardly anyone had a clear understanding of the bigger picture. The electrical engineer knew about the future components. The marketing guy knew about buying behavior. The CFO knew what growth projections they had to hit long term.

By spending 20 minutes drawing the product ecosystem and competitive environment on a whiteboard, we were able to solicit the information and share it in an accessible way. If they had simply looked at the growth indicators, they would have continued to invest in a platform that couldn't ever pay back the investment. Instead, they made a pivot to a much better platform that took the emerging realities into account.

SOP #3: Make Robust Lateral Communication a Part of Company Policy

Aligning a team on innovation goals requires more than shared context. It also takes open, high-volume communication channels that are in constant use.

Tim Winkler raises pigs near where I live in the Bay Area. And not just any pigs, but 400-pound, furry monsters called Mangalitsas.

They're among the most valuable and sought-after heritage breeds, worth thousands of dollars each. They range free over acres of forest, raising the serious problem of defending them against both thieves and coyotes.

Tim's nutty, brilliant solution was to use a pack of domesticated wolves. Raised around pigs from early on, the wolves defend them tirelessly, and they're very good at their job. They also provide an opportunity to observe some of the most effective teamwork in the animal kingdom.

One day, over the course of an hour, I watched as each wolf took turns in different roles: a sentry would sit back several hundred feet, another would walk the forest perimeter, and two more would pretend to not pay attention, wrestling with each other or resting on the lawn.

Wolves work collaboratively to understand and monitor changes in the operating environment. They play fight to reduce stress and resolve conflict. They change behavior based on the actions of the others. They are in constant, subtle communication. Most importantly, they do this without a steering committee or an org chart.

Learning how to think together is a force multiplier. Humans do this by having meetings, but very few human teams achieve the level of coordination of a wolf pack, no matter how many meetings they have. This isn't so much a failing of the team, but of the way meetings are conducted.

Meetings fail because leaders tend to focus on the content of their agendas instead of orchestrating the way the team thinks together. The wolves may not have written agendas, but they always know what the shared goal is, who is in charge, and what role each of them is playing at any moment.

Human leaders can achieve this level of coordination by putting the right processes in place. This starts by clarifying the goals of the meeting and the roles of everyone involved.

Goals

Most meetings fall into one of six categories, depending on what they're trying to achieve:

1. **Networking:** Building trust through informal interaction
2. **Information:** Sharing the commander's intent and coordinating activity
3. **Exploration:** Identifying baseline reality and options
4. **Alignment:** Synthesizing differing views and data to enable a decision
5. **Selection:** Choosing a path forward
6. **Execution:** Delivering on experiments

Roles

Most teams work through seven types of tasks. Each requires its members to assume and carry out different roles:

1. **Ideation:** Providing new input
2. **Coordination:** Helping parties come together
3. **Defense:** Protecting a position
4. **Offense:** Attacking a position
5. **Judgment:** Deciding what to do
6. **Learning:** For junior team members, this is its own job
7. **Execution:** Delivering on decisions

Meeting Process

Clarifying intent is necessary, but not sufficient. You also need to develop standards for how your team thinks together. There are entire books written on this subject, but here are a few basic recommendations that help keep meetings productive:

- **Have multiple notetakers.** Otherwise, you end up with a record of what interested the notetaker, not what was said.
- **Keep the extroverts in check.** Make sure that everyone (whether online or in person) has a chance to speak. Ideally, keep it all online or all in person, so no one's at a disadvantage. At the end of the meeting, go around the group and ask each person what they know that you don't, but didn't say.

- **Confirm decisions, assign next steps, and schedule a firm follow-up.** The more unclear the situation is, the more important it is to ensure that the team is actually aligned, and not just smiling and nodding.

By being clear about your goals and where you are in the innovation process, you give your team more freedom to hunt for the right solution.

PLAYING BASKETBALL ON A FOOTBALL FIELD

When you shift from executing a predefined strategy to evolving one dynamically, you have to change the way you organize activities. To use a sports analogy, you need to move from playing football to playing basketball.

At first glance, American football may look like a bunch of large men ramming into each other on a big lawn. In fact, it's one of the most highly structured, strategic games in modern sports. The quarterback calls a play, and each member of the team performs his predefined task. There are a variety of specialized players on the bench, like the kicker and the punter (which are different roles), who play for just one or two minutes per game. In many cases, the point spread at the end of the contest can be between 30 and 50 percent. There is a clear winner, and the win is often the result of strategy.

If football is like a nineteenth-century infantry battle, basketball is closer to a melee. The ball moves around the court at lightning speed. Roles are ambiguous. In an instant, the forward is suddenly playing defense. The defenders are suddenly taking three-point shots. The game is dynamic and agile, just as business is becoming today. The spread at the end of a typical basketball game is just 2 or 3 percent. The slam dunks and heroic longshots sell the fans, but the wins are often the result of the small stuff. A fake left or right, passing the ball a little faster or slower, can change the course of the game. Often, the most important plays don't show up in the stats on the big board.

Basketball is at least as strategic as football, but in a very different way. Basketball teams are inherently agile, and thrive through a combination of alignment and independence.

Winning the Game by Playing the Stats

By nearly any metric, Shane Battier was a mediocre basketball player, yet he spent his career redefining the game. Fans rarely paid attention to him because he didn't look the part. Battier couldn't dunk and wasn't a particularly effective guard. The owner of the Houston Rockets, Leslie Alexander, once charitably said that Battier's stats "weren't great."

Yet, when he joined the Memphis Grizzlies, their win rate doubled. When he joined the Rockets, their win rate went up 60 percent. When he joined the Miami Heat, one of the best teams in the history of the NBA, their game improved, too—even though he was sharing the court with superstars like Lebron James and Dwyane Wade.

So what did Battier do differently? His retirement job gives us a clue: he's now the statistics geek for the Houston Rockets.

While still a player, he would spend every night before a game poring over the statistics of the players on the opposing team. When he was on the court, he used his knowledge to gauge the probability that superstar Kobe Bryant would fake left or right and got ahead of it. Then he'd push Kobe to shoot from his weakest position on the court. Instead of relying on athleticism, Battier relied on his mind.[12] He used the dynamics of the game to force the other team into vulnerable situations and his own into strong ones.

Something funny would happen when Battier's team played the Lakers: the Lakers did better if Kobe took the night off.

Battier didn't so much play the game as play the probabilities. He used a version of the VEGAS technique to spot weaknesses and the 5Ds to game the play. And since he taught the teamates to play probabilistically, their games improved, too.

Look for Icebergs, Not Stars

Bold leaders like Shackleton are easy to spot; they stand out like the dawn on the horizon.

But what made Shackleton effective wasn't his charisma. It was his understanding of team dynamics. In challenging times, it's natural to look for a bold, high-profile leader. Often, what you really need is a problem solver, like Shane Battier. Much like the iceberg that struck the Titanic, most of Battier's genius wasn't on public display. But if you break it down, his approach consisted of a few key components:

- **Data-driven decision-making:** Battier focused on likelihoods and used them to tilt situations in his favor.
- **Self-awareness:** He didn't just play to his strengths, he avoided his own weaknesses.
- **Perspective:** He recognized the other teams' habits and encouraged them, but only to weaken their position on the court.
- **Context:** He played differently against every player and every team.
- **Communication:** He taught his teams how to hunt as a pack.

In business, team players like Battier go unrecognized much of the time, yet they are the secret weapon that makes the difference between great players and great teams. You can often identify them by the questions they ask, instead of the questions they answer. They are constantly encouraging their teammates to think like they do and share their insights, asking questions like:

- What is your perspective on what we are doing?
- What are we missing?

- What leads you to think that?
- What are your concerns about that subject?
- Can you tell me more about this issue?
- What else do you know about this issue that I don't?
- How do we prepare for what happens after?

Many times, these kinds of leaders need to be actively identified because they look very different from the titans of prior eras. They're often mistaken for gofers or dilettante networkers. But this perception comes from a very valuable task they're performing: making sure that the silos each have all of the information they need to coordinate, instead of telling them how to do their jobs.

Many organizations either passively or actively discourage this behavior in their managers. It makes senses to do that if your goal is to manage lemmings. But if you're trying to evolve your organization into an octopus and create a future-proof culture, you need to do the opposite. You must:

- Flatten your organization
- Make sure your Shane Battiers have enough context to play the probabilities
- Get your teams managing day-to-day coordination with each other instead of through you
- Incentivize group performance on learning faster and your commander's intent, instead of individual performance on your executional order

How to Get Your Tentacles Working as a Team

To my mind, Steph Curry of the Golden State Warriors is the best team leader in the National Basketball Association. He's charismatic. He's a great shooter and a near-perfect athlete. But what his coaches and teammates say about him isn't what you might expect when you think Superstar. All of them focus on what he does for others, rather than for himself.

Assistant Coach Bruce Fraser says, "He's definitely gone out of his way to try to get others involved, while sacrificing his own numbers." This likely costs Curry millions in performance bonuses.

Teammate DeMarcus Cousins says, "He's opened my game up. He takes all the attention away and lets me be me."

Damion Lee, another player, talks about Curry's intense empathy, saying, "Even if he hasn't been in your shoes, he can try to put himself in your shoes. That's huge."

Teammate Draymond Green says, "He was keeping his finger on every single situation as opposed to coming in after something goes wrong."[13]

There are numerous anecdotes about Curry popping over to someone's house to smooth the waters when things are rough, or showing up at a rookie's house with barbecue from his wife's restaurant to welcome him to the team.

While Steph is one of the greatest shooters in the game, what makes the Warriors win is the culture of trust and sharing on the team that Curry's done so much to build. He doesn't do it through KPIs or orders. He does it by example. After all, who wouldn't want to be like Steph Curry when they grow up?

What we see in his leadership is a focus on values. It's not what he does with the ball. It's how he shares it. He doesn't give up shots on net because he's stupid. He knows that giving is what creates teams. He knows that teams win championships and that's what creates real wealth.

You Can't Wrangle an Octopus

In New Zealand, Rambo is a celebrity. Not the Sylvester Stallone character from the 1980s; Rambo is an octopus. She's also one of Auckland's most popular portrait photographers. The Sea Life Aquarium's staff put a camera in her tank on a lark to see what would happen. What happened was she figured out how to take pictures of visitors.[14]

This is interesting because octopods are not known for being easy to teach. You'll notice that nobody's ever trained an octopus to perform acrobatics or do tricks on command, as similarly intelligent creatures like dolphins and dogs have been. Instead, the aquarium staff had simply given Rambo the tool—a camera—and let her figure it out for herself. There's a great lesson here for leaders: the most creative teams are more like octopodes than dolphins.

Successfully leading an octopus is all about providing the commander's intent and letting the octopus find the solution. When the environment is dynamic, the people closest to the problem need freedom to respond as they see fit. The challenge is that, as the environment becomes more complex, the coordination of your team needs to be tighter, too.

Paradoxically, you can't achieve this through planning. You need to do this by creating the right situation. You don't win by having the best plan or the best players. You win by having the best team.

SPEAKING IN KOANS

Just as in basketball, trust, sharing, and autonomy are the characteristics that make the difference for companies looking to increase their agility and speed. Few organizations have more top-down cultures than Japanese heavy manufacturing firms. So when I began working with Tom Matano, Mazda's former chief designer, it was a surprise to encounter all of these characteristics.

Tom had lifted Mazda from a regional competitor to a global juggernaut through the creation of iconic products like the Mazda Miata and the RX-7. His studio delivered six hit products in a row for the company. His success wasn't a fluke.

I asked him how he managed to create such consistent breakthroughs within such a massive, operations-driven culture. The answer was that he was lucky enough to have a boss like Steph

Curry—who let him lead like Steph Curry himself. He freed Tom's hands by locating him in Los Angeles, far from the politics and prying eyes of his Japanese superiors. At a time before industrial design was cool, his boss flattened the chain of command, acting as his direct conduit to the CEO and board.

Everyone I know who works for Tom calls him Yoda. He's an old, wise man who speaks in koans—little riddles meant to provoke enlightenment. He never tells you directly what to do, but structures your path forward by communicating a clear intent. The experience is frustrating and freeing at the same time.

When I got to know Tom, it was later in his career. We were building the Academy of Art's fledgling Automotive Design program into an industry powerhouse. Somehow, in a world without staff meetings, he kept 400 lunatic students and faculty (including me) marching in the right direction. No one was ever completely clear on how he did this.

I finally worked out that every week, he had one-on-one conversations with nearly all of us, in which he expressed how his intent had changed and suggested who should talk to whom. Though he hid it, I was later told that he kept notes. None of the conversations were random, and there was a reason he knew to check in on how your conversation with David or Carol went.

When I was working for him, I asked him how to be a better manager. It took me 15 years to understand what he meant when he said, "If you want to create a beautiful stone, you don't chisel it. You change the flow of the water." His words stayed in my mind as I moved from junior faculty to executive leader. This is the power of a great koan: it continues to resonate long after it is spoken.

This is how you manage an octopus. You can't tell creators what to do, but you can embody discipline and communicate the high-level objectives and uncertainties. You can discuss similar challenges you have faced, and you can manage the flow of information. Most importantly, you can create a culture of giving and trust by modeling that behavior yourself. This is how you create a high-performance culture that can act autonomously.

LEAD: The Four Messages Your Octopus Needs to Hear

Both Steph Curry and Tom Matano lead by example, and in doing so, they ward off the behaviors that tend to break teams. They build alignment with their explicit messaging, but even more so with their approach. That approach has several key qualities, which can be summarized with the acronym LEAD (Figure 8.4).

Figure 8.4 **LEAD: The Four Messages That Matter**

Logic

Empathy

Authority

Deadline

Logic: They are brutally honest about the facts and logic of the situation. They clarify to everyone in the team:

- What is and isn't under their control
- Why their options are viable and why they could work

If you listen to Steph Curry at a press conference after a game, he is always clear about his personal weaknesses, the team's weaknesses in the game, and the next steps, whether the night went their way or not. The interesting thing isn't necessarily the words. It's how dispassionate he is. He follows the logic of the situation and he never loses his cool.

Empathy: They demonstrate that they understand the values and beliefs their team members hold, as well as their concerns. Then they demonstrate how their values align.

Through their words and actions, they regularly confirm, "I hear you, and here's why you can follow me." They demonstrate and discuss values with broad resonances, such as care, fairness, and loyalty (see Jonathan Haidt's Moral Foundations Theory[15] for a deeper investigation of this topic). A vivid example of this can be seen in the name of Steph Curry's film production company: Unanimous Media, which *Sports Business Daily* describes as a "faith-based studio."[16]

Authority: Many leaders tend to skip past Logic and Empathy and start here instead. But durable, flexible authority is based on those qualities, and they make team members more open to messages about why you're the right person to lead them. Once you've demonstrated that your decisions are sensible and your values are aligned, it's easier to convince them that your intentions are pure, and your proposed solutions, while not perfect, are often the best way forward.

Deadline: There is nothing that brings a team together like a deadline, whether it's the last three minutes of the game or presenting your proposals to the head of design at a car company. In Tom's case, you always knew he would pop by sometime in the next week, so you had to be ready with a drawing, and to tell him how your conversation went with Carol. Effective leaders make it clear why the issue demands attention now, when new information will become available, and what they want to learn next time they see you.

In times of change, people are inevitably some combination of upset, panicked, worried, angry, and most of all, confused. Logic, empathy, authority and a deadline are the keys to success. Removing the pathways of division makes way for love. Love for each other is what pulls teams together. And love is how you lead an octopus.

SUMMARY

Create a Culture of Experimentation

1. **Incentivize smart failure.**
   - Encourage innovative experiments, not safe success.
   - Reward employees who deliver quality experiments, not preordained results (*ex ante* incentives).
   - Incentivize your team to kill their own projects.

2. **Build an experimental mindset.**
   - Make room for experimentation.
   - Push others to explore the full range of options before making decisions.
   - Create a process for problem solving in your organization.
   - Incentivize experimentation and disincentivize the failure to participate.

3. **Devolve communication and decision-making.**
   - Create a common mental model.
   - Encourage people at all levels to report the impact of changes in ways that everyone can comprehend.
   - Empower individuals to coordinate experiments without excessive intrusion from above.

4. **When possible, be a coach instead of a captain.**
   - Make sure everyone understands the context they are working in and the team's overall goal.
   - Motivate every team member, both personally and financially, to see the goal achieved.
   - Build a rapid feedback loop between team members and yourself.
   - Assign risk at the right level, and make the risk parameters clear.

5. **Eliminate unnecessary risks.**
   - SOP #1: Actively listen to all of your team members' ideas.
   - SOP #2: Involve the entire group when building system models.
   - SOP #3: Make robust lateral communication a part of company policy.

6. **Use LEAD messaging.**
   - **Logic:** Explain what can and can't be controlled and the range of viable options.
   - **Empathy:** Articulate your understanding of the needs and concerns of the group.
   - **Authority:** Share why you, while maybe not the perfect messenger, offer the best path forward.
   - **Deadline:** Communicate why it is important to pay attention now.

Today's To-Dos for Tomorrow

- **Define risk bands at each level of your organization.** Set explicit parameters for risk-taking and protect anyone who works within their upper and lower limit.

- **Ask junior staff to find blockers that decrease agility.** Ask the most junior members of your team where your controls are making them inefficient and what's constraining their agility. Make sure to do this in a neutral setting (not your office, maybe the lunch area).

- **Remove blockers.** Assign and fund a senior sponsor to help employees remove inefficiencies, following the employee's lead wherever possible.

- **Identify where KPIs are disincentivizing innovation and communication.** Assign a sponsor to assess where mismeasurement is causing the wrong balance of short-term and long-term payoffs, and of reliability and risk-taking.

- **Build more frequent formal and informal alignment processes.** Focus on installing procedures and incentives that keep people in communication, informed about changes in context, and aligned on shifts in objective.

- **Use incentives and tracking to drive desired behavior.** Assign a sponsor to identify where better incentives, training, and tracking tools can free up employees to take risk while delivering reliability.

- **Teach your leaders to coach and listen.** Invest in leadership training that encourages improved messaging, coaching, and lateral communication across your organization.

CONCLUSION

Driving Resilient Growth in Your Organization

It takes time to transform from an organization that reacts to radical change to one that prepares for and leverages it. In my experience, the transformation occurs in four stages.

PHASE I: AWARENESS

In the first phase of change, you're likely to see an explosion of beautiful new PowerPoint decks as team members try to signal their commitment to this new approach. Often, these are old insights dressed up and presented as new experiments.

While this isn't necessarily effective, it's an understandable response to yet another program designed to make employees more "innovative." Everyone has been through many of these "initiatives," and people are likely to be skeptical but still play along.

The good news is that just by going through this process, you're opening up communication. Having open conversations about your organization's shared context, where it's in denial, and how it can be changed by experimentation is a crucial first step. But talk does not automatically lead to sustained effort.

You're likely to see pushback, including verbal degradation of the people and projects associated with experiments, sabotage, and subversion. There are several ways to deal with this:

- Celebrate both successes and failures—all attempts, in fact—especially if team members are killing off their own obviously unsuccessful projects.
- When you analyze opportunities, talk through your thought process out loud with the team and come to an honest agreement about their probability of success.
- Use "sink or swim" messaging to establish a sense of urgency: "If you don't take care of this, it's going to impact the whole team."

This phase is successful if it:

- Convinces people on the team that there is a genuine problem
- Creates a common language for discussing experiments
- Gets people thinking about how to tell the story of an experiment and how to bring its possible outcomes to life
- Expands the range of possibility

PHASE II: BEHAVIOR CHANGE

In the second phase, the pirates start trying to run the ship. You'll know you've gotten to this point when groups of people within your organization stop sneakily trying to divert money to run experiments and start requesting budgets to perform them. This is a crucial point because your team members are essentially asking you if you're serious about this.

This phase can yield some useful innovations, but rarely ones that can be scaled up to the whole organization. That takes more practice and broader buy-in from the company as a whole.

Pushback during this phase is similar to that in Phase 1: disparaging, sabotage, subversion. But your response should look a little different:

- Assign high-level executives to sponsor and protect initiatives.
- Provide modest resources for a few people on an ongoing basis.
- Don't kill programs after a single failure.
- Provide systems that allow the small groups to remain agile while interfacing successfully with the larger organization.

This phase is successful if it:

- Gets small teams on the edge of the organization producing solutions that are adopted by the core
- Starts developing a system for making this kind of solution transfer common

PHASE III: CULTURE CHANGE

In this phase, experiments are happening often enough that you can start getting picky about which ones to maintain. Cutting internal projects is something that should be happening routinely, based on predefined, commonly agreed-upon metrics. These might include proof of market or the performance of prototypes.

You can start developing systems for scaling up successful experiments once you have a reliable, defined process that runs *outside* of your regular day-to-day operations. This requires people with the expertise to oversee the transfer, a budget to make it happen, and a system of governance to keep it running. You won't yet have a full-fledged operating unit, but you will have a steady source of new ideas and see a noticeable impact on organizational performance.

This doesn't mean pushback goes away. You'll still have naysayers, but they'll be more focused on the adoption aspect of the experiments. One response is to make a policy that a certain percentage of internal innovations must be adopted. This shifts the conversation from *whether* to adopt any to *which* ones best balance present and future needs.

It helps to identify high potential employees with experimental mindsets at the edge of your business and rotate them through the central organization. This will give them the chance to learn about the levers of power and an opportunity to make others more receptive to the approach.

Not all innovations are meant to help you survive and profit from radical change. Incremental process and feature improvements are also necessary. It's a classic management trap to get so excited about one that you neglect the other. You'll know this phase is successful when you can demonstrate an improvement in your organization's ability to innovate for both performance and optionality.

PHASE IV: RESILIENT GROWTH

The final phase of the change process is when you start to see broad and proactive support from the C-suite. This means there's active backing for experimentation and reliable resourcing for it. With this in place, you'll generally see organization-wide participation—not everyone, but a network of people from throughout.

You'll know this phase is successful when you can point to a portfolio of impacts, not just experiments. This means measurable improvements in performance and resilience that can be directly attributed to internally developed innovations. Resilient growth comes from recognizing that balance.

EPILOGUE

There is a tide in the affairs of men,
Which, taken at the flood, leads on to fortune;
Omitted, all the voyage of their life
Is bound in shallows and in miseries.
On such a full sea are we now afloat,
And we must take the current when it serves
Or lose our ventures.

—BRUTUS, *JULIUS CAESAR* (ACT 4, SCENE 3)

If you've read this far, chances are good that you're concerned about uncertainty and suspect that traditional strategy and management tools make companies brittle to radical change. Perhaps you've already suffered a major setback because of an unexpected event. Maybe you've had a stroke of good luck and want to understand how to make the next one come sooner. Perhaps you just pay attention and realize that business as usual won't cut it for much longer.

Whatever brought you here, hopefully, these principles and examples make it clear that you don't need a crystal ball to survive and profit from uncertainty. And that black swans rarely are. While you can't prepare for every possible change, you know that you can prepare for categories of radical change and that the right small nudges can turn systemic threats into outsized opportunities. The recurring analogies of waves, surfing, and exploration are intentional: the fate of a ship, a kayak, or a surfer in rough seas depends heavily on where they're positioned when each wave breaks and on their ability to buoy themselves when they take water.

We've explored the broad range of mental models that enable resilient growth, but where do you start? If I had to pick one piece of advice, it would simply be to *understand the game you're playing before you choose a strategy*:

- If you understand the game, and you see a possibility of winning, then take steps to uncouple your threats from your opportunities, like Pixar did.
- If you can't win, then don't play the game, like Bill does when considering startup investments.
- If you can't avoid the game, then figure out how to game the system, like OPFORS did in the Millennium Wargames.
- And if you can respond to a situation that your competitors can't—like Elon Musk did when starting SpaceX—then you win.

Regardless of whether or how you prepare, more rogue waves are rolling in. The undercurrents are converging too quickly; their forces are too powerful to ignore.

Change that used to be irrelevant—because it was too far away, too slow, or too small in scale—is suddenly earthshaking. In 2019, few Fortune 500 CEOs believed that someone sneezing in Wuhan could quickly crush their business on the other side of the world. Issues that used to be contained at different levels of the economic, technological, and social stacks are moving between and across them more frequently. The concerns of governments are now impacting companies, and issues that affected individuals are suddenly affecting institutions. The economy, technology, and society are boiling in the same stormy seas.

You can't escape any of this, any more than you can outpaddle an oncoming wave. But if you paddle the right amount, in the right direction, at the right time, you may be able to ride it.

In light of this growing uncertainty, smart investors and managers are increasing their focus on resilience. It's hard to read the news without feeling a sense of urgency that you need to be better prepared for the next upheaval. But books and articles about resilience often gloss over a crucial, uncomfortable fact: many strategies for resilience are inherently inefficient. You can add armor to your hull, but you can't expect to be as nimble. That's not how armor works.

There are other ways to be resilient, though. Instead of trying to armor an organization against every threat, it's often more efficient to focus on recovering quickly or compartmentalizing the damage. You want to flip your kayak faster than your competition, instead of trying to build an unsinkable ship.

Amazon did this in the first months of Covid, using its structural advantage to reconfigure and scale up faster than the many brick-and-mortar competitors who went bankrupt. Terrorists and insurgents often use similar fluidity to great effect, letting their assets dissolve when under threat, then reassembling later. Big, old companies that survive systemic upheavals have used it, too; for example, in the 1990s, IBM sold off many of its hardware divisions, and then reinvented itself in the 2000s as a B2B services company.

This kind of resilience comes from better decision-making and adaptive leadership at all levels of your organization. It's hard to armor yourself against future uncertainty—much less take advantage of it—when all you've got to go on are current realities. But awareness works well against the unknown when paired with the behavior and culture of resilient growth.

HOW TO SEE CLEARLY

Observation is the most valuable skill of the coming decades.

It's always been important to see things clearly in business, government, and other organizations, but it's never been this hard. There's more to pay attention to than ever before, but there are also more structures and systems designed to reinforce your biases. Whatever perspective you've formed through your own experience, there are others out there who share it. Customized content, social media, and a fractured information space have made it incredibly easy for others to wrap their perspective around you until you believe it's the only one.

The true captains of modern business see a more complete reality. They look outward as well as inward. They listen broadly and they read more than recent history. They constantly look for corollaries, and they're intensely skeptical anytime someone says this has never happened before. Often, they've had some training in an academic discipline that balances abstract thinking with the finding of objective truth, such as applied mathematics, physics, computer science, economics, or law (Jeff Bezos, Elon Musk, Warren Buffett, Charlie Munger, and Peter Thiel come to mind).

They also tend to be comfortable with ambiguity, and can base decisions on stacked-up probabilities as well as on certainties. We've talked a lot in this book about "probabilistic decision-making" which, at the end of the day, simply means continuing to make good decisions even when you don't know as much as you'd like to. When you know what's most likely and what's less likely but also plausible, you can plan for a range of possible futures and invest in making your preferred outcomes more likely.

WINNING WITH A RESILIENT GROWTH STRATEGY

So how do these captains of tomorrow, with their better-than-average awareness and their probabilistic thinking, spend time and money to shape their future?

There are many examples of successful responses to uncertainty in Chapters 6, 7, and 8, but they're hard to summarize because each response depends heavily on context. But here's what's common: zombie assumptions—a blind adherence to what's worked in the past—are what get us into trouble.

The winners in the rogue wave era know how to act quickly because they already have the right tools, the nudges and impact amplifiers in place, and they've modeled the Four FOES of Growth before the wave welled up. They've short-circuited the threats that come with radical change and built systems that maximize their upside. They've given their people tools that simultaneously increase autonomy and coordinate action. They know how to balance resilience and growth and have rejected the false claim that they can sustain one without the other.

Is your organization like that? Are you one of these captains of tomorrow? If not, then I urge you to course correct. Bigger waves mean bigger risk and more unexpected threats, but they also contain immense power, which presents immense opportunity. With the right awareness, behavior, and culture, you can do more than just avoid drowning. You can enjoy a ride more thrilling and more rewarding than any that's come before.

ACKNOWLEDGMENTS

This book wouldn't have happened without the help of a massive and dedicated team. Thank you so much to my family, Rebecca, Lora, Margot, Sarah, Cooper, Lee, Kathy, and my late father, Ken Brill.

An incredible core team that guided me through this journey: Casey Ebro, James Levine, David Lavin, Mike Nardullo, Mark Fortier, Steve Wunker, Charlotte Desprat, Lilian Halstrom and Lene Andersen of Teleportec, Byron Kaufman, Robin Harris of TechnoQWAN, Charles Yao, Dorie Clark, Steve Straus of THINK Book Works, and Arthur Goldwag—this book literally couldn't have happened without your acumen. A special thanks to Alvin Ho Young, who took me through many aspects of the design of the book.

I'm especially indebted to Carl Alviani, who spent the better part of two years teaching and guiding me through the writing process.

I'm also deeply grateful to the leadership at HP who sponsored the multiple years of research that form the foundation of this book: Shane Wall, CTO and Global Head of HP Labs; Andrew Bolwell, Head of HP Tech Ventures; Doug Warner, SVP of Innovation; Chandrakant Patel, Chief Engineer; and CEO Dion Weisler.

The Singularity University community has also been central in helping shape the story, in particular, Christyna Serrano, Molly Pyle, James Del, and Ben Bode, who were there at the beginning.

An incredible team of reviewers supported the development of *Rogue Waves*. I can't thank you enough for your selfless contributions, especially Charlotte Desprat, Byron Kaufman, and Lilian Hallstrom, who read the manuscript multiple times.

A large team advised on the broad topics covered in the book. On geopolitics, I leaned heavily on Nicholas Butts of HP, Ansgar Baums of Zoom, and Nick Cosmas of the US Defense Threat Reduction Agency. A large team advised on issues related to China over many years, including Teddy Lo of Light Engine, Horacio Miranda and Jason Rodriguez of HP, Robert Griffith and Stephen Liang of Vertiv, Gary Liu of the *South China Morning Post*, Lorenzo Scazziga, Liming Yu, and Angel Chang. On other rapidly evolving markets, I'm grateful to Okkie Esterhuizen, Andre Bodson, Peter Apeltauer, David Rozzio, Daniel Mason, and Mark Hibbert of HP for insight into Greater Asia, Africa, and the Middle East; to Steve Dashiell and Sorapol Chawaphatnakul for expertise on Thailand; and to Barbara Silva for wisdom on South America.

On topics related to science, a tip of the hat to Daniel Rosenberg, Harvard University's big brain hidden in the basement. On topics related to technology, I owe deep debts to Kevin Gorey, Ed "Steak Frites" Davis, Stephanie Dainow, Brian Rieger, Chet Chambers, Tommy Gardner, and Luke "Earthshaker" Thomas. NYU's Michael Diamond offered insights into the data economy, and the team at Frost & Sullivan have provided ongoing support. On topics of biotechnology, thank you to Andrew Hessel and Jane Metcalfe of Neo.Life.

On economics and statistics, Richard Wong, HP's Chief Economist, was a patient tutor, and Rakan Mosely of Oxford Economics was generous with access to data. On strategy issues, I'm deeply grateful to Steve Wunker of New Market Advisors, Pär Eden of KPMG, Doug Warner, and Robin Harris of TechnoQWAN, and David Frigstad of Frost & Sullivan. On decision-making and logic, I'm grateful to my colleagues Daniel Ginter, Jonathan Daves, Anant Garg, Cameron Vine, Paul Burman, and Chris Clearfield. On social issues, Michael Gresty and Deborah Kattler Kupetz were vital contributors. On finance, I'm grateful to James Clark of Apogee, Marie Myers of HP, Terry Purcell of AECOM, Cynthia Rock of Bank of the West, and Peter Demarzo who taught me at Stanford. For insights into intellectual property, I'm indebted to Peter Yennadhiou of HP and Cindy Yang of Duane Morris. The foundational research on operations was built on work with Christine Hawkins and Jose Llano, Isabelle Ranc, and David George of HP and Patrick St. Laurent of Expeditors.

On innovation process, thanks to Tony Lewis of HP's AI and Emerging Compute Lab. My longtime collaborators JD Cole and Ted Selker made editorial contributions; and Tip Sempliner, Keith Moore, Tom Wujec, Steve Caney, and HP's Chandrakant Patel, Spike Huang, and Guayente Sanmartin were all instrumental to my understanding of this topic.

The chapter on leadership was strongly informed by colleagues Dorie Clark, David and Mary of Ask the Sherwins, and Robert Ellis who developed the leadership program at Singularity. Much of it comes from executive training programs developed with Brittany Conant, Nikki Rivera, and Cathy Brett of HP and Melissa Swift at Korn Ferry; global workforce skills analysis done with Konstantin Mudrack, Jose Llano, Oanh Phuong, Amanda Regan, and Greg Blythe of HP; and courses at Stanford developed by Sarah Soule and Neepa Acharya. Perhaps most of all, it is the result of exceptional leaders I've met, including Jamie Simpson, Andrew Bolwell, Tom Matano, Kent Langley, and Bob and Lee Jones.

Thank you to my fellow travelers along this journey: Courtney Hohne of X, Mary Glenn, Steve Brown of Intel, Mario Chamorro of Coursera, Kirsten Andelman, Sharbani Roy of Amazon, Winslow Burleson, Tony Cordero, David Moore, John Girard, Gil Penchina, Aaron and Ana Hankowski, Mimi Almeida, Anne Devlin of JP Morgan, Jim Harley, Arthur Kremer, Jan Newell-Lewis, Ali Vassigh, Christiano Abrahao, Luisa Ruge, Ali Vassigh, Matt Connors, Colin Owens, Thomas Jensen, Norm Schwab, Matt Ward, Lukas Svec, Roy Hague, Scott Hagen, Charles Faulkner, Greg Beck, and Otilia Barbuta.

NOTES

INTRODUCTION

1. European Space Agency. "Ship-sinking Monster Waves Revealed By ESA Satellites." ScienceDaily. ScienceDaily, 21 July 2004. https://www.sciencedaily.com/releases/2004/07/040721084137.htm.
2. Michael Porter, *Competetive Strategy* (HBR Press, 1980).
3. Carl Icahn, "Open Letter to HP Inc. Shareholders," December 4, 2019, https://carlicahn.com/open-letter-to-hp-inc-shareholders/.
4. John Antioco, "How I Did It: Blockbuster's Former CEO on Sparring with an Activist Shareholder," Harvard Business Review, April, 2011 https://hbr.org/2011/04/how-i-did-it-blockbusters-former-ceo-on-sparring-with-an-activist-shareholder (accessed February 27, 2021).
5. Ari Levy, "Netflix was the best-performing stock of the decade, delivering a more than 4,000% return," CNBC, December 23, 2019, https://www.cnbc.com/2019/12/23/netflix-was-the-top-stock-of-the-decade-delivering-over-4000percent-return.html.
6. Carl Icahn, Open Letter to Shareholders, https://carlicahn.com/open-letter-to-hp-inc-shareholders/ (accessed March 1, 2021).
7. Xerox Releases Fourth-Quarter and Full-Year Results, February 10, 2020, https://s3.amazonaws.com/cms.ipressroom.com/84/files/20210/4Q2020-XRX-News-Release.pdf.
8. https://www.cdc.gov/polio/what-is-polio/polio-us.html; "Age and tenure in the C-Suite," Korn Ferry, https://www.kornferry.com/about-us/press/age-and-tenure-in-the-c-suite-korn-ferry-institute-study-reveals-trends-by-title-and-industry.
9. https://www.euro.who.int/en/health-topics/communicable-diseases/poliomyelitis.
10. Will Feuer, "Trump says everyone knew the coronavirus was airborne in February: It's 'no big thing," CNBC, September 10, 2020, https://www.cnbc.com/2020/09/10/trump-says-everyone-knew-the-coronavirus-was-airborne-in-february-its-no-big-thing.html
11. Kristen Aiken, "How to make a coronavirus face mask out of a t-shirt," April 13, 2020, https://www.huffpost.com/entry/how-to-make-t-shirt-face-mask-coronavirus_1_5e8f2f06c5b6b371812d15af
12. Claudio Aporta, "Inuit Orienting: Traveling Along Familiar Horizons", Sensory Studies, https://www.sensorystudies.org/inuit-orienting-traveling-along-familiar-horizons/ (accessed January 12, 2021).

CHAPTER 1

1. Bjarne Røsjø, Kjell Hauge, Science Norway, "Proof: Monster Waves Are Real," Norwegian Geotechnical Institute, November 8, 2011, https://partner.sciencenorway.no/feature-forskningno-geography/proof-monster-waves-are-real/1435235.

2. Peter Janssen and Werner Alpers, "Why SAR Wave Mode Data of ERS and ENVISAT Are Inadequate for Giving the Probability of the Occurrence of Freak Waves," http://earth.esa.int/workshops/seasar2006/proceedings/papers/s1_5_jan.pdf (accessed January 12, 2021).

3. Mark A. Donelan and Anne-Karin Magnusson, "The Making of the Andrea Wave and Other Rogues," *Nature*, March 8, 2017, https://www.nature.com/articles/srep44124.

4. "Rogue Waves," Wikipedia, https://en.wikipedia.org/wiki/Rogue_wave #Modern_knowledge_since_1995 (accessed January 12, 2021).

5. M. Onorato, S. Residori, U. Bortolozzo, A. Montina, F. T. Arecchi, "Rogue Waves and Their Generating Mechanisms in Different Physical Contexts," *Physics Reports* 528, no. 2 (July 10, 2013), 47–89.

6. Nic Fleming, "Terrifying 20m-Tall 'Rogue Waves' Are Actually Real," Earth, May 12, 2017, http://www.bbc.com/earth/story/20170510 -terrifying-20m-tall-rogue-waves-are-actually-real.

7. Frank Tang, "China overtakes US as No 1 in buying power, but still clings to developing status," South China Morning Post, May 21, 2020, https://www.scmp.com/economy/china-economy/article/3085501/china -overtakes-us-no-1-buying-power-still-clings-developing.

8. HP analysis, based on Oxford Economics data.

9. Condoleezza Rice and Amy B. Zegart, *Political Risk: How Businesses and Organizations Can Anticipate Global Insecurity* (Twelve, 2018).

10. "Perceptrons," Wikipedia, https://en.wikipedia.org/wiki/Perceptron (accessed January 12, 2021).

11. Declan Butler, "Engineered bat virus stirs debate over risky research," Nature November 12, 2015, https://www.nature.com/news/engineered -bat-virus-stirs-debate-over-risky-research-%201.18787

12. Robert G. Webster, "Wet Markets—a Continuing Source of Severe Acute Respiratory Syndrome and Influenza?," *Lancet* 363, no. 9404 (January 17, 2004): 234–6, doi: 10.1016/S0140-6736(03)15329-9.

13. HP and Deloitte Analysis based on sustained change in risk ratio of Fortune 1000.

14. A. J. P. Taylor, *War by Time-Table* (Macdonald & Co, 1969; Lume Books, 2019), Kindle.

15. Taylor, *War by Time-Table*.

CHAPTER 2

1. "RIP CURRENTS", United States Lifesaving Association, https://www .usla.org/page/ripcurrents.

2. David E. Irvine, "Extreme Waves in the Agulhas: A Case Study in Wave-Current Interaction," *Johns Hopkins APL Technical Digest* 8, no. 1 (1987),

https://www.jhuapl.edu/Content/techdigest/pdf/V08-N01/08-01 -Irvine.pdf.

3. Michel Olagnon, *Rogue Waves: Anatomy of a Monster* (Bloomsbury, 2017), 49; "A List of Freaque Wave Encounters," *Freaque Waves* (web blog), July 20, 2006, http://freaquewaves.blogspot.com/2006/07/list-of-freaque -wave-encounters.html.

4. Echo Huang, "In China, a Robot Has Started Delivering Packages to People," Quartz, June 19, 2017, https://qz.com/1009155/chinas -second-largest-ecommerce-company-jd-jd-just-used-a-robot-to-deliver -packages/.

5. Institute for Energy Research (web blog), "India's Electricity Demand Expected to Explode as Air Conditioning Proliferates," January 2, 2019, https://www.instituteforenergyresearch.org/international-issues /indias-electricity-demand-expected-to-explode-as-air-conditioning -proliferates/.

6. Arjun Kharpal, "Amazon CEO Jeff Bezos Has a Pretty Good Idea of Quarterly Earnings 3 Years in Advance," CNBC, May 8, 2017, https:// www.cnbc.com/2017/05/08/amazon-ceo-jeff-bezos-long-term-thinking .html.

7. Jenny Howard, "Plague Was One of History's Deadliest Diseases— Then We Found a Cure," *National Geographic*, July 6, 2020, https:// www.nationalgeographic.com/science/health-and-human-body/human -diseases/the-plague/.

8. "The Great Bullion Famine," Wikipedia, https://en.wikipedia.org/wiki /Great_Bullion_Famine (accessed January 12, 2021).

9. "The Quickening," *McKinsey Quarterly*, https://www.mckinsey.com /business-functions/strategy-and-corporate-finance/our-insights/five -fifty-the-quickening (accessed January 12, 2021).

10. "Consumption as a Percentage of GDP Around the World," TheGlobalEconomy.com, https://www.theglobaleconomy.com/rankings /consumption_GDP/ (accessed January 12, 2021).

11. "World Population Prospects, Profiles of Aging 2019," United Nations, June 2019, https://www.un.org/en/development/desa/population/events /pdf/other/35/Key%20Findings_28JUNE19.pdf.

12. Sungki Hong and Hannah G. Shell, "Factors Behind the Decline in the U.S. Natural Rate of Interest," *Economic Synopses* 2019, no. 11 (April 19, 2019), St. Louis Federal Reserve, https://research.stlouisfed.org /publications/economic-synopses/2019/04/19/factors-behind-the-decline -in-the-u-s-natural-rate-of-interest.

13. David E. Bloom, David Canning, and Günther Fink, *Implications of Population Aging for Economic Growth*, NBER Working Paper No. 16705, January 2011, https://www.nber.org/system/files/working_papers /w16705/w16705.pdf.

14. Institute of Medicine (US) Committee on the Long-Run Macroeconomic Effects of the Aging U.S. Population, *Aging and the Macroeconomy: Long-Term Implications of an Older Population* (Washington, DC: National

Academies Press, December 10, 2012), 9, "The Outlook for Fiscal Policy," https://www.ncbi.nlm.nih.gov/books/NBK148823/.

15. Thomas Piketty, *Capital in the Twenty-First Century* (Harvard University Press, 2014).

16. Sarah Bohn, *California's Need for Skilled Workers*, Public Policy Institute of California, September 2014, https://www.ppic.org/content/pubs/report /R_914SBR.pdf.

17. Yannick Binvel, Michael Franzino, Alan Guarino, Jean-Marc Laouchez, and Werner Penk, *Future of Work: The Global Talent Crunch*, Korn Ferry, 2018, https://www.kornferry.com/content/dam/kornferry/docs/article -migration/FOWTalentCrunchFinal_Spring2018.pdf.

18. Luís M. A. Bettencourt, José Lobo, Dirk Helbing, Christian Kühnert, and Geoffrey B. West, "Growth, Innovation, Scaling, and the Pace of Life in Cities," *Proceedings of the National Academy of Sciences* 104, no. 17 (April 2007): 7301–7306, doi: 10.1073/pnas.0610172104, https://www .pnas.org/content/104/17/7301; Luis Bettencourt and Geoffrey West, "A Unified Theory of Urban Living," *Nature* 467 (October 20, 2010), 912– 913, https://doi.org/10.1038/467912a, https://www.nature.com/articles /467912a#ref-CR4.

19. Parag Khanna, *Connectography: Mapping the Global Network Revolution* (New York: Orion Publishing, 2016).

20. Mark Arax, "A Kingdom from Dust," *The California Sunday Magazine*, January 31, 2018, https://story.californiasunday.com/resnick-a-kingdom -from-dust.

21. Yuan Yang "China's Big City Populations Shrink as Caps Take Effect," *Financial Times*, March 24, 2018, https://www.ft.com/content/be687eea -2790-11e8-b27e-cc62a39d57a0.

22. Bill Gates, "5 Questions to Ask About Any Climate Change Solution, from Bill Gates," ideas.ted.com, February 17, 2021, https://ideas.ted .com/5-questions-to-ask-about-any-climate-change-solution-from-bill -gates/.

23. Amy Hawkins, "The Grey Wall of China: Inside the World's Concrete Superpower," *The Guardian*, February 28, 2019, https://www.theguardian .com/cities/2019/feb/28/the-grey-wall-of-china-inside-the-worlds -concrete-superpower.

24. David Reinsel, John Rydning, and John F. Gantz, "Worldwide Global DataSphere Forecast, 2020–2024: The COVID-19 Data Bump and the Future of Data Growth," IDC, April 2020, https://www.idc.com/getdoc .jsp?containerId=US44797920.

25. Sarah Buhr, "George Church's Genetics on the Blockchain Startup Just Raised $4.3 Million from Khosla," TechCrunch, August 29, 2018, https://techcrunch.com/2018/08/29/george-churchs-genetics-on-the -blockchain-startup-just-raised-4-3-million-from-khosla/.

26. John Hawksworth and Richard Berriman, "Will Robots Really Steal Our Jobs?: An International Analysis of the Potential Long Term Impact of Automation," PwC, 2018, https://www.pwc.com/hu/hu/kiadvanyok /assets/pdf/impact_of_automation_on_jobs.pdf.

27. Ben Frost, Alan Guarino, and Mark Thompson, *Future of Work: The Salary Surge, Putting a Price on the Global Talent Crunch*, Korn Ferry, 2018, https://www.kornferry.com/content/dam/kornferry/docs/pdfs/KF-Future-of-Work-Salary-Surge-Report.pdf.

28. N. Case, "How to Become A Centaur," *Journal of Design and Science*, January 8, 2018, https://jods.mitpress.mit.edu/pub/issue3-case.

29. Joseph Nye Jr., "After the Liberal International Order," ProjectSyndicate.org, July 6, 2020, https://www.project-syndicate.org/commentary/biden-must-replace-liberal-international-order-by-joseph-s-nye-2020-07.

30. Global Fortune 500 Rankings, https://fortune.com/global500/2019/search/ (accessed January 12, 2021).

31. HP analysis, based on Oxford Economics data.

32. Wolfgang Fengler and Homi Kharas, "A Golden Age for Business? Every Second Five People Are Entering the Global Middle Class," The Brooking Institution, July 27, 2017, https://www.brookings.edu/blog/future-development/2017/07/27/a-golden-age-for-business-every-second-five-people-are-entering-the-global-middle-class/.

33. Jared Diamond, "What's Your Consumption Factor?," *New York Times*, January 2, 2008, https://www.nytimes.com/2008/01/02/opinion/02diamond.html.

34. HP Annual Megatrends 2019, February 26, 2019, https://www.jonathanbrill.com/recent/hp-2019-megatrends-report.

35. Philip Citowicki, "China's Control of the Mekong," *The Diplomat*, May 8, 2020, https://thediplomat.com/2020/05/chinas-control-of-the-mekong/; Prashanth Parameswaran, "Southeast Asia and China's Belt and Road Initiative," *The Diplomat*, May 15, 2019, https://thediplomat.com/2019/05/southeast-asia-and-chinas-belt-and-road-initiative/.

36. Ronald O'Rourke, *China Naval Modernization: Implications for U.S. Navy Capabilities—Background and Issues for Congress*, Congressional Research Office, December 17, 2020, https://fas.org/sgp/crs/row/RL33153.pdf; Jeremy Page, Gordon Lubold, and Rob Taylor, "Deal for Naval Outpost in Cambodia Furthers China's Quest for Military Network," *Wall Street Journal*, July 22, 2019, https://www.wsj.com/articles/secret-deal-for-chinese-naval-outpost-in-cambodia-raises-u-s-fears-of-beijings-ambitions-11563732482.

37. 2011 Census of India, https://censusindia.gov.in/2011census/ (accessed January 12, 2021).

38. David I. Auerbach and Arthur L. Kellermann, "How Does Growth in Health Care Costs Affect the American Family?," Rand Corporation Research Briefs, 2011, https://www.rand.org/pubs/research_briefs/RB9605.html.

39. Narrow money (M1), OECD Data, https://data.oecd.org/money/narrow-money-m1.htm (accessed January 12, 2021)

40. Sungki Hong and Hannah G. Shell, "Factors Behind the Decline in the U.S. Natural Rate of Interest," Economic Synopses, Economic Research, Federal Reserve Bank of St. Louis, 2019, No. 11, posted April 19, 2019,

https://research.stlouisfed.org/publications/economic-synopses/2019
/04/19/factors-behind-the-decline-in-the-u-s-natural-rate-of-interest;
Carlos Carvalho, Andrea Ferrero, and Fernanda Nechio, "Demographic
Transition and Low U.S. Interest Rates," Federal Reserve Bank of San
Francisco FRBSF Economic Letter, 2017-17, September 2017, https://
www.frbsf.org/economic-research/publications/economic-letter/2017
/september/demographic-transition-and-low-us-interest-rates/.

41. "Deflation," Wikipedia, https://en.wikipedia.org/wiki/Deflation
(accessed January 12, 2021).

42. Andrew McAfee, "Technology, Deflation and Economic Stagnation,"
Financial Times, April 30, 2015, https://www.ft.com/content/a2b78c71
-b4a2-3888-8bea-9473fc1b75c2.

43. Tingyi Chen, "The Cross-Border Payment War of WeChat Pay and
Alipay," WalktheChat, February 25, 2019, https://walkthechat.com/the
-cross-border-payment-war-of-wechat-pay-and-alipay/.

44. Josh Spero and Nicole Bullock, "Can Air Miles Points Be Securitised?,"
Financial Times, June 10, 2019, https://www.ft.com/content/a0d46b95
-5ac1-3663-844c-b93d61dc874c.

45. James Areddy, "China Creates Its Own Digital Currency, a First for
Major Economy," WSJ, April 5, 2021, https://www.wsj.com/articles
/china-creates-its-own-digital-currency-a-first-for-major-economy
-11617634118.

46. Eltjo Buringh and Jan Luiten van Zanden, "Charting the 'Rise of the
West': Manuscripts and Printed Books in Europe, A Long-Term
Perspective from the Sixth Through Eighteenth Centuries," *The Journal
of Economic History* 69, no. 2 (2009): 409–445.

47. David Woodward, "Techniques of Map Engraving, Printing and
Coloring in the European Renaissance," History of Cartography, Volume
3, pp. 591-610, https://press.uchicago.edu/books/HOC/HOC_V3_Pt1
/HOC_VOLUME3_Part1_chapter22.pdf

48. Heidi Vella, "5G vs 4G: What Is the Difference?," May 15, 2019, https://
www.raconteur.net/technology/4g-vs-5g-mobile-technology.

49. Source: HP internal research.

50. Y. A. Chen, Q. Zhang, T. Y. Chen, et al., "An Integrated Space-to-
Ground Quantum Communication Network over 4,600 Kilometres,"
Nature 589 (2021): 214–219.

51. Mike Mueller, "Nuclear Power Is the Most Reliable Energy Source and
It's Not Even Close," U.S. Department of Energy, Office of Nuclear
Energy, March 24, 2021, https://www.energy.gov/ne/articles/nuclear
-power-most-reliable-energy-source-and-its-not-even-close.

52. Ray Kurzweil, *The Singularity Is Near* (Penguin Books, 2006).

53. Soumitra Dutta, Bruno Lanvin, and Sacha Wunsch-Vincent, eds., *Global
Innovation Index 2020*, World Intellectual Property Organization, 2020,
https://www.wipo.int/edocs/pubdocs/en/wipo_pub_gii_2020.pdf.

54. OECD Triadic Patent Families Database, https://data.oecd.org/rd
/triadic-patent-families.htm (accessed January 13, 2021).

55. Hepeng Jia, "China's Citations Catching Up," *Nature Index* 30 (November 2017), https://www.natureindex.com/news-blog/chinas-citations-catching-up (accessed January 13, 2021).

56. "Number of Master's and Doctor's Degree Students Enrolled at Public Universities in China from 2009 to 2019," Statista, https://www.statista.com/statistics/1101469/number-of-postgraduate-master-doctor-students-at-universities-in-china/ (accessed January 12, 2021).

57. Hepeng Jia, "China's Citations Catching Up," Nature Index, November 30, 2017, https://www.natureindex.com/news-blog/chinas-citations-catching-up.

58. "New Education Policy Recommends Multidisciplinary System, Single Regulator for Higher Education," *Indian Express*, July 29, 2020, https://indianexpress.com/article/education/new-education-policy-recommends-multiple-disciplines-system-single-regulator-in-higher-education-6529385/.

59. Robert J. Gordon, *The Rise and Fall of American Growth: The U.S. Standard of Living Since the Civil War* (Princeton University Press, 2016).

60. Andrew McAfee, *More from Less* (Scribner, 2019).

61. "New Additive to Enhance Surface Cleanability," Paint & Coatings Industry, June 5, 2003, https://www.pcimag.com/articles/84991-new-additive-to-enhance-surface-cleanability.

62. Kristen V Brown, "Covid-Sniffing Robots Offer Testing Alternative," October 1, 2020, https://www.bloomberg.com/news/articles/2020-10-01/covid-sniffing-robots-offer-a-testing-alternative-startup-bets?.

63. 4D Knit Flyknit™ Shoe Construction, The Sneaker Factory (Web Log), October 24, 2017, https://www.sneakerfactory.net/2017/10/4d-knitting-flyknit-shoe-construction/.

64. "FDA Approves Combination Insulin Pump, Continuous Glucose Monitor," Healthline, https://www.healthline.com/health-news/fda-approves-combination-insulin-pump-glucose-monitor-121214 (accessed January 12, 2021).

65. XXII Group, "VR EXPERIENCE with EEG + HTC VIVE," January 14, 2019, YouTube video, January 14, 2019, https://www.youtube.com/watch?v=A_MOaz_wVoE.

66. Ana Swanson, "U.S. Delivers Another Blow to Huawei with New Tech Restrictions," *New York Times*, May 15, 2020, https://www.nytimes.com/2020/05/15/business/economy/commerce-department-huawei.html; "GDPR Fines and Penalties," Nathan Trust (blog), April 6, 2020, https://www.nathantrust.com/gdpr-fines-penalties; Ryan Brooks, "United States Data Protection Laws: State-Level Approaches to Privacy Protection," Netwrix (blog), August 27, 2019, https://blog.netwrix.com/2019/08/27/data-privacy-laws-by-state-the-u-s-approach-to-privacy-protection/; Sarah Rippy, "US State Comprehensive Privacy Law Comparison," IAPP, The International Association of Privacy Professionals, March 22, 2021, https://iapp.org/resources/article/state-comparison-table/.

CHAPTER 3

1. Peter Dizikes, "When the Butterfly Effect Took Flight," *MIT Technology Review*, February 22, 2011, https://www.technologyreview.com/2011/02/22/196987/when-the-butterfly-effect-took-flight/.

2. "Global Wine Manufacturing Industry—Market Research Report," IBIS, https://www.ibisworld.com/global/market-research-reports/global-wine-manufacturing-industry/.

3. Dina Fine Maron, "Many Prisoners on Death Row are Wrongfully Convicted," *Scientific American*, April 28, 2014, https://www.scientificamerican.com/article/many-prisoners-on-death-row-are-wrongfully-convicted/.

4. "Rumsfeld / Knowns," CNN, March 31, 2016, YouTube video,0:26, https://www.youtube.com/watch?v=REWeBzGuzCc.

5. "I am Elon Musk, CEO/CTO of a Rocket Company, AMA!," Reddit, May 27, 2009, https://www.reddit.com/r/IAmA/comments/2rgsan/i_am_elon_musk_ceocto_of_a_rocket_company_ama/.

6. NBC Nightly News, February 1986, https://www.youtube.com/watch?v=raMmRKGkGD4.

7. "How to Taste Wine Like a Master Sommelier - Wine Oh TV," September 13, 2013, YouTube video, https://www.youtube.com/watch?v=A6tfug8PM2E.

8. C. Bushdid, M. O. Magnasco, L. B. Vosshall and A. Keller, "Humans Can Discriminate More Than 1 Trillion Olfactory Stimuli," *Science* 343, no. 6177 (March 21, 2014): 1370–1372.

9. Nola Taylor Redd, "What Is Dark Matter?," Space.com, July 19, 2019, https://www.space.com/20930-dark-matter.html.

10. Steven Lee Myers, Jin Wu, and Claire Fu, "China's Looming Crisis: A Shrinking Population," *New York Times*, updated January 17, 2020, https://www.nytimes.com/interactive/2019/01/17/world/asia/china-population-crisis.html.

11. "Does China Have an Aging Problem?," China Power, February 15, 2016, updated March 19, 2021, https://chinapower.csis.org/aging-problem/.

12. Nicholas Eberstadt, "China's Demographic Prospects to 2040: Opportunities, Constraints, Potential Policy Responses," Governance in an Emerging New World, Fall Series, Issue 218, Hoover Institution, https://www.hoover.org/research/chinas-demographic-prospects-2040-opportunities-constraints-potential-policy-responses.

13. Rick Merritt, "Moore's Law, China vs. Team USA," EE Times, July 27, 2018, https://www.eetimes.com/moores-law-china-vs-team-usa/; Justin Hodiak and Scott W. Harold, "Can China Become the World Leader in Semiconductors?," The Diplomat, September 25, 2020, https://thediplomat.com/2020/09/can-china-become-the-world-leader-in-semiconductors/.

14. Chip Heath and Dan Heath, *Decisive: How to Make Better Choices in Life and Work* (Crown Business, 2013).

15. Gil Morrot, Fréderic Brochet, and Denis Dubourdieu, "The Color of Odors," *Brain and Language*, doi:10.1006/brin.2001.2493, http://www.daysyn.com/Morrot.pdf.

16. Gary Klein, "The Curious Case of Confirmation Bias," Seeing What Others Don't, *Psychology Today*, May 5, 2019, https://www.psychologytoday.com/us/blog/seeing-what-others-dont/201905/the-curious-case-confirmation-bias.

17. Elon Musk, transcript of interview at TED Conference, March 2013, https://www.ted.com/talks/elon_musk_the_mind_behind_tesla_spacex_solarcity/transcript?quote=2101.

18. Julian Zubek et al., "Performance of Language-Coordinated Collective Systems: A Study of Wine Recognition and Description," *Frontiers in Psychology* 7, no. 1321 (September 27, 2016), doi:10.3389/fpsyg.2016.01321.

19. Sherman Kent, "Words of Estimative Probability," *Studies in Intelligence*, Fall 1964, posted March 19, 2007, last updated July 7, 2008, Central Intelligence Agency, https://web.archive.org/web/20190428102759/https://www.cia.gov/library/center-for-the-study-of-intelligence/csi-publications/books-and-monographs/sherman-kent-and-the-board-of-national-estimates-collected-essays/6words.html.

20. *New York Times*, July 23, 1914, https://timesmachine.nytimes.com/timesmachine/1914/07/23/issue.html (accessed March 2013).

21. *British Army & Navy Gazette*, Saturday, July 25, 1914, https://www.britishnewspaperarchive.co.uk/viewer/BL/0001394/19140725/001/0001 (accessed March 2020).

22. Jean de Bloch, "The Future of War in Its Technical Economic and Political Relations," The World Peace Foundation, 1914, https://www.armyupress.army.mil/Portals/7/combat-studies-institute/csi-books/Future-of-War.pdf (accessed January 21, 2021).

23. Jonathan R. Treadwell, Scott Lucas, and Amy Y. Tsou, "Surgical Checklists: A Systematic Review of Impacts and Implementation," *BMJ Quality & Safety* 23, no. 4 (April 2014): 299–318, doi:10.1136/bmjqs-2012-001797, https://www.ncbi.nlm.nih.gov/pmc/articles/PMC3963558/.

CHAPTER 4

1. Sharon Lerner, "Whistleblower details how Trump's bureaucrats refused to secure N95 masks as pandemic loomed", May 7 2020, The Intercept, https://theintercept.com/2020/05/07/coronavirus-whistleblower-hhs-n95-ppe/.

2. Peter Demarzo, "Financing Innovation: Common Mistakes Even Great Investors Make," Stanford University Online, August 13, 2013, YouTube video, 52:33, https://www.youtube.com/watch?v=I-JgtIiwX4M&t=782s.

3. "Ray Dalio Discusses How He Was Able to Foresee the 2008 Debt Crisis," Yahoo Finance, February 20, 2019, YouTube video, 7:10, https://www.youtube.com/watch?v=JhRBrLNXTsQ.

4. Cloe Pogoda, "Methods and Logic: Gregor Mendel Experiments in Plant Hybridization," February 19, 2014, http://dosequis.colorado.edu/Courses /MethodsLogic/Docs/Mendel.pdf.

5. Gregor Mendel, "Experiments in Plant Hybridization," *Proceedings of the Natural History Society of Brünn*,1865, 1–39.

6. Jim Cantrell, "How Did Elon Musk Learn Enough About Rockets to Create and Run SpaceX?," Quora, June 7, 2016, https://www.quora.com /How-did-Elon-Musk-learn-enough-about-rockets-to-create-and-run -SpaceX/answer/Jim-Cantrell?ref=forbes&rel_pos=1 (accessed January 12, 2021).

7. Ashlee Vance, *Elon Musk* (Ecco, 2015), 108, Kindle.

8. "Elon Musk - CEO of Tesla Motors and SpaceX | Entrepreneurship | Khan Academy," April 22, 2013, YouTube video, 48:41, https://www .youtube.com/watch?v=vDwzmJpI4io.

9. "Impaired Driving: Get the Facts," Centers for Disease Control and Prevention, https://www.cdc.gov/motorvehiclesafety/impaired_driving /impaired-drv_factsheet.html (accessed January 12, 2021); "2016 Data: Alcohol-Impaired Driving," NHTSA's National Center for Statistics and Analysis, October 2017, https://crashstats.nhtsa.dot.gov/Api/Public /ViewPublication/812450.

10. "Blockbuster LLC," Wikipedia, https://en.wikipedia.org/wiki/Block buster_LLC.

11. "Number of Netflix Paid Subscribers Worldwide for 1st Quarter 2013 to 4th Quarter 2020," Statista, https://www.statista.com/statistics/250934 /quarterly-number-of-netflix-streaming-subscribers-worldwide/.

12. Elisabeth Bumiller,"We Have Met the Enemy and He Is PowerPoint," *New York Times*, April 26, 2010, https://www.nytimes.com/2010/04/27 /world/27powerpoint.html.

CHAPTER 5

1. Shannon Forrest, "What Happened to Crew Resource Management?," Flight Safety Foundation, October 26, 2018, https://flightsafety.org/asw -article/what-happened-to-crew-resource-management/.

2. Chris Clearfield and Andras Tilcsik, *Meltdown* (McClelland & Stewart, 2019).

3. Jeremy Bogaisky, "Here's Who May Be Teaching Your Airline Pilot to Fly: In Air Travel Boom, CAE Soars," *Forbes*, February 27, 2019, https:// www.forbes.com/sites/jeremybogaisky/2019/02/27/heres-who-teaches -your-airline-pilot-to-fly-cae-is-cashing-in-on-the-boom-in-air-travel/.

4. Dan Parsons, "Full Flight Simulators Incorporate VR for Next Generation of Pilots," *Aviation Today*, August 1, 2019, https://www .aviationtoday.com/2019/08/01/training-brain-mind/.

5. Interactive charts and tools, Blackrock Capital, https://www.blackrock .com/institutions/en-zz/insights/charts (accessed January 12, 2021).

6. "Our Team," B612 Foundation, https://b612foundation.org/our-team/ (accessed January 12, 2021).

7. Jonathan Abrams, "What were the key mistakes that Friendster made?", Quora, December 7, 2011, https://www.quora.com/What-were-the-key-mistakes-that-Friendster-made/answer/Jonathan-Abrams?ch=10&share=6641efb3&srid=5M5mg

8. Gary Klein, "Performing a Project Premortem," *Harvard Business Review*, September 2007, https://hbr.org/2007/09/performing-a-project-premortem.

9. Matthew Shaer, "Is This the Future of Robotic Legs?, November 2014, "https://www.smithsonianmag.com/innovation/future-robotic-legs-180953040/

10. https://vimeo.com/303534231.

11. Gideon Gil, Matthew Orr, "Pioneering surgery makes a prosthetic foot feel like the real thing", May 30, 2018, https://www.statnews.com/2018/05/30/pioneering-amputation-surgery-prosthetic-foot/.

12. Data from https://www.investing.com/equities/jd.com-inc-adr-ratios (accessed April, 21, 2021).

13. Harry Jones, "The Recent Large Reduction in Space Launch Cost," International Conference on Environmental Systems, July 8, 2018, https://ntrs.nasa.gov/archive/nasa/casi.ntrs.nasa.gov/20200001093.pdf.

14. Micah Zenko, "Millennium Challenge: The Real Story of a Corrupted Military Exercise and Its Legacy," War on the Rocks.com, November 5, 2015, https://warontherocks.com/2015/11/millennium-challenge-the-real-story-of-a-corrupted-military-exercise-and-its-legacy/.

15. Malcolm Gladwell, *Blink* (Little, Brown, 2005), 99–146.

16. Thom Shanker, "Iran Encounter Grimly Echoes '02 War Game," *New York Times*, January 12, 2008, https://www.nytimes.com/2008/01/12/washington/12navy.html.

17. D. Moriña, I. Serra, P. Puig, et al. "Probability Estimation of a Carrington-like Geomagnetic Storm, *Scientific Reports* 9, no. 2393 (2019), https://doi.org/10.1038/s41598-019-38918-8, https://www.nature.com/articles/s41598-019-38918-8.

18. Amazon staff, "Amazon Has Hired 175,000 Additional People," Amazon.com, April 13, 2020, https://www.aboutamazon.com/news/company-news/amazon-has-hired-175-000-additional-people.

19. "Maginot Line," Wikipedia, https://en.wikipedia.org/wiki/Maginot_Line (accessed January 12, 2021).

20. "Ardennes," Wikipedia, https://en.wikipedia.org/wiki/Ardennes. (accessed January 12, 2021).

21. "Battle of Dunkirk," Wikipedia, https://en.wikipedia.org/wiki/Battle_of_Dunkirk#Evacuation (accessed January 12, 2021).

22. "Commander's Handbook for Attack the Network," United States Joint Forces Command," May 20, 2011, https://www.jcs.mil/Portals/36/Documents/Doctrine/pams_hands/atn_hbk.pdf.

23. Francis Horton, "The Lost Lesson of Millennium Challenge 2002, the Pentagon's Embarrassing Post-9/11 War Game," Task and Purpose, November 6, 2019, https://taskandpurpose.com/opinion/millenium-challenge-2002-stacked-deck; Zenko, "Millennium Challenge: The

Real Story of a Corrupted Military Exercise and Its Legacy," War on the Rocks.com, November 5, 2015, https://warontherocks.com/2015/11/millennium-challenge-the-real-story-of-a-corrupted-military-exercise-and-its-legacy/.

24. Micah Zenko, *Red Team: How to Succeed by Thinking like the Enemy* (Basic Books, 2015).

25. Taylor Soper, "Amazon's Secrets of Invention: Jeff Bezos Explains How to Build an Innovative Team," Geekwire, May 17, 2016, https://www.geekwire.com/2016/amazons-secrets-invention-jeff-bezos-explains-build-innovative-team/.

CHAPTER 6

1. Amerigo Vespucci, *Letter to Piero Soderini, Gonfaloniere: The Year 1504*, trans. George Tyler Northup (Princeton University Press, 1916), https://books.google.com/books?id=boQKAQAAIAAJ.

2. https://news.microsoft.com/innovation-stories/project-natick-underwater-datacenter/.

3. Emelia J. Benjamin et al., "Heart Disease and Stroke Statistics—2018 Update: A Report from the American Heart Association," *Circulation*, January 31, 2018, https://www.ahajournals.org/doi/full/10.1161/CIR.0000000000000558.

4. Mark Landler, Germany Debates Subsidies for Solar Industry, *New York Times*, May 16, 2008, https://www.nytimes.com/2008/05/16/business/worldbusiness/16solar.html; Erik Kirschbaum and Christoph Steitz, "Germany to Cut Solar Subsidies Faster Than Expected," Reuters, February 23, 2012, https://www.reuters.com/article/us-germany-solar-incentives/germany-to-cut-solar-subsidies-faster-than-expected-idUSTRE81M1EG20120223.

5. Caroline Donnelly, "Zoom Signs Multi-year Preferred Cloud Provider Deal with AWS," December 1, 2020, https://www.computerweekly.com/news/252492929/Zoom-signs-multi-year-preferred-cloud-provider-deal-with-AWS.

6. Tanner Callais, "How Much Money Carnival Corporation Lost in 2020," January 28, 2021, https://cruzely.com/how-much-money-carnival-corporation-lost-in-2020/.

7. "The 20 Reasons Startups Fail," CB Insights, 2019, https://www.cbinsights.com/reports/The-20-Reasons-Startups-Fail.pdf.

8. Katie Roof, "RIP Juicero, the $400 Venture-Backed Juice Machine," September 1, 2017, https://techcrunch.com/2017/09/01/rip-juicero-the-400-venture-backed-juice-machine/; David Gelles, "A $700 Juicer for the Kitchen That Caught Silicon Valley's Eye," *New York Times*, March 31, 2016, https://www.nytimes.com/2016/04/03/business/juicero-juice-system-silicon-valley-interest.html?mcubz=0&_r=0.

9. "Why Do So Many Hardware Startups Fail?," CB Insights, https://www.cbinsights.com/research/report/hardware-startups-failure-success/ (accessed January 12, 2021).

10. https://www.nytimes.com/2016/04/03/business/juicero-juice-system-silicon-valley-interest.html.

11. "Here's Why Juicero's Press Is So Expensive," April 24, 2017, https://blog.bolt.io/juicero/.

12. https://www.nytimes.com/2016/04/03/business/juicero-juice-system-silicon-valley-interest.html.

13. Juicero Investors, https://www.crunchbase.com/organization/juicero/company_financials (accessed January 12, 2021).

14. "Analysis of Titanic's Safety Features and Failures," Ultimate Titanic, https://www.ultimatetitanic.com/titanics-safety-features (accessed January 12, 2021).

15. Bill Sanderson, "More Than $100M in Art Lost in 9/11 Attacks," *New York Post*, September 15, 2011, https://nypost.com/2011/09/15/more-than-100m-in-art-lost-in-911-attacks/.

16. Source: Interview with parent.

17. Michael Lewis, "How the Eggheads Cracked," *New York Times Magazine*, January 24, 1999, https://www.nytimes.com/1999/01/24/magazine/how-the-eggheads-cracked.html.

18. Maria Konnikova, "Poker and the Psychology of Uncertainty," *Wired*, June 23, 2020, https://www.wired.com/story/poker-psychology-uncertainty/.

19. Peter Coy, "Ray Dalio's Seven Bubble Indicators Are 'Flickering But Not Flashing,'" *Bloomberg Businessweek*, September 12, 2018, https://www.bloomberg.com/news/articles/2018-09-12/ray-dalio-s-seven-bubble-indicators-are-flickering-but-not-flashing.

CHAPTER 7

1. "Bay Model," Wikipedia, https://en.wikipedia.org/wiki/U.S._Army_Corps_of_Engineers_Bay_Model (accessed January 14, 2021).

2. CC BY-SA 2.0 License: https://creativecommons.org/licenses/by-sa/2.0/; https://www.flickr.com/photos/bastique/3024070104/in/photostream/.

3. Mark Arax, "A Kingdom from Dust," *The California Sunday Magazine*, January 31, 2018, https://story.californiasunday.com/resnick-a-kingdom-from-dust.

4. John King, "Let's Dam the Bay! How Daydream Got Sold as Grand Solution," November 28, 2016, https://www.sfchronicle.com/bayarea/place/article/Let-s-dam-the-bay-How-daydream-got-sold-as-10636884.php; L. H. Nishkian, "Report on the Reber Plan and Bay Land Crossing to Joint Army-Navy Board," San Francisco, August 12–15, 1946.

5. Geoffrey A. Vanderpal, "Impact of R&D Expenses and Corporate Financial Performance," *Journal of Accounting and Finance* 15 (2015): 135–149, https://www.researchgate.net/publication/321242843_Impact_of_RD_Expenses_and_Corporate_Financial_Performance.

6. Clyde Winters, "Did the Portuguese Have Secret Knowledge About Brazil Before the Treaty of Tordesillas?," Ancient Origins, updated October 27, 2016; J. H. Parry, *The Age of Reconnaissance: Discovery, Exploration, and Settlement 1450 to 1650* (University of California Press, 1981), 155, https://books.google.com/books?id=6l5rXRkpkFgC&pg.

7. D. Satava, "Columbus's First Voyage: Profit or Loss from a Historical Accountant's Perspective," *Journal of Applied Business Research* (*JABR*) 23, no. 4 (2007), https://clutejournals.com/index.php/JABR/article/view /1375/1357.

8. "Gregor Mendel," Wikipedia, https://en.wikipedia.org/wiki/Gregor _Mendel (accessed January 14, 2021).

9. "Iridium Satellite Constellation," Wikipedia, https://en.wikipedia.org /wiki/Iridium_satellite_constellation (accessed January 14, 2021).

10. Rolfe Winkler and Andy Pasztor, "Exclusive Peek at SpaceX Data Shows Loss in 2015, Heavy Expectations for Nascent Internet Service," *Wall Street Journal*, January 13, 2017, https://www.wsj.com/articles/exclusive -peek-at-spacex-data-shows-loss-in-2015-heavy-expectations-for -nascent-internet-service-1484316455.

11. Meghan Bartels, "SpaceX Launches 10 Iridium Satellites Into Orbit, Then Sticks Rocket Landing," Space.com, January 11, 2019, https://www .space.com/42977-spacex-rocket-launches-final-iridium-satellites-then -lands.html.

12. Dr. James Grime, "The Inner Workings of an Enigma Machine," Perimeter Institute for Theoretical Physics, June 23, 2014, YouTube video, 14:03, https://www.youtube.com/watch?v=mcX7iO_XCFA.

13. "Apple Store," Wikipedia, https://en.wikipedia.org/wiki/Apple_Store (accessed January 14, 2021).

14. Marianne Wilson, "The Most Profitable Retailers in Sales Per Square Foot Are . . . ," *Chain Store Age*, July 31, 2017, https://chainstoreage.com /news/most-profitable-retailers-sales-square-foot-are.

15. Steve Chazin, "The Secrets of Apple's Retail Success," https://www .marketingapple.com/Apple_Retail_Success.pdf (accessed January 14, 2021).

16. Siegfried Flügge, "Kann der Energieinhalt der Atomkerne technisch nutzbar gemacht werden?," *Die Naturwissenschaften* 27, no. 23/24, 402– 410 (June 9, 1939).

17. https://www.osti.gov/opennet/manhattan-project-history/Events/1939 -1942/einstein_letter.htm#:~:text=Roosevelt%20(right)%20wrote %20Einstein%20back,he%20had%20chosen%20a%20direction.

18. Jon Tate Self, "An Analysis of Success and Failure: The Manhattan Project and German Nuclear Research During the Third Reich," 1994, Honors Thesis, Ouachita Baptist University, https://scholarlycommons .obu.edu/cgi/viewcontent.cgi?article=1146&context=honors_theses.

19. Bruce Cameron Reed, "From Treasury Vault to the Manhattan Project," *American Scientist* 99, no. 1, January–February 2011, https://www .americanscientist.org/article/from-treasury-vault-to-the-manhattan -project.

20. Neel V. Patel, "Why the CDC Botched Its Coronavirus Testing," *MIT Technology Review*, March 5, 2020, https://www.technologyreview.com /2020/03/05/905484/why-the-cdc-botched-its-coronavirus-testing/.

21. *Lost in La Mancha*, 2002 documentary; "*The Man Who Killed Don Quixote*," Wikipedia, https://en.wikipedia.org/wiki/The_Man_Who_Killed_Don _Quixote.

22. Frank Pallotta, "How Napkin Sketches During a Pixar Lunch Meeting Led to Four of the Studio's Greatest Movies," *Business Insider*, April 29, 2014, https://www.businessinsider.com/pixar-movies-thanks-to-napkin -sketches-at-lunch-meeting-2014-4.

23. "*Toy Story* (1995) Awards," IMDB, https://www.imdb.com/title /tt0114709/awards (accessed January 14, 2021).

24. *General Magic*, 2018, documentary, https://www.generalmagicthemovie .com/ (accessed January 14, 2021).

25. "Spurious Correlations," https://tylervigen.com/view_correlation?id= 29006.

CHAPTER 8

1. Ernest Shackleton, *South: Endurance Expedition* (Signet Books, 1999).

2. F. A. Worsley, *Shackleton's Boat Journey* (Wakefield Press, 2000), 61, https://books.google.com/books?id=EgjJdLKFarEC.

3. Henry Nicholls, "The Truth About Norwegian Lemmings," BBC Earth, November 21, 2014, http://www.bbc.com/earth/story/20141122-the -truth-about-lemmings.

4. Dominic Sivitilli and David Gire, "Researchers Model How Octopus Arms Make Decisions," Astrobiology Science Conference, June 25, 2019, https://news.agu.org/press-release/researchers-model-how-octopus-arms -make-decisions/.

5. Signe Dean, "Octopus and Squid Evolution Is Officially Weirder Than We Could Have Ever Imagined," Science Alert, March 17, 2018, https:// www.sciencealert.com/octopus-and-squid-evolution-is-officially-weirder -than-we-could-have-ever-imagined.

6. Katherine Harmon, "Octopuses Reveal First RNA Editing in Response to Environment," *Scientific American*, January 5, 2012, https://blogs .scientificamerican.com/octopus-chronicles/octopuses-reveals-first-rna -editing-in-response-to-environment/.

7. "The World's 25 Biggest Oil Companies," *Forbes*, January 2, 2013, forbes .com/pictures/em45gmmg/7-royal-dutch-shell-3-9-million-barrels-per -day/?sh=737a109d2f17.

8. "The Operation Order - OPORD," Army Study Guide, https://www .armystudyguide.com/content/army_board_study_guide_topics/training _the_force/the-operation-order-opord.shtml (accessed January 14, 2021).

9. https://www.youtube.com/watch?v=CBYhVcO4WgI.

10. https://www.dco.uscg.mil/Portals/9/OCSNCOE /OCS%20Investigation%20Reports/NTSB%20Marine%20Accident %20Reports/Ocean%20Ranger%20NTSB%20Report.pdf?ver=2017-10 -05-073744-570.

11. "Marine Accident Report, Capsizing and Sinking of U.S. Mobile Offshore Drilling Unit Ocean Ranger Off the East Coast of Canada 166 Nautical Miles East of St. John's, Newfoundland," National Transportation Safety

Board, February 15, 1982, 73–77, https://www.dco.uscg.mil/Portals /9/OCSNCOE/OCS%20Investigation%20Reports/NTSB%20Marine %20Accident%20Reports/Ocean%20Ranger%20NTSB%20Report.pdf.

12. Michael Lewis, "The No Stats All Star," *New York Times*, February 13, 2009, https://www.nytimes.com/2009/02/15/magazine/15Battier -t.html.

13. Mark Medina, "How Stephen Curry Helped the Warriors Keep Everything Together," *The Mercury News*, March 27, 2019, https://www .mercurynews.com/2019/03/27/how-stephen-curry-helped-the-warriors -keep-everything-together/.

14. " 'Rambo' The Octopus Shoots Photos of Tourists at New Zealand Aquarium," *All Things Considered*, NPR, April 15, 2015, https://www .npr.org/2015/04/15/399937693/rambo-the-octopus-shoots-photos-of -tourists-at-new-zealand-aquarium.

15. https://moralfoundations.org/.

16. Tyler Everett, "Inside Look at Stephen Curry's Unanimous Media Projects, Vision," *Sports Business Journal*, November 13, 2019, https://www .sportsbusinessdaily.com/Daily/Issues/2019/11/13/SMT-Conference /Unanimous-Media.aspx.

INDEX

Page numbers followed by *f* refer to figures.

ABOUT THE AUTHOR

Jonathan Brill prepares organizations to profit from radical change. He is a renowned expert on resilient growth and decision-making under uncertainty.

He was a senior leader and the Global Futurist at HP (Hewlett-Packard), where he directed long-term strategy programs, a creative director at frog design, and the managing partner of innovation firms that created over 350 products.

He is a board member at Frost & Sullivan, a major market intelligence firm with offices in 46 countries. He develops products for both fictional heroes and real people as the Futurist-in-Residence at Territory Studio, the creative visionaries behind the sci-fi tech in *Ghost in the Shell*, *Blade Runner 2049*, and Steven Spielberg's *Ready Player One*.

He advises globally on product innovation and resilient growth strategy with clients, including Samsung, Microsoft, Verizon, PepsiCo, the United States government, and the MIT Media Lab. He is an in-demand thought leader, speaker, and contributor to TED, Singularity University, Korn Ferry, JPMorgan Chase, *Forbes*, and *Harvard Business Review*.

He holds a degree in industrial design from Pratt Institute and has done extensive management training at Stanford University.

For more information, please visit jonathanbrill.com.